The Yod Book

The
Yod
Book

Including a complete
discussion of
unaspected planets

Karen Hamaker-Zondag

SAMUEL WEISER, INC.

York Beach, Maine

First published in 2000 by
Samuel Weiser, Inc.
P. O. Box 612
York Beach, ME 03910-0612
www.weiserbooks.com

Library of Congress Cataloging-in-Publication Data
Hamaker-Zondag, Karen.
    [De jod figuur : en ongeaspecteerde planeten. English]
    The yod book : including a complete discussion of unaspected planets /
    Karen Hamaker-Zondag.
        p. cm.
    Includes bibliographical references and index.
    ISBN 1-57863-163-7 (pbk. : alk. paper)
    1. Zodiac. 2. Astrology. I. Title.

    BF1726.H345 2000
    133.5'2—dc21   00–027020

EB

Our thanks to the translator, Wanda Boeke, TransAtlantic Translations, who rendered the Dutch into English.

Typeset in 10.5/12.5 Palatino

Printed in the United States of America

07 06 05 04 03 02 01 00
8   7   6   5   4   3   2   1

This book is dedicated to
Christina, Esther, Gemma, Helen, Jannette, and Jacqueline

Contents

PREFACE ix

1. What Is a Yod?—Technical Background of the Yod
   Configuration 1

2. Unaspected Planets 19

3. Family Themes and the Generation Problem 35

4. Effects of Yods and Unaspected Planets 47

5. Interpreting Yod Configurations 69

6. Interpreting Unaspected Planets and Duets 93

7. The Shadow and Evil 103

8. Unaspected Planets and Temporary Yods
   by Progression and Transit 123

9. How Should We Deal with
   Yods and Unaspected Planets? 135

10. Yods and Unaspected Planets in the
    Astrology of Relationships 145

11. Yods, a Duet, and Unaspected Planets 161
    Diana, 162
    Charles, 170
    Camilla, 173

12. Yods and Unaspected Planets in Action 183
    Monica Lewinsky, 183
    Linda Tripp, 194
    Kenneth Starr, 203
    William Jefferson Clinton, 213

13. Life and Death 219

14. Yods and a Duet in C. G. Jung's Childhood 237

15. Case Files of Yods and Unaspected Planets 253
    Helen—Temporary Yods in Transit, 253
    Jacqueline—From External Structure to Internal Flows, 260
    Christina, 266

16. Gemma—Your Own Form within
    the Generational Theme 275

17. Living with a Number of Yods—Esther's Experience 289

18. In Conclusion 313

BIBLIOGRAPHY 319

INDEX 321

ABOUT THE AUTHOR 324

Preface

For me, the years between 1975 and 1978 can be characterized in retrospect as an important turning-point in my life. Many things happened during that period of time—lots of sorrow and pain, emotions, turbulent events, health and family problems. Everything was piling up, and fast, until I got to the point where I felt I had to leave a particular life behind me and start all over again. These were also years when, despite two master's degrees, I decided to say goodbye to the university world and start making my living with astrology. It is difficult to describe what one goes through at times like this, and naturally I tried to analyze it all astrologically.

Now, years later, I understand very well what was going on, both psychologically and astrologically. At the time, however, I was still unacquainted with the yod aspect. Although I knew inconjuncts existed, I had been taught that an inconjunct was a minor aspect and that it wouldn't have much effect on my life. Now I know better!

In 1975, Pluto approached by primary progression an inconjunct to my Ascendant and at the same time, it was inconjunct Jupiter—a yod. In 1976, Pluto did the same thing, but this time by transit. At the end of 1976, Neptune in Sagittarius was sextile Pluto, also forming an inconjunct with my Jupiter—a double yod. And right after this, in January and February of 1977, Saturn in Leo by transit formed an inconjunct with my Ascendant, while Saturn also stood sextile to Pluto by transit—the third yod. And in 1977–1978, primary Mars from my natal chart had entered Pisces, and from that point made a progressed inconjunct with Pluto, *and* Neptune, *and* Saturn in my natal chart—two more yods! So five yods in short order, which partially overlapped during that time.

Everything I was experiencing made me change quickly. My dream life was intense, and these yod years were years when I was very involved with Jungian psychology. This meant confrontations, digesting, and having to look at myself honestly.

In 1978, I married Hans, an important turning-point in my life. I got to know him during the "yod years" and if one compares our horoscopes using synastry, they form quite a few yods between them! The extremes couldn't have been any greater than they were during these years: deep sorrow about things from the past that had to be worked out, and great happiness in love. I began suspecting that this horoscope configuration, this yod, might very well have something to do with it, so I decided to study this configuration in depth. A whole world opened up for me! And as if the heavens wanted to help me do this, no sooner did I mention that I wanted to research this configuration more, than the next nineteen requests for horoscopes came from clients all of whom had a yod configuration in the natal chart. Well, I could ask the clients questions, and listen to how life was turning out for them!

In looking for the meaning of the yod configurations, I also stumbled on a theme of unaspected planets. Part of the underlying dynamic is the same for both, which is why I address them together in this book, even though they are two different horoscope factors, and so I will also clearly show the differences between them.

When an image of the profound and far-reaching meaning of yods and unaspected planets slowly began to unfold, I started carefully telling clients about how the energy manifests, letting them know that I was still studying. I will never forget the first client with whom I shared my findings. Right in the middle of what I was saying, she grabbed my hand and said, with tears in her eyes, "This is the first time I've had the feeling that somebody really understands me. . . ." That moment I decided I would someday, after having gathered lots of data, write a book about this. I started writing in 1989, but it took a lot of time and energy. It was Christmas 1998 before the book was really finished.

Now, twenty years after I began my study of yods and unaspected planets, I offer my experiences in this book. I have often noticed that while I'm writing a book, I experience the theme on which I am working to a heightened degree inside as well as outside myself. It was no different with the yod book! Needless to say, during the preparation and writing of this book, I had the requisite yods by transit and progression. But now things are different. I understand much better what's going on, and have learned to be flexible about it. I hope this book will contribute to improving insight into the whys and wherefores of particular feelings of uncertainty, but especially that it will help you enjoy more of the here-and-now.

In the first part of the book, I have tried to clarify the background and dynamics of yods and unaspected planets as much as possible, and to indicate what needs attention when interpreting the natal chart, by progression and transit, and relationship charts. The second part of the book consists of examples, including examples that made history, like the relationship between Charles and Diana, and between Bill Clinton and Monica Lewinsky. In the light of yods and unaspected planets, we can see what kind of dimension is playing in the background. These are examples of how yods and unaspected planets can lead to all kinds of complicated situations in the world at large. In addition, I have included a number of examples that reflect the kind of inner feelings and emotions connected to yods and unaspected planets. Jung wrote an impressive description of this in his book, *Memories, Dreams, Reflections*, which I bring into perspective using his horoscope. I also work out the connection between feelings, emotions, and events in the day-to-day life of people like you and me, to show how yods and unaspected planets feel and gain form in daily reality.

As always, I owe many thanks to my husband, Hans, who is both my biggest support as well as my biggest critic. I would also like to take this opportunity to thank my sister-in-law, Yvonne, who cheerfully took on a lot of administrative work and so gave me more space to write, and with whom it's such a pleasure to work. In particular, my thanks also to the many people who shared their experiences with me so openly and honestly, clients as well as workshop participants, thereby enabling me to comprehend yods and unaspected planets. A number of them worked very actively on this book. I was allowed to publish their experiences and stories, including their horoscopes. Their stories were all corrected, supplemented, and approved prior to publication. They chose the names that are used in the book, and so I cannot use their real names here to thank them. Words cannot express the gratitude and pleasure I had working with their stories in this book, and I am very grateful to them for their cooperation, support, and openness. It is to them that I dedicate this book.

—Karen Hamaker-Zondag

CHAPTER ONE

What Is a Yod?—
Technical Background
of the Yod Configuration

A yod is an aspect configuration where one planet (MC, Ascendant, or a planet) forms an inconjunct with two other zodiacal points, while these two planets form a sextile between them. In a yod either the MC or the Ascendant can participate, but because we don't draw aspects between the MC and the Ascendant, they can never be involved in a single yod at the same time. [Jod comes from the Hebrew word יֹד, 'jod' = hand.]

Astrology recognizes a number of different aspects that form a "closed" configuration; for instance, we recognize the grand trine (whose points connect three signs of a single element), or the grand cross (or square), whose points connect the four signs of a single mode, and so on. The direction the interpretation of any aspect configuration takes is determined, for one, by the meaning of the kinds of aspects involved, and by the planets involved. More is going on though. In order to understand thoroughly what aspects are all about, aspect configurations in general, and the yod in particular, we will sidestep a bit and look at other astrological rules and interpretive factors so we can bring these together later on at a deeper level in discussing the yod configuration.

Aspects

Technically speaking, an aspect is an angle a planet forms in relation to another in the sky, as seen from Earth. There are countless possible angles, but history has taught us that particular angles exhibit a clear effect and others do so less or not at all. After Kepler, classification according to so-called major and minor aspects was recognized; the major aspects were traditionally the conjunction (0°), sextile (60°), square (90°), trine (120°), and opposition (180°). These are all angles divisible by 30, the number of degrees comprising a whole sign. At that time, aspects were considered exclusively with reference to sign. The only two aspects missing from this list of major aspects that are also divisible by 30 are the semi-sextile (30°) and the inconjunct (150°). These used to be minor aspects.

By combining music and numerology with the concept of astrological aspects, Kepler created many new aspects. He was familiar with the inconjunct (also called a quincunx), but also made totally new ones. Because Kepler came up with quite a few aspects whose angles were no longer divisible by 30, the problem arose, for instance, that you could get a quintile (72°) between the signs Aries and Cancer (i.e., a planet at 29° Aries, and the other 72° further at 11° Cancer), but also one between Aries and Gemini (i.e., a planet at 2° Aries, and the other 72° further at 14° Gemini). He gave aspects their own meaning based on music and numerology, and the angles that belong to the aspects were, from Kepler's time on, pretty much considered from a strictly mathematical point of view, rather than from the sign where the planets were placed. This meant changing the traditional manner of reading the chart, where a planet was inseparably linked to its sign and where the sign was of considerable importance when thinking of aspects.[1] In the old days, as Greek sources report (think of Ptolemy), it was even the case that aspects were not seen as having an orb, but only used as "whole-sign" aspects.

For example: every planet in Aries, regardless of the degree was considered to be sextile to every planet in Aquarius, again regardless of the degree in which that planet was located. The reason for this was that Aries and Aquarius are sextile, and any planets located in these signs, because of their background, will also have a sextile-tendency to each other.

However, if you ignore the background sign when interpreting aspects, you will arrive at very strange combinations and encounter conflicting readings. For example: if you only look at the angle (the distance in degrees) as a mathematical given, then you'll see the 120° angle (with an orb, of course) between 29° Aries and 1° Virgo as a trine because the aspect is 122°, and falls within the effective range due to the allowed orb. However, the planets involved never work on their own; they are also colored by the sign in which they are placed.

Although Mercury always remains Mercury as such (representing such things as our way of talking, combining facts, and thinking), it will inevitably exhibit itself differently and express

---

[1] Walter Koch, *Aspektlehre nach Johannes Kepler* (Hamburg, 1952).

itself differently in Aries than it will in Taurus. So when interpreting an aspect, we can't just say that Mercury is in this or that aspect, but must first describe Mercury in greater detail in connection with its sign.

Let's say that in our example, we have Mercury at 29° Aries and the Moon at 1° Virgo.[2] What are these planets doing? Mercury in Aries will talk and think in the way of fire—rapidly and in broad terms. This is a Mercury that wants to take the world by storm, sees countless possibilities, smells adventure, and in this way combines facts and comes up with ideas. This Mercury will almost stumble over words when speaking, which he does enthusiastically, at full throttle, and with zeal. He might even blurt out all kinds of things. Details and the concrete material world are completely lost sight of. But not Moon in Virgo. This Moon will feel the most comfortable if it can direct itself at concrete reality, at what is tangible and can be experienced by the senses—at that which offers security. This Moon in Virgo has the most trouble with the insecurity of adventure and chasing after countless still intangible possibilities. A Moon in Virgo feels safe if it can calmly weigh things mentally and act cautiously. In fact, it is totally different and, with respect to feelings, even *in conflict* with Mercury in Aries. What are the implications for the trine without reference to sign?

A trine is always described as a harmonious and flexible connection between two planets that also work well together. But how is a taking-the-world-by-storm, adventuring Mercury in Aries supposed to work together flexibly and "go well with" an in his eyes inhibiting, sober Moon in Virgo with both feet on the ground who abhors adventure? Mercury in Aries' tempestuous thoughts and wrestling with possibilities are the very things that make cautious Moon in Virgo's hair stand on end! The chance that these two patterns of needs would have lots of trouble with each other and cause tensions in each other is overwhelming. However, had the Moon been located in the last degree of Leo, we would have had a trine whereby both the Moon and Mercury would be working from a fire basis. Aries and Leo are both fire signs, after all. In this case, the Moon would be truly able to appreciate Mercury's need for adventure and new possibilities, in addition to Mercury's enthusiastic way of talking about things. Okay, Leo is a fixed sign and therefore needs a bit more time than Aries, which is a cardinal sign. However, they have so much in common (fire) in terms of

---

[2] We all know that the Sun and Moon are not planets, but for the sake of easy conversation, we shall call them planets.

their orientation toward life, that they can tolerate a lot from each other. This situation certainly reflects the flexibility of a trine. This flexibility will, however, be missing from trines if there is no reference to sign. If an aspect like this, without reference to sign, no longer fits its basic meaning, is it still that aspect? In other words, can a trine, described as being flexible, still be a trine if it directly elicits tension and irritation? In my view, no, and I think we have to return to the older views, whereby the sign the planet is in is of overriding importance when interpreting an aspect.

Background Sign, Element, and Mode

Planets involved in aspects and aspect configurations are located in a sign, and therefore when interpreting these planets, the sign the planet is in plays a significant role. A sign in turn owes a great deal of its meaning to the fact that it belongs to a particular element, mode, and polarity (positive or negative sign).

Elements form ways of looking that, in Jungian terms, represent the functions of consciousness. Looking at things this way (automatically), is a big help when orienting ourselves in terms of the outside world. Even before we've thought about it, we're already busy ordering and labeling the facts and phenomena coming at us so we can give ourselves a handle on the world. Jung discovered in practice that consciousness has four different ways of orienting and looking, and they turn out to match the astrological elements perfectly. Although Jung was active in astrology, if we study the way he developed his typologies, we see very clearly that he did not derive his four function types from the astrological elements. It is therefore even more archetypal that they correspond so closely.

The four possible functions of consciousness that Jung distinguished we can clarify as follows:

—*Sensation Type* : Accepting something as it is and looking at how it is, for example: hard, sharp, warm, etc. Perception is primary. Considering anything not perceivable with the senses offers no handle for this way of seeing things, for this type is focused on the security of the concrete world and of the here and now: the future obviously cannot be grasped. This corresponds to the earth element.

—*Thinking Type*: Asking what the thing perceived actually is and how it can be classified in the current frame of reference. This type likes to look at things theoretically and strictly logically. The actions of those around, as well as this type's own actions, are seen from logical reasoning, and everything is rationally thought out and motivated as much as possible. This corresponds to the air element.

—*Feeling Type*: Imagining and experiencing all that is evoked by what is perceived, in the way of feelings of pleasure and displeasure, on the basis of which something will be accepted or rejected. Emotional values are important. This way of seeing also entails absorbing very subtle things of which this type is not necessarily always aware. A mood or intention will quickly be detected, and this becomes part of weighing issues. This corresponds to the water element.

—*Intuition Type*: (Unaware) Knowing or "imagining" where what is perceived comes from and/or how it will develop (as a possibility). In doing so, the object, as such, is often not even experienced with awareness. This is a kind of "grasping" or "seeing" of backgrounds. This is why Jung called it intuition, which is not the same as the astrological Uranus. The intuitive type is always in search of possibilities, backgrounds, and space. This corresponds to the fire element.

Planets located in a single element all orient themselves in the same way in terms of the outside world. In this respect, there is, in fact, a great mutual understanding among planets in the same element. Even when there is no question of a real trine within the allowed orb, a planet in Leo will feel comfortable with a planet in Sagittarius because they have the same orientation toward the world, and order the world around them in the same way. In earlier times, astrologers already remarked on this, and there was a time when all planets in Leo were considered to be trine to all planets in Sagittarius, due to their mutual understanding and the similarity in their way of looking, even though things were described differently back then.

However, Leo and Sagittarius each belong to a different mode. Each element consists of three signs, and these three signs all belong to different modes. Modes are involved in the way we tackle the problems we encounter, in our ways of coping with things, and in the flow of our psychic energy. There are three:

—*The Cardinal Mode*: Signs that belong to this mode cope with their problems best by insuring their place in their environment and/or by directing themselves toward the outside world or to those around them. The ways in which their environment plays a role can, however, vary greatly. For instance, you might need people around you in order to rebel against them, or to play a little contest with them (Aries), in order to be able to experience the impetus of emotions (Cancer), in order to effect compromises (Libra), or to execute them (Capricorn), just to give you a couple of simplified examples.

—*The Fixed Mode*: Copes precisely by withdrawing inwardly and shutting out the environment outside, so completely opposite to the cardinal mode. Fixed signs can psychically or literally "shut themselves up" and sit and brood until they come out of it. As long as they haven't come out of it, they won't bother about whether they're being "sociable" or "taking those around them into account." Fixed signs are definitely not asocial or antisocial, but need both time and space with problems to collect themselves again. It is not a question of unwillingness if something doesn't work; their inner world just hasn't become activated yet.

—*The Mutable Mode*: Mutable signs tend to seek out all kinds of ways first, so they can move on, and run the risk of thinking that their problems are already (almost) solved the moment they spot them. Or else they are so busy "clearing rubbish" that they forget to stop and consider the seriousness of their problems. They are capable of continuing quickly and picking up the thread again, but often after the fact will suddenly become aware, on a deeper level now, of what was actually wrong, and may still have to cope with it.

Planets that are located in different signs, but in the same mode, will cope with their problems in the same ways, but they will see their problems differently, because seeing depends on the element of the sign. Let's consider the signs Aries and Capricorn. They look at the world totally differently. However, if they have problems, they will both, each in their own way, want to do something in or with their environment in order to feel good again, and to have the feeling they can handle the world again.

Between Aries and Capricorn, there is another difference at work: Aries is a positive sign and Capricorn is a negative sign. The difference between the polarities is:

—*Positive*: Tends to take the initiative and to proceed to action. This polarity symbolizes the need to do something and to handle it instead of waiting. Likes to have the helm in hand. This polarity represents a facet of yang. Signs: fire and air signs.

—*Negative*: Tends to acquire an idea of what all is wrong, first. Needs time and feels more comfortable looking around first, and then responding. This polarity therefore waits for the first action, then proceeds to action—reactive, in other words, instead of taking the initiative. This polarity represents a facet of yin. Signs: earth and water signs.

It is always the case with an aspect that if your psyche is doing something with one kind of subject matter (meaning one planet), and harnesses it, as it were, all the other planets with which it is in aspect will be jumping to join in. And they will quickly start interfering, and so start to color the action or effect of the subject matter you harnessed. The books describe Moon in Taurus as being tranquil, but you should see when a person with Moon in Taurus has Uranus in an aspect to the Moon. Then, most definitely, restlessness and speediness come into play!

So, except when a planet is an unaspected planet, it never stands alone, and will always be involved in other energies. Those other planets, however, aren't located in a void. Their effect bears the stamp of their placement in an element, in a mode, and in a polarity. Then the question is which of the planet's signs will "color" the aspected planet and which will not. In an aspect pattern or configuration, such as a grand trine, a grand square, a kite, or a yod, to name only a few, it comes down to a complicated interaction of all kinds of factors that determine the interpretation.

Backgrounds of Aspect Configurations or Patterns

The planets in a grand trine are always located in a particular element. There are four elements. This means that we have four kinds of grand trines: a fire, an earth, a water, and an air variety. Two of these elements belong to the positive signs and two to the negative. As a result, two of the four possible grand trines belong to the "positive" variety and two to the "negative." The words positive and negative should not be considered in the popular sense, but in the sense of action— yang (positive), and reaction—or yin (negative). If we are talking about the grand trine, we should always keep in mind that there are various kinds, which of course have consequences for interpretation.

Another example: In a grand square, the four planets involved are located within the same mode, so therefore in a cardinal, fixed, or mutable mode. The signs involved, though, are all in different elements. A grand square involves two positive and two negative signs. The structure of a grand square is therefore different in its make-up from that of a grand trine.

Planets' signs are an important component of interpretation, and are an essential part of reading an aspect pattern. When an aspect pattern has a similar orientation, the effect of that pattern will be flexible. Planets involved in a grand trine all have the same orientation to the world because the signs the planets are in involve the same element. And all three will have either an active or a reactive approach, depending on whether the grand trine is in positive or negative signs. The only thing that differs in a grand trine is how the planets cope with things: the modes are different. But, if orientation and the way of reacting lie in the same line, there is coordination without friction, so that very little tension is elicited. Considering that modes primarily have to do with coping, the fact that no tension is elicited will insure that the presence of three different modes in a grand trine doesn't necessarily lead to problems. (See figure 1, page 9.)

The situation presented by a grand square is very different. Here we have four different ways of looking at a situation because there are four different elements taking part. (See figure 2, page 10.) This also means that one of the four always belongs to the inferior or unconscious function. Four different orientations imply tension and conflict. Although it is true that the signs involved in a grand square belong to a single mode, so that the tension will be approached and coped with in a single way, within that grand square we have two signs that are positive (yang), and two that are negative (yin). Consequently, some of the participants in a grand square will immediately want to proceed to action (yang) and some will want to wait and respond to coming impetuses (yin). In the tension among the various ways of seeing and coping, there is some fishtailing between the tendency to proceed to action in actuality or just not right away.

These examples of the grand trine and the grand square show that simply by looking at the role of the background signs of the planets involved, we can gain good insight into the meaning and effect of aspect patterns.

The Inconjunct and the Yod

A yod consists of two inconjuncts with a sextile at the base, and one of the points involved can be the Ascendant or the MC instead of a planet. The inconjunct, also sometimes called the quincunx (Lat.: five-twelfths), plays an important part. It is an aspect where the planets or points involved are at a distance of 150° from each other, and where only a small orb is allowed.

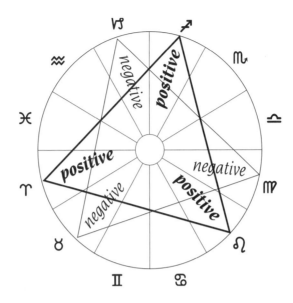

Figure 1. The grand trine. The positive (or yang) trine is a grand fire
trine and the negitive (or yin) trine is a
grand earth trine.

It is remarkable that this aspect simply was not studied, or
was considered to be minor for so long, although this has fortunately changed over the last decades. This aspect is not new. Johannes Kepler referred to the 150° aspect and describes it as
"cutting sharply." Koch, who analyzed Kepler's study of aspects,
describes the aspect as a "clearly splitting tendency that sets both
possibilities in clear-cut opposition to each other."[3] In his view, it
indicates limitations and disappointment, because the situation
insists on a decision.[4] With the quincunx, we would tend to look
only at the opportunity that was missed, and not at the one that
was realized. We will have to understand the inconjunct if we
want to be able to interpret a yod.

An inconjunct is formed by two planets (or by the MC, ASC,
or a planet) that are five signs apart (a sign is 30°, and 5° x 30° =
150°). These signs will belong to different elements, different qua-
druplicities, and different polarities: if the one "leg" is negative,

---

[3] Walter Koch, *Aspektlehre nach Johannes Kepler*, p. 319. Also *Sonderdruck der Astrologis-
chen Montatshefte* (Hamburg: Kosmobiosophische Gesellschaft e. V.), p. 89.
[4] There have also been more modern publications about the inconjunct, such as Sakoian and Acker's (1972) and Alan Epstein's (1984; 1996).

then the other will be "positive." Take the sign Cancer, for instance, to start with. From there, two inconjuncts can be formed: one to Sagittarius and one to Aquarius (five signs to the right and to the left). Cancer is a negative sign, a sign that waits and responds. The two signs with which Cancer can make an inconjunct, Sagittarius and Aquarius, belong to the positive signs, those that don't want to wait, but want to be the first to proceed to action.

As far as the elements are concerned: Cancer is water, Sagittarius is fire, and Aquarius is air. No similarity in orientation here, because the background elements are different. And as far as the modes are concerned: Cancer is a cardinal sign, Aquarius is a fixed sign, and Sagittarius is mutable. The result is that the difference in orientation (the background element) and the difference in positive/negative nature can lead to tensions. In order to be able to handle that stress and to cope with problems, it's best to use one of the modes. Each of the modes copes in its own way. In an inconjunct there are two modes, however, and each of the points involved wants to tackle the problems in a different way, which causes the stress to increase. Based on the analysis of the background signs involved, we conclude that the inconjunct is a combination of signs that are not compatible and that tends to step up the tension even more.

I have noticed that the role of the distinction between positive and negative signs in aspect configurations is significant, more significant than often appears from the literature. Just look at the sextile. It consists of two signs that are different regarding element as

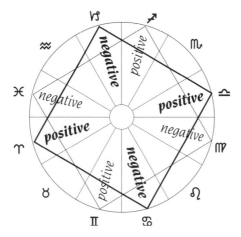

Figure 2. A grand square. The heavy lines indicate a
cardinal square and the lighter lines show a mutable square.

well as mode. But they have a similar nature, either positive or negative. That agreement in proceeding to action immediately or not helps compensate for the difference in orientation. A sextile is always between air and fire (positive signs) or water and earth (negative signs). The sextile also has some tension because of the differences in orientation (element) and coping (mode), which is also noticeable in the discussion of the sextile. It is true that it is seen as a friendly or harmonious aspect, but sometimes it is seen as an aspect that lends insecurity, and what it promises we won't get for free. We'll still have to work hard for it, unlike with the trine where it all comes together more rapidly.

An inconjunct is therefore a troublesome aspect. We might say that the planets involved don't understand each other's worlds at all. Those who work from the Jungian study of elements distinguish two kinds of inconjuncts: those where the signs involved relate in an inferior-superior way and those where that is not the case. Jung emphasized in his practice that that there are four ways in which people orient themselves in the world outside. Not only are these four mutually exclusive, but each type of orientation or function of consciousness results in its opposite remaining unconscious. He distinguished the following four functions, which are linked in astrology to the following four elements:

Thinking = *Air*
Feeling = *Water*
Sensation = *Earth*
Intuition = *Fire*

For a thinking type (air), the orientation of feeling (water) keeps working from the unconscious; for a sensation type (earth) the orientation of intuition (fire) is unconscious. Jung referred to a superior function where the type that we "are" is concerned, or the orientation of consciousness (astrologically reflected by the Sun). The psychological function opposing this, which remains in the unconscious, he called the inferior function.

Astrologically, we get the following polarity if we work from the Jungian view: air versus water and fire versus earth. (For a detailed analysis and further explanation of this, see *Psychological Astrology* and *Elements and Modes as Basis of the Horoscope*.[5]

---

[5] Both Books were published by Samuel Weiser. *Psychological Astrology* (1990) was also issued by the Aquarian Press in London; *Elements and Modes as the Basis of the Horoscope* is now included in *Foundations of Personality* (1994).

This way of looking at things has major consequences for an inconjunct, because an inconjunct that has air-water or fire-earth as background signs will have an even harder time of it than when air-earth or fire-water background signs are involved. So in our example using Cancer, the inconjunct between Cancer (water) and Aquarius (air) is more troublesome than the one between Cancer (water) and Sagittarius (fire). Although the latter pair is under sufficient tension simply because an inconjunct happens to be that way.

A yod, as we saw, is an aspect configuration with two inconjuncts from a single point, with a sextile forming the base. Let's take a look at the signs involved to gain more insight into the tension in a yod:

- A yod links three planets that are each in different elements.
- A yod links three planets that are each in different modes.
- The top of a yod always belongs to a different polarity (positive or negative) than do the points linked by the sextile at the base.
- Of the two legs of a yod, one always has the extra superior-inferior stress.

If we consider Cancer, again, as an example (see figure 3, page 13) we see the following: three modes are involved in the Yod, so three different motivations and needs for coping; Cancer is negative and prefers to wait, Aquarius and Sagittarius are positive and would prefer to proceed to action right away.

We know that all the planets that are in aspect to a planet, or a point, have the tendency to interfere as soon as we activate or "harness" the planet or point involved. However, as we were able to see above, a planet does not work with its own pure energy, but with an energy that gets channeled through the sign in which it is located. For a yod, this means that should the planet in Cancer be activated, to stick to our example, the other two "legs" of the yod, those in Aquarius and Sagittarius, want to join in and intervene. If the planet in Cancer wants to see based on its own feeling and experience, the planet in Aquarius will object and will intentionally place a mental vision in the foreground. With a Cancer background, the planets in this sign tend to become more conservative and direct themselves at their immediate environment. And this again is something that the Sagittarius background resists, because it really wants to see things in a broad perspective, and to look farther than the end of its nose.

We see the same kind of problem with a T-square: for instance a planet in Aries (fire) square a planet in Cancer (water) oppose a planet in Libra (air). There are three elements here as well. This always provides a solid basis of tension, and as soon as stresses and problems start occurring, two other mechanisms come into play: the necessity of coping (the modes) and the necessity to do something actively, or positively (the positive/negative polarity).

The T-square is similar to the yod in that the positive/negative polarity is also under tension. After all, for both the yod and the T-square, one of the points involved is in another polarity than the other two. In our example of the yod, Cancer is negative, and Sagittarius and Aquarius positive. In the example of the T-square, Cancer is negative, Aries and Libra positive. For both the yod and the T-square this adds inner tension, because one part of the aspect wants to proceed to action and go at it, while the other part wants to wait and see which way the wind is blowing.

So, double tension in a yod (as well as in a T-square) is due to the combination of three elements and the tension of polarities. This strengthens the necessity of coping inwardly and coming to terms with the dynamic that arose. And therein lies the big difference between a T-square and a yod: in a T-square all the points

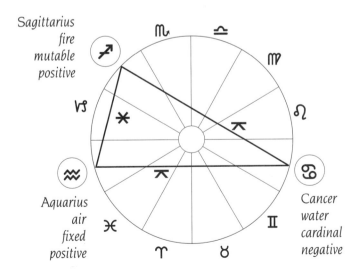

Figure 3. A yod is formed between a sextile and two inconjuncts.

involved are in the same mode, and will cope with and mull over a problem in the same way. In our example, Aries, Cancer, and Libra are all in the cardinal mode, and someone with this T-square will cope in a "cardinal" way. In order to deal with problems, people with this T-square will direct themselves at the outside world and want to experience and affirm their role there, after which they will be able to cope again. With a yod, things aren't that simple. Here the three points of the yod are each in a different mode. Therefore, if the first point is cardinal (Cancer, in our example), this point will want to direct itself at the outside world and want to do something in it, even if only to make things more sociable. The positive feedback will then give it a feeling it can move on again. But the fixed point (Aquarius, in our example) is directly opposed, and will want to force the participants in the yod to turn inward and not pay any attention to those around them. This point *has* to mull and brood in order to cope again, and the "cardinal" leg makes it nervous, because it makes it lose its center. The "cardinal" leg, however, is made nervous precisely by the "fixed" leg, because the fixed mode wants to pull it to its inner world and that isn't something that makes the cardinal mode feel comfortable, and is certainly not a mechanism for being able to face something. On the contrary, this only makes it feel worse. And the mutable leg (Sagittarius here) can offend the other two by either acting as if nothing's wrong, or ending up in all kinds of escapist activities that have nothing at all to do with the problem, getting around to coping only later. And just as the other two are starting to come out of it, it will cause problems.

Even though this explanation may seem a little black and white, it does describe the essence of the problems with a yod: there is no agreement, none whatsoever, among the three participants. The ways of looking differ (the elements), the tendency to action or reaction differs (the polarities), and if something needs to be coped with, the participants will be all over one another! So, turbulence and agitation, insecurity, and instability are the result. If we tally it all, there are three elements, two polarities, and three modes. Three plus two plus three is eight. In fact, the three participants in a yod are located in eight different "worlds"!

Once we understand how signs are constructed and how they color the effect of the planets, we will immediately gain additional insight into the effect of aspect patterns. In the literature on yods it is occasionally claimed that a yod might have a kind of 6th-8th-house meaning: from Aries, both of the other legs are located in Virgo and Scorpio, the 6th and 8th signs, after all. And even aside from the fact that you could also take starting points other than Aries and get very different meanings, I think the dynamics of a yod can be understood a lot better from the structure of the signs involved.

Orbs

Another important technical issue is the question of orbs. An orb is the allowable deviation in degrees to either side, measured from the exact point within which the aspect is still valid, or still works. There is no unequivocal opinion about orbs in astrology, but with regard to yods there are a couple of things we need to consider.

The aspect reflects an angle of 150°, five whole signs. It has been consigned to the minor aspects for a long time, but nowadays is considered major by many. This is why this aspect is also granted an orb appropriate for a major aspect, an orb that is much bigger than that granted the minor aspects. Table 1, below, lists the aspects by their angles, so we can see see which problems the 150° presents concerning orbs.

Now imagine that you give the inconjunct an orb of 6°. Thus it is supposed to work between 150° − 6° and 150° + 6°, so it has a reach from 144° to 156°. However, if we look on the list of minor aspects, then we see that 144° is a biquintile, and that this

Table 1. Major and Minor Aspects and Orbs.

DEGREES	MAJOR ASPECTS	ORB	DEGREES	MINOR ASPECTS	ORB
0°	CONJUNCTION	6°	18°	VIGINTILE	1°
60°	SEXTILE	4°	30°	SEMI-SEXTILE	2°
90°	SQUARE	6°	36°	DECILE	2°
120°	TRINE	6°	40°	NOVILE	2°
180°	OPPOSITION	6°	45°	SEMI-SQUARE	2°
			51°25′43″	SEPTILE	1°
150°	INCONJUNCT	. . .	72°	QUINTILE	2°
			108°	TREDECILE	2°
			135°	ONE-AND-ONE-HALF SQUARE	2°
			144°	BIQUINTILE	2°

aspect has an orb of 2°. In other words: the biquintile (with a totally different meaning and interpretation) works from 144° – 2° to 144° + 2°, and has a reach from 142° to 146°.

So, if we grant the inconjunct an orb of 6°, then it overlaps considerably with another aspect, the biquintile. Epstein, in his book about the inconjunct, even grants this aspect an orb of 8°, so that the inconjunct completely overlaps and swallows up the biquintile. He believes a larger orb is also possible.

There is, therefore, a large theoretical problem here, and we must be aware of it before we start working with an inconjunct. Duly considered, there are two possible choices:

- Either we leave the minor aspects totally out of consideration and allow a large orb for the inconjunct;
- Or else we take the minor aspects seriously and allow a small orb for the inconjunct.

So we can only allow a large orb for the inconjunct if we consider the minor aspects to be ineffective, unimportant, or unnecessary. In all other cases there is a maximum limit for the inconjunct of 4 degrees of orb: 150° – 4° = 146°, and this is the outer limit of the biquintile. There is still always the question as to whether there is a blank zone between two aspects, so a zone without aspect effects, or whether there is a sharp border. If we assume a blank zone, the inconjunct can take an orb of a maximum of 3° to 3.5°.

Personally, I use an orb of three degrees. That's safe, and in practice we see the inconjunct working itself out very clearly with this orb. However, I have a number of examples where an orb of 3.5° still showed indications that agreed with my experiences of an inconjunct—where one of 4° no longer did. This means that I hover between an orb of 3° and a maximum of 3.5°, but for reasons of safety I will not go any farther than 3° in this book. And as I already pointed out, I work with aspects exclusively with reference to sign.

The Points

In investigating and working with yods, it has consistently been the case that the yod exhibits its characteristics particularly when the points involved are planets. One of the three may be the Ascendant or the MC. Planets are psychic motivators and dynamics that provide the needed movement. This movement is brought out through the angles, or more specifically, the MC or the Ascendant.

Horoscope factors, such as the nodes or the Part of Fortune, are of a very different order; in any case, they are not psychically dynamic. My experience is that these last cannot be full-fledged participants in a yod configuration. As my knowledge about and insight into yod configurations grew, it became clear to me that yods limit themselves to planets, the ASC, and the MC. This is the reason why I do not discuss the nodes and angles as "legs" of a yod in this book. I particularly doubt that they have any effect in this aspect pattern.

CHAPTER TWO

Unaspected Planets

Major Aspects, Minor Aspects, and Orbs

Aspects form a vital component of the interpretation of the natal chart. They link the planets that are the active and dynamic factors of the horoscope. Each link means that a piece of our psychic energy is making contact with another part, and that these parts not only influence each another and can work together (or work against each other), it is also particularly true that they *see* each other and experience each other consciously. This makes it possible for us to get to know ourselves.

It does, however, happen that one or more planets do not receive or make any major aspects. They stand apart, and are therefore unintegrated. They have no direct influence on other planets (or psychic dynamics), and are themselves also not influenced, so they can exhibit extremes in their effects. We notice this particularly in an all-or-nothing attitude: quick to exaggerate, or precisely the opposite: not responsive in the least. In any case, whether a planet is unaspected depends particularly on the question of how large an orb we use. If we allow very large orbs, then there is little chance of having unaspected planets. If, however, we allow very small orbs, there is in fact a greater chance of having one or more unaspected planets. So, if we want to involve unaspected planets in our interpretation, we will first need to think about the question of orbs. And with this issue, unaspected planets can be of service to us.

The characteristics of an unaspected planet are very specific. If a planet in its expression also bears the characteristic of an unaspected planet, then it is likely that it is not, in fact, making any aspects. If you allow large orbs, for instance of 10° or more, as was still occasionally customary some time ago, then this planet may possibly still make one or more aspects, which would not exist using a smaller orb. However, if the planet is working as an unaspected one, we will obviously need to use smaller orbs. On the contrary, it is likewise true that if a planet is unaspected when using very small orbs, but the person in question doesn't reveal the characteristic expression of this in practice, we know we will have to allow somewhat more leeway in orbs. In studying aspects, I have looked at both major and minor aspects. Whenever planets made exclusively minor aspects (see chapter 1 for an overview), they seemed to work like unaspected planets. This is why, in my experience, a planet is unaspected if it makes no major aspects. The minor ones evidently do not play a part in this.

Researching the effect of unaspected planets finally also led me to particular orbs for aspects, and these are the orbs I will be using. (See Table 2, below.) With unaspected planets, the issue is about aspects made to other psychic dynamics, meaning planets. If a planet aspects the Ascendant or the MC, but not other planets, it will in practice turn out to have the characteristics of an isolated planet. We will, of course, learn to recognize a planet in aspect with an angle, meaning with the ASC or the MC, a bit sooner.

General Characteristics of Unaspected Planets

If we have an unaspected planet in the horoscope, it is very likely that we aren't really very aware of all the things we do with it and how strongly we bring this planet to expression in daily life. An unaspected planet manifests itself unmistakably though! However, just to clear up a couple of misconceptions right off the bat: an unaspected planet is *not* weak, *not* insignificant, and *not* bad. On the contrary, many people who have achieved extraordinary things turn out to have had help in doing so from an unaspected planet in the horoscope. With unaspected planets, the question is not, therefore, whether we can achieve anything with them, because we definitely can. Instead, the question is how we go about it and how that feels inside.

Table 2. Aspects and Orbs.

Aspect	MC, ASC, Planets in Relation to One Another	Sun and Moon in Relation to Each Other and to Other Planets
Conjunction	6°	8°
Sextile	4°	6°
Square	6°	8°
Trine	6°	8°
Inconjunct	3° (possibly 3.5°)	3° (possibly 3.5°)
Opposition	6°	8°

In Search—Preoccupation

An isolated planet has to do everything by itself. At first it even seems like the other subject matter inside us doesn't see this piece of us. That's why we don't get to know it very quickly. Somewhere, though, deep inside, we do know it's there. This isn't so much a conscious knowing, but more an implicit knowing. It makes us tend to keep searching for that piece of ourselves, that planet. To our feeling, it is a "faraway" given, and if this concerns a skill or activity, we'll have the idea that we aren't ready to do it by a long shot and "maybe never will learn," without there being any demonstrable proof of this. That inner feeling is usually pretty strong, and if one little thing goes wrong, we tend to lend it a lot more weight than necessary.

So, we go off in search of the subject matter of that planet. Some domains that are appropriate to that planet even hold a sort of magical or mysterious kind of attraction. Once I met a boy with an unaspected Mercury who, at a very early age, was fascinated by pencils and pens (objects appropriate to Mercury). Whenever his parents couldn't find any, all they had to do was go to his room and that's where they would find just about all the writing utensils they had in the house! He simply couldn't keep his hands off them. No matter what his parents did—from asking in a friendly way to leave the pens where they belonged, to giving him a big set of his own pens, to punishing him—nothing worked. Each pen had its own fascination. Mercury can, of course, also entail lots of other things, so a fascination can also lie in other Mercury domains. For this boy, it was pens.

Precisely because of this fascination and our "being in search of," we will be preoccupied with an unaspected planet, but won't ourselves be aware of it at all. The problem is, namely, that there are no other planets that provide any contact with this isolated planet, so that at first we don't see all the things we do with it. We simply don't recognize it, and aren't able to place it, like the boy with his pens. He simply didn't understand that he had a few too many of them in his room. It's as if everything we do with that planet somehow or other isn't to be fathomed, knows no moderation, or isn't to be controlled. This, by the way, doesn't have to be the case forever. Over the course of life we will have several chances to gain insight into this: other planets will naturally start creating aspects with it in transit and progression, and in those periods will make contact with that subject matter. Then we suddenly take a big step forward and see what we're doing, or come closer to deeper longings and character traits. And the unaspected planet itself will start creating aspects in progression and transit as well. So there will be plenty of chances to learn moderation and to figure ourselves out. Initially, though, things will be tough.

However, it seems as if our unconscious wants to help in every way to start seeing the subject matter of that unaspected planet. If we are preoccupied with the energy or domain of that planet, the chance that various things will start getting through to us is better, of course, and we will also begin to recognize this kind of planet sooner that way. But a long running start is still needed for this, and in the meantime we are not aware to what extent those around are confronted by this unintegrated planet. Our emphasizing it means those around us will already have experienced the full weight of it and will have to endure more before we have even the slightest inkling of what we're up to. In fact, if we hear remarks or criticism about it, we will in all honesty not have a clue what they're talking about.

For example: A client has a son with an unaspected Mars. He is an extremely lively and active little boy, so maybe the description "the height of restlessness and energy" would be better. He sleeps little and is always nearby making lots of noise. He is a radiant child who is clearly enjoying life. He (still) isn't aware of how much difficulty his parents are having with this. They are understanding and patient (and love their peace and quiet!), but often he's too much for them. They were unable to grasp that even after years of asking him if he couldn't just sit *still* at the table, he still always kicked, danced, and knocked things over due to the restlessness of his movements. His mother told me once that her son, while yelling, was drumming on the table with his silverware, barely missing his plate, and thereby creating a situation where his parents were unable to say a single word to each other. Mars was clearly active. When she finally exclaimed, "Now, can't you sit still for just one minute?" her son looked at her in utter surprise and even denied that he had made any noise or done anything. This is a critical problem for children with unaspected planets. Every parent who knows something about unaspected planets will know that a child doesn't *really* see what he or she is doing, and the boy in this case may honestly be *totally* surprised at his mother's remark. It is very possible that he felt he hadn't even begun to drum and shout. It unmistakably remains a fact, however, that he was already at it and producing a barrelful of noise. Most parents would react with some form of annoyance—after all, why is the child denying this? Does the child also want to be contrary? And why does the child keep denying it? After all, it's obvious he is doing it! Sure, for *outsiders* it's clear that he was doing it. He is the only one who doesn't see it.

The fascination that an unaspected planet exerts on its "owner," coupled with an orientation toward the domain of that planet,[1] largely contribute to the development of the talent that particular planet promises. Unnoticed, we develop many facets of this energy by continually being preoccupied with it, but as soon as we start understanding and recognizing this energy a little more, it holds even more potential. The fascination and the quest give us focus on—and at the same time an orientation toward—a particular domain. Frequently, people choose the domain of the unaspected planet as their profession, or otherwise use the energy of this planet in their daily lives. This is certainly possible, and can be done with great joy and very consciously. I once saw a sports teacher (she has an emphasized 5th house) with an unaspected Venus finally change profession: she became a cosmetologist.

Insecurity and the Unaspected Planet

Another hallmark of unaspected planets is that they are often accompanied by feelings of insecurity. This insecurity is connected to a number of things. In the first place, the idea of "being in search of," that often expresses itself in a kind of restless feeling, I sometimes try to describe as a feeling of "hunger," or "yearning," or "being unfulfilled" in the area of that planet. A longing, too, but for *what* we don't know. It can't be described; it is diffuse and vague, and we can't really make anybody see what it's all about. Even if we have everything our hearts desire, this feeling can *still* be there. So it has absolutely nothing to do with external circumstances or with whatever we've achieved in life.

An unaspected Moon, for instance, can have a deep longing for security and a profound need for warmth, and even run the risk of not seeing the warmth that is there (but this is not on purpose!) because of a gnawing feeling that overrides it.

Or, to give an example of Venus: A couple of years ago a couple consulted me and asked for an astrological analysis of their relationship. They had been married almost thirty years, but the woman was in a kind of crisis. She didn't know if she loved her

---

[1] I have used the word "domain" to describe the world of the planet: each planet "rules" some aspect of life, certain material things, and carries its own energy. For example, Saturn rules parts of the body, mining, land, feelings of lack, etc., and any part of life touched by this planet is in its "domain."

husband, or if she had ever loved him, and claimed she didn't really know what love actually was. Her husband didn't take this personally. His commentary was simple and honest, "We've gotten along very well together all these years, and I just know she loves me, and I love her. So something else must be going on, and that's why we're here." His wife, however, had gotten hold of the nagging thought that she didn't know what love was, and therefore also didn't know if she loved her husband.

Her Venus created no aspects whatsoever! After I had explained what an unaspected planet meant in general, and how an unaspected Venus works in particular, something finally clicked in her. She understood that the unfulfilled and searching feeling was inside herself and had nothing to do with her marriage. "If I look back at it that way," she said, "then we have in fact gotten along very well together all these years, and I wouldn't want to be without my husband." There was a moment of silence, and then she said, "Maybe that's what love is. Maybe I shouldn't be getting myself so worked up about it anymore, and accept that I can't catch or grasp it all." This is a nice example of how, with an unaspected planet, we can run the risk of misjudging a situation because with all that "searching" we begin to mull and fret. Just as often, though, all that searching has yet another result, namely the idea that we "aren't there yet," or can't do certain things. In the case of the unaspected Venus, this can express itself in a feeling that others don't think we're nice, or that we weren't cut out for love, or that we feel inferior because of our looks and/or emotions. In every instance this feeling does not corroborate the real situation or talents and capabilities. Once again though, the fact is that we don't see it *at first.* And even with an unaspected Venus, we *can* be very sweet, mediate very well, and have a finely tuned sense of harmony! Hidden in an unaspected planet like this is a great talent waiting to be discovered.

All or Nothing with the Unaspected Planet

Since an unaspected planet has no contact with other planets, this means that its energy can go in any direction, and cannot always be coordinated. Planets can influence the energy of another planet through aspects, twist it, even possibly funnel it, or else stimulate it. However, with aspects there is always a situation in which the planets have to take one another into account, as it were. With an unintegrated planet, this isn't the case, and this is why such a planet can express itself extremely one minute and be completely absent the next, which is actually the other extreme.

When is a planet like this absent? Precisely at all those times when it's needed! If we want to call on this energy, we will have to "harness" it. But it can also be the case that at a critical moment we "can't find" it. Just then when we *have to* do something, it seems to have disappeared, to return a short while later when it isn't needed anymore. In this way, athletes with an unaspected Mars might be very good athletes and win a lot of competitions, as long as everything is treated like a game and they aren't put under pressure. But the moment others start expecting them to win, and they "have to harness Mars," Mars can disappear suddenly just like that and they won't have the fighting power or the energy at hand to make something of the competition. An unaspected planet is allergic to being forced! And just when the newspapers start reporting how crazy it is that these athletes brilliantly managed to win all the unimportant races, but remained inexplicably below par in major events, they will have a tremendous burst of energy at another major event and outdo themselves. Then Mars suddenly lets its opposite side be seen. Thus unaspected planets are characterized by a kind of all-or-nothing reaction, whereby the "nothing" happens quite a lot when there should be something, and the "all" just when a little less would have done.

This doesn't have to remain the same all throughout life, though. We can learn to live with it. After all, an unaspected planet often turns out to be a talent, and we can learn to use it as such, as long as we look at our feelings of restlessness in a different way.

Let 's look at another example. A client with an unaspected Sun was working for a midsize company when economically hard times hit and things began to go wrong. She confessed that she was really bothered by feelings of inferiority and preferred to stay in the background. She couldn't understand why some of her colleagues called her domineering or said that whenever *she* was there, she was always palpably there or wanting attention. According to her this was absolutely not the case. I also noticed during the consultation that the woman had "something" that gave me the feeling she was domineering. She had come to me because she was in a panic. She had been offered a leadership function in the company and was at her wits' end regarding the offer. She was convinced that she was absolutely not up to being in a leadership role, and that this offer had to be based on some terrible mistake. Exactly! An unaspected Sun: one of its talents is leadership! She didn't see that though. I asked her if in the past she hadn't exhibited an ability to tackle things and make decisions quickly and satisfactorily. This was indeed the case.

During the company's rapid downswing, she had spontaneously and very directly made a number of decisions and told colleagues what they should do. She had stimulated others to tackle things instead of throwing in the towel, and in fact had clearly evinced leadership and organizational talents. She said this, however, as if she were talking about somebody else, and when I pointed out to her that this really had been her, and that she had been successful, her evasive answer was, "Yes, but that success was an accident . . ." Just as if she just *couldn't* see that she had simply been valuable during that time. At that time, however, she had not been asked to do anything, and her actions had come about spontaneously. Now something was being asked of her Sun, and now it seemed to be crawling away.

If something like this happens and we have an unaspected planet, the best thing to do is simply relax and to realize that this insecurity, and even the denial, are simply hallmarks of the effect of an unaspected planet, but this doesn't mean that we can't do anything! So it shouldn't hold us back. We should simply accept that we will have to move on through a phase of insecurity with steps like this, but after that it'll turn out that we are very capable. Learning to trust the energy of an unaspected planet is therefore a very important step.

It took some time to make it clear to this woman that her unaspected Sun was actually a good thing, and she was denying her qualities in the affiliated domain. Finally she admitted understanding that she had, in fact, done important things for the company. With shaky knees she accepted the leadership position, and now she's doing fine. She has learned to relax and learned to accept her restlessness and insecurity regarding this point.

Ambivalence

In spite of the problems we have discussed, we can have lots of fun in the area of an unaspected planet. Think again of the boy with his pens. He thought it was awesome, and he was in seventh heaven when he was busy with them. Children are absorbed in their play, and children with unaspected planets are just the same. The result is that when the atmosphere is relaxed, feelings of happiness, pleasure, and joy are associated with that unaspected planet, and this will automatically make children feel good. Even when we are older this is a possibility! Usually, though, it requires that there are no pressures, obligations, or demands, but a natural flow of energy and a relaxed atmosphere. Then we see that a planet like this very much "becomes itself," and can express it-self totally according to its own nature. This also feels nice.

In the other example, the boy with the unaspected Mars was having lots of fun with the noise he was making, just as the woman who claimed she didn't know what love was still expressed her Venus in a real Venusian way in her life. After all, without it she would never have been able to have had a good marriage lasting over thirty years. Also the woman who finally accepted a leadership position managed to remember after some reflection that she had felt pretty good when she had been so active tackling the problems the company was having. Everyone who has an unaspected planet will experience clearly positive expressions of it. What strikes me from time to time is that the hallmarks of such a planet are so recognizable and come out so purely. Of course there's a reason for this, and that is that the unaspected planet does not undergo any influence from other planets. The only thing that colors it is the background of the sign in which it is located. So an unaspected planet can be itself to a very significant degree.

We can experience many happy moments with our unaspected planets. This is why it is so difficult to cope with the fact—and also so absurd—that with the same energy, but under other circumstances, we can suddenly lose our way, snap shut, become insecure, and be confronted by a lack of self-confidence. Sometimes a number of those difficult experiences can overshadow the positive ones. Then we identify more with recurring difficult expressions that seem unpredictable, and meanwhile forget that there are so many fine things to be experienced with that planet.

Those who begin to see what's going on will notice another ambivalence, because they are starting to *see* some of the reactions, attitudes, expectations, and actions connected with the unaspected planet, but other parts not at all, yet. It's just as if we have to conquer an unaspected planet bit by bit every time another piece is added to the puzzle. Each time we tend tentatively not to identify at all with this new piece, so that what still needs to be "conquered" stays out of sight.

On the one hand we will have the feeling that we have that energy in our sights, while the same energy can still present an all-or-nothing attitude in particular domains, and can be accompanied by searching or insecurity. Don't get discouraged. Maybe it's good to realize that if we are aware that insecurity can be the price of a talent, it means that we're already on the way to getting the hang of an unaspected planet!

Relating to the Energy

The central theme that came out of all the previous examples was that when we have an unaspected planet, we need to learn to relate to that energy, which means seeing that energy in relation to ourselves. This is absolutely essential. As long as we don't do this, and also don't see how we behave, our unconscious will confront us with the theme, and that means that we will encounter it by projecting it on others, as well as experiencing it in the circumstances and events of our lives. I even ran into this very literally, as the following example will illustrate.

Mars has traditionally been associated with everything that is sharp. Wasps also fall under Mars. In my practice I have had various clients with an unaspected Mars, and they have all had some problem or other with wasps. A couple of them turned out to have a wasps' nest in their homes. One had a nest hanging in the attic and he discovered this because he kept hearing a strange soft humming noise. The nest had to be removed by local exterminators—it was one of the biggest ones that had ever been found in a private home in the Netherlands!

So, with unaspected planets it takes longer before we see what we want and what we are doing. This will entail quite a few problems from the point of view of raising children. Children with unaspected Jupiters will have a strong tendency to exaggerate on all fronts. If given a piece of candy, they will usually ask for another one right away, as if they think that they didn't get enough. However, asked why they want another piece of candy, they won't be able to answer. This is not a question of greed or of feeling short-changed. The unaspected Jupiter seems to want to multiply everything, including the number of candies the children get.

For parents, it is difficult to understand what's really going on, because they keep seeing that the child wants more. If we know nothing about unaspected planets or what they do, the obvious conclusion is that the child is greedy, or is only thinking of himself or herself, and so on. So the parents decide to approach the child about this behavior, because it's not appropriate. If their efforts turn out to have no effect, and the child simply keeps up the old behavior, the parents won't understand that the child's not doing this on purpose. After all, it is abundantly clear what's happening! And so the child is placed under more and more pressure and gets into trouble, when the child has no clue about the issue. This is not only very confusing for the child, it can also have harmful consequences farther down the line.

Just imagine the world of experience of that child. The child doesn't see what he or she is doing, and so can't understand the scolding. The child feels misunderstood. If punishments follow because "the child just doesn't want to listen," the child will feel rejected, and there is a big chance that he or she will begin to feel unsure, misunderstood, and insecure. Many problems that we have as adults with unaspected planets are not so much locked up in these unaspected planets as such, but derive from what we experienced around their themes when we were young. We can't, however, blame or find fault with the parents for what went wrong. After all, they honestly tried to civilize their child to protect it from social problems later on. And where that polishing seems to succeed with other children, it won't catch on or much less so with the child who has an unaspected planet. For this child, the situation arises where he or she may feel desperate under all that polishing, because he or she doesn't have a clue, while the parents feel equally desperate because they can't do a thing with this child. Insight into unaspected planets can help us stay out of this spiral.

However, insight into a child's unaspected planets will also create new problems. If we have an understanding of the expressions of the child's unaspected planet, we will tend to tolerate the extremes in behavior a lot more. We understand what's involved, and want to give the child safety and security above all. Certainly if we understand that a child can experience these crazy contradictions regarding an unaspected planet—on the one hand great joy and pleasure, on the other the frequently arising insecurity—we will try to give the child a feeling of security and stimulate it in the area of the unaspected planet. What will happen? The child will (unintended and unconsciously) start to exaggerate that planet even more, and we'll have a lot of trouble on our hands. As a parent, we will encounter new dilemmas. In this way, a child with an unaspected Sun can manifest itself very powerfully, pretty domineeringly even, and in a way that doesn't leave much room as an adult. At the same time, the child will often feel unsure and won't be aware of his or her behavior. So, if, as a parent, we give a child extra attention and try to develop self-confidence, he or she will unconsciously behave even more domineeringly, and can then start sucking up all the attention. This can easily happen at the expense of other children, or lead to unpleasant situations, such as when many adult family members come to a birthday party for one of the parents, and the child turns out to dominate the entire atmosphere. This will certainly result in commentary from the rest of the family. Result: the child feels a split—understanding on the part of the parents, and rejection on the part of a number of family members. An unaspected planet is very sensitive particularly to these kinds of experiences! And if we try to redirect the child a little at that party, there is the chance he or she won't understand what's going on, and so feel misunderstood anyway, by the parents as well. So, a dilemma in raising such children!

Unaspected planets require patience and understanding on the part of parents. Time and again parents will need to explain the child's behavior to the child. Camcorders are a big help here! If a child who is a bit older looks at scenes taken years before, he or she can see objectively the behavior in question. I have witnessed at various times that children slowly began to understand from this what was going on. But don't start filming troublesome situations on purpose, that will only elicit more stress! Explaining and talking, over the course of years, will really help a child with one or more unaspected planets on its way. In the meantime, though, the child will still feel jerked around a lot, and no matter what we do as parents and no matter how good our intentions are, we simply can't get around this. So it makes no sense to feel guilty about it. Realize that the child has a number of exceptional talents, but needs to be patiently guided to create a safe basis from which those talents can develop. The more we help the child to connect with that "loose piece," the sooner he or she will be able to develop these natural talents in a *conscious* way.

Synastry and Unaspected Planets

Children with unaspected planets may not act them out in the way I have described earlier. People don't exist all by themselves, but are a part of a family and a community. Every horoscope has its own dynamics and need patterns, but the expression of our planets is also influenced by the aspects and planets in *other people's* horoscopes, as well as our own! If a child has an unaspected planet, but there are planets in the parents' horoscopes that create an aspect to it, the energy of the child's unaspected planet can "out itself" through the parents. Such a parent will unconsciously become very important for that child, of total importance if it is a harmonious aspect. After all, the child feels more relaxed and safe around that parent, without knowing why and without there even being any external reason for this. It's as if that parent had a "direct connection" with that child.

For the child this makes it easier in the sense that the parent involved is better equipped to help, guide, and give the child insight into situations. The child can teach himself or herself to see through the eyes of that parent. It will become clear that this also entails risks. For, if the parent has a distorted image as a result of her or his own problems, the parent will transfer a distorted view to the child, and the child will later be confronted by two problems: a possible confrontation with the unaspected planet anyway, plus wrestling to incorporate the erroneous view. Another risk is a certain dependence of the child on that parent, which can cause problems in the family. And should the parent involved live above all "through and for the kids" so that the children are a kind of justification for and give substance to that parent's existence, then this parent can feel very flattered by the bond with the child, which doesn't help the child very much. In such a case, the parent will have no clue to what's really going on.

A child, through the bond with such a parent, can, relatively speaking, temporarily have less trouble with an unaspected planet, and the situation will remain this way until the child steps out into the world. For, as long as a child is at home regularly and experiences the parent physically, the aspect between the horoscope of parent and child will remain active. However, if the child goes to live somewhere else, the meaning of that aspect will be less, and at oncoming adulthood, the child will suddenly be confronted full force with the unaspected planet in his or her horoscope.

This will include the insecurity, the ambivalence, the all-or-nothing expression, and the lack of perspective on this. Such a child will then suddenly seem to change very much. After all, the child is showing sides that were slumbering till then, and which nobody knew existed. In essence something is now surfacing that should have surfaced a long time ago! Parents may then lament the fact that their child has changed so much, and that they tried so hard to do their best, and now look! Something like this can come across as incomprehensible to those around, particularly if the child significantly lived through the parent who provided his or her unaspected planet with an outlet. In such a case, the child may opt to choose a field of study that is in line with that parent's expectations, only to get into trouble once he or she has moved and started college. Then a turnaround to giving life an entirely different substance is possible.

Of course, all of this doesn't have to happen as problematically as I have just outlined it. A lot depends on the extent to which such children have learned to build self-confidence, as well as on the understanding of their parents. Should a child have aspects with both parents' horoscopes, then it is of the greatest importance that the parents respect and guide the child, and also look closely at themselves and ask themselves *why* they want certain things from their child, and *why* they expect certain things. Then the child will be able early on to gain experience with the effect of an unaspected planet, and will later face surprises that won't be so big.

If a child with an unaspected planet has an obvious hobby, then nine times out of ten this will have something to do with the area of that planet. Parents can stimulate the child in this hobby, and possibly even join in to share in the child's experience (as long as there is no question whatsoever of any form of competition or authority here!). It is very possible that this hobby will, unnoticed, be a fine preparation for the child's future profession, and even give the child an advantage over others. However, parents will be confronted by another dilemma: stimulating the child in this area can lead to lots of fun, on the one hand, but due to the orientation of the unaspected planet, the child won't have much of an interest in homework or other things anymore. If such a child falls behind in school, this usually has nothing to do with intelligence, but with an orientation toward certain things, and homework unfortunately won't be part of that.

If the issue is aspects to someone else's horoscope, a brother or sister, or an instructor at school, this can fulfill a special function if one of the planets makes a harmonious connection with the child's unaspected planet. On the other hand, an unaspected planet will be more sensitive to tension if planets in somebody else's horoscope form a tense aspect with that planet. A square of either parent's Saturn to the child's unaspected planet can make this child extremely sensitive to the inhibiting and structuring side of that parent—much more than the other children in the family.

In short: the aspects that a child's unaspected planet receives from other horoscopes play an important part in the way in which an unaspected planet develops for a child. This also makes it very important to imagine what the people involved have done with that planet (meaning, with that piece of the psyche).

If the parent involved in the Saturn example refuses to take responsibility and always blames everything and everybody else when things go wrong, Saturn won't have much backbone. This parent will give the child a whiny, limiting, distrusting, and maybe even fearful Saturn. On the other hand, if the parent has a balanced awareness of the law of cause and effect, and is prepared to take responsibility for his or her own actions, then the child will gain structure, strength, equanimity, and modesty through this Saturn. This is true as such for all synastry, but in particular for aspects made by one person's planets to another's unaspected planets.

Duet

A duet, in the musical sense, requires two participants who play music together. In astrology, too, we have a so-called duet: two planets that "dance" together, exclusively with each other, apart from other planets. This is the case whenever two planets only aspect each other, and neither creates a major aspect with any other planet. It is possible that one of the two or both form an aspect with the MC or the Ascendant, but as we have seen, this does not count when judging unaspectedness. So we have two planets that are involved only with each other, and stand apart from the rest of the horoscope. This is what we call a duet. An "unaspected aspect" in fact. Practice teaches that both planets will behave as if they were unaspected. So they each bear the previously mentioned hallmarks of unaspected planets, and aside from this we can also see the influence of each on the other.

A duet can be linked by any aspect, so it doesn't matter if it is a trine, a square, or a conjunction, to name just a few. What's important is that neither planet creates any aspects to any other planet.

Reception

If an unaspected planet is receptive to another planet, the unaspected planet will be drawn out of its isolation. In practice we see that the characteristic expressions of an unaspected planet occur only in severely diluted form. Something will linger, but compared with a true unaspected planet, nothing to speak of. The receptive partner is very important and significantly influences the function of the unaspected planet. So it makes a big difference with which planet a reception is formed. For instance, the Moon in Aquarius (ruler Uranus) and Uranus in Cancer (ruler Moon), and the Moon is unaspected. Uranus will then be the receptive partner, and will "liberate" the Moon to a large degree. However, the Moon will thereby gain a Uranian tint, it seems a little like an aspect between the Moon and Uranus, even though we aren't supposed to formulate it that way. However, as soon as this person is active in the area of the Moon, a mixing will take place with the freedom-loving, original, and restless sides of Uranus.

If you have the Moon in Capricorn and Saturn in Cancer, and your Moon is unaspected, then Saturn will be the liberator in this case. Now, however, the expressions of the Moon are colored by Saturn as well, and as soon as you are active in the area of the Moon, you will experience a mixture of equanimity and seriousness, and possibly a little restraint.

Of course the background sign of the Moon contributes; Moon in Aquarius is, after all, different from Moon in Capricorn. However, the flashiness and simultaneously whimsical effect of Uranus can easily be distinguished in the Moon-Uranus reception, and those are characteristics that are more appropriate to Uranus than to Aquarius.

So it is important with unaspected planets to pay attention to receptions; they will soften the effect considerably.

Despite the fact that an unaspected planet will initially behave like a loose piece, this is certainly no indication of psychic problems, such as schizophrenia or multiple personality disorder! It really has nothing to do with anything like this. Practice teaches that in the course of our lives we can learn to live with unaspected planets very well; we can learn to work with them, develop talents, and even become famous because of them! It is not unusual for an unaspected planet to drive a person to great achievements.

CHAPTER THREE

Family Themes and the Generation Problem

Yod configurations and unaspected planets don't just crop up in a natal chart. They turn out to play a very important part in the way in which family themes gain form and work themselves out over several generations. As if by chance, I stumbled on a number of remarkable phenomena, both in my research on families over several generations (a kind of astrological genealogy) and in talking to people with unaspected planets and yods.

Several times I heard from people who had a yod that they had the feeling of having to answer questions that weren't their own. Some of them indicated family problems directly. Those who had unaspected planets sometimes also formulated it this way. It was in particular in the second half of their lives, when they were able to look back with more perspective, that people came up with these insights. I do have to admit that the majority of people with these factors in their horoscope didn't spend much time thinking about this kind of thing, although they were very caught up in wrestling with the themes linked to the yod or the unaspected planet. Still, these remarks stayed in the back of my mind, and they were unexpectedly confirmed in my research on generational phenomena.

The planet Uranus turned out to play a dominant role in one of the families I researched. Uranus was at grandpa's MC and grandma's Ascendant. Their daughter also had Uranus in a prominent place in the 1st house in aspect to the Sun. This daughter married a man who had Uranus on the Ascendant. They also had a daughter with Uranus as an unaspected planet. This fascinated me, and I asked the granddaughter, the woman with the unaspected Uranus, what she had seen and experienced in her childhood regarding the Uranus of her parents and grandparents. To my surprise she said, "Nothing." Her parents had led a life that the daughter described as being "normal" and "middle-class," and her grandparents also lived in the pattern that had been expected of them in their day. No personal substance given to Uranus, but a Uranus that hid behind the expectations and patterns of the times and the environment in which these people lived. Neither her parents, nor her grandparents, turned out to have had any Uranian hobbies; at any rate she couldn't recall anything of that kind. So it is very likely that both the parents, as well as the grandparents, repressed the Uranian part of themselves, although it is so pronounced in their horoscopes. This isn't so strange in itself. Society at the beginning of the 20th century was more structured and well defined than it is now. There were clearer rules for what was appropriate and what was not, and social control was much greater. Deviating from the norm still had major consequences at that time, much more than nowadays.

Uranus does not have to gain form in "contrariness" or "provocation," though; we can also express it in a profession (from pilot, or electrical technician, or engineer, to astrologer or acupuncturist), or in a hobby (such as model trains or computers). In the beginning of the 20th century, of course, we had to be able to obtain or subsidize an education to become an engineer, for instance, or have money for a technical hobby, to mention just one example. If we were born in poor circumstances, there was usually no money and we could forget substantiating these ambitions, and thus giving form to the diverse domains appropriate to this planet as well. As women, we had even fewer possibilities.

Repressed contents continue as an issue unconsciously, however, and will somehow ask for an outlet. With Uranus this can be in the form of tension, of unconscious irrational behavior, irritations, and actions that aim at the least amount of ties and most amount of freedom possible, although we are not aware of this. If we have repressed contents, we will give our children a kind of double message: what we say and think will not always be confirmed or supported by our actions, and a child can end up with problems because of this. If that child in turn represses those contents, he or she will in doing so perpetuate, as it were, the patterns of the parents. This is how it can come about that a dominant planet in the horoscopes of family members of consecutive generations can remain rather invisible or unconscious in terms of its effect. In those families where, over several generations, I have encountered a theme that has not undergone any development and has been repressed, a child will be born sooner or later with precisely that theme unavoidably in her or his horoscope in the form of an unintegrated planet or a yod. It's as if that child had been "appointed" to tackle the issues of past generations and to find a solution, whether the child wants to or not. An "unlived theme" over several generations can thus manifest as an unaspected planet or a yod. In addition, issues that come out over several generations but that have not really been solved or that have not found appropriate expression, will end in yods and unaspected planets in later generations. Also very unbalanced or extreme expressions of particular themes, again over various generations, will lead to yods and unaspected planets. Thus the insight arose that whenever a particular energy in a family is seeking to manifest itself in form, this will not be limited to one family member or to one generation, but will come out as a theme in consecutive generations. So significantly, even, that the consecutive family members will often also marry partners who have a similarly prominent theme as well. Just as if fate wanted to say, "There's no escaping, it has to be worked on *now*. You are going to feel it or encounter it in all possible ways." Evidently wherever that theme does not come out, or comes out in an unbalanced fashion, in whatever way, tension will build and express itself in the form of yods and unaspected planets.

If you are preoccupied with family patterns and with astrological research of various generations, you will be confronted by the fact that you cannot see yourself separately from your background. You will see how particular themes and patterns are to be found again and again in many horoscopes, and how your horoscope might very well look like your grandmother's or great-grandfather's. Due to the current Western way of looking, we have started to see ourselves more and more as separate and isolated individuals with our own identity and individuality. We have forgotten that we are connected by countless invisible threads to our past and to the people who went before us. Our lives express patterns that these people also had in their horoscopes, and in our lives we may have to answer questions that our grandparents already had on their minds. If these are pressing questions or dominant patterns, yods and unaspected planets may form.

In the previous chapters we saw that both a yod and an unaspected planet (and of course a duet) are difficult horoscope factors. They are accompanied by a lot of insecurity and are initially incomprehensible. On top of this, both a yod and an unaspected planet suck a lot of energy toward themselves and are constantly demanding attention. In the light of family themes it seems as if unbalanced expressions or problems that remained unsolved for several generations will manifest themselves in one or more children as a pervasive personal problem that can no longer be avoided. Due to the energy that these horoscope factors suck toward themselves, this piece will no longer be able to be repressed. It will always be there, loud and clear, though demanding and longing for an answer. Since this primarily has to do with unsolved or unbalanced family themes, the children usually have no role models. Even if they did have one, they wouldn't be able to follow it because yods and unaspected planets tend to make you search for your very own, very individual answer, and will have you take an equally singular direction in life, often significantly deviating from the pattern of your origins. It has often been my experience with people who have yods or unaspected planets that the second half of life differed distinctly from the first.

What does it mean to be a child with a yod or unaspected planet? In many cases I encountered yods and unaspected planets in children whose parents, grandparents, uncles, aunts, or other family members were stuck in old patterns and opinions, and who were not (or did not want to be) conscious of the call of their inner selves. But I have also encountered yods and unaspected planets in children whose parents were already busy sailing a different course, finding their own expression for the issues dwelling in *them* as well, and who had sometimes already arrived at a new, dynamic, and satisfying style of life. Still, they would have one or more children with a yod, a duet, or an unaspected planet. This seems absurd, but the absurdity primarily depends on what standpoint you take.

If you think in terms of "guilt" and "cause," you will quickly tend to say that parents who "don't do the job well" may saddle their child or grandchild with a yod or an unaspected planet. This view also implies that you could prevent yods and unaspected planets. It gives the illusion that if you just followed "the rules of life" closely, you could keep everything in hand. This is not how it works though, and it is very important to realize that whenever yod configurations and unaspected planets appear, this is not a question of guilt or whether you went about things in the right way. Just look at all the possibilities that you have in your horoscope. Are you up to realizing all of them within this single lifetime? Sometimes I have the feeling I need at least seven lives to do everything that's in my horoscope! Besides, there are certain facets of everybody's horoscope that have no possibility of developing, given the birth culture or life circumstances. What do you do with Mars–Uranus–Pluto aspects if you are born in a country where collectivity is highly regarded and individuality is seen as undesirable? What do you do with all your possibilities if you have to grow up in a country where a dictator swings the scepter, restricting all kinds of possibilities, or where religious fanaticism has gained the upper hand and imposes countless radical restrictions? Or if you have to grow up in the commonly considered free Western world, where the pressure to achieve and the rat-race atmosphere also have a restrictive effect on particular horoscope factors? Result: there will *always* be a particular bit of your horoscope that you will not be able to shape, partially because of the situation in which you were born, live, and work, and partially because of your own choices.

In studying family patterns another couple of matters struck me regarding yods and unaspected planets. Once they pop up in a family, they tend to do this over several generations, regardless of whether there are people in that family who have meanwhile been able to substantiate the themes fully and in balance. So once a kind of "intersection in time" originates in the pattern of many generations, which is expressed by yods or unaspected planets, they will form, however they do, even if at some point there has been some movement in the theme.

Several times I have also seen the theme skip a generation, to come out later all of a sudden in the form of a yod or an unaspected planet. Sometimes parents won't have that theme with much emphasis in their own horoscopes, for instance (although other members of the family will), while it inevitably comes out suddenly in one or more of their children. In practice, this amounts to a lot of confusion and problems raising those children.

If parents or grandparents are busy, or if they have been busy giving these themes their own, individual substance and making them visible, they can be a great help to their children and grandchildren who have yods or unaspected planets. This may even cause them to be able to gain a deep and special bond with their descendants, and they will help to achieve that which yods and unaspected planets *really* are—enormous talents that are ready to burst! I cannot shake the impression that what previous generations repress causes an energy to brew that can be expressed as a tremendous force and a great talent during the life of the person who has a yod or unaspected planet. As difficult and confrontational as yods and unaspected planets are on the one hand, their constructive and positive side is equally strong. Considered positively, we can assume that a yod or an unaspected planet in the horoscope of your child is the birth of a great talent, which can be developed through that child and/or through future generations. It may even make them famous!

Naturally, quite a lot of children who have unaspected planets or yods are born into families where the parents have little insight into the deeper family pattern. Often the parents (forced by external circumstances or not) live a pattern that doesn't fit them, or they have not heeded the deep urge every person has to develop. Jung called that urge the process of individuation. In this climate the family may seem to be a normal family, unconscious of what is at the point of breaking through.

If a child with a yod or an unaspected planet is born, he or she will express from day one, in some way or other, the unspoken, repressed, or unbalanced theme of generations. If that theme is also suppressed in the parents, or emotionally charged, the parents will have a great deal of difficulty with this child. For such children are, in fact, doing nothing less than giving form to the shadow-side of their parent(s), and since this concerns an entire family theme, there is a big chance that the child's yod or unaspected planet will also be expressing the shadow for grandparents, uncles, and aunts.

Yod children, or children with unaspected planets, simply *cannot* live the well-groomed life of their parents and act as if there is nothing going on. Doing this will not be enough for these children's inner restlessness to disappear. They will start looking, but won't know what for. The restlessness, the searching, the insecurity, and the exaggerations that go together with this can cause (lots of) friction with those around, and of course with the very family members who were dealt the same problematic potential, but who have managed to suppress it.

How would you feel as the adult who has succeeded, with a lot of effort, in forcing those gnawing feelings into the background, or in suppressing character traits so you don't see them anymore (or see that you still express them in a particular way, either)? You would be susceptible to exposure and confrontation. If there is a child with whom you interact in some way, whether this child is a member of your own family or of your extended family, and that child unconsciously, but in an unmistakable way, shows you exactly what your weak spot is, you will have a lot of trouble with this child. It will seem as if the child has taken on an undermining role. In fact, there is a big chance that a number of adults will believe the child is "worthless," put him or her down, and will turn the child into the black sheep of the family. This is not intentional, as it happens, but is inspired by the deep-seated fear and projection that in the unconscious mind happens to accompany the shadow.

It may be, though, that one or more family members do understand what's going on, or what's more likely, see the child do something that they themselves had wanted to do but never dared. The child then represents their unlived longing, which can cause negative jealousy as a result. However, there is an equally big chance that they will *adore* the child, worship the child, and even sing the child's praises everywhere. They will broadcast it all over the place, "Just you wait, this is a very exceptional child and he or she is going to go far. . . ." They mean it, and they may be absolutely right.

Although this seems like it would be stimulating for the child, it can easily lead to the opposite if the party who is singing the praises is one of the parents. Whenever the child symbolizes something for a parent that is very important to the *parent*, but of which the parent is unaware (or is insufficiently aware), this will generate an intense projection on the part of that parent onto the child. The parent won't see the child as he or she is, but through the eyes of his or her own projection. If it is a "can-do-no-wrong" projection, then the dark side of the child won't be seen. I have witnessed cases where such a child was able to act out the shadow side almost without restraint, without the parent seeing it. Sometimes the parent will interpret these expressions in such a way that the idolized image of the child can remain intact. For the balanced upbringing of a child, such projections are extremely harmful. Other members of the family will see the child in a more realistic light, in behaviors that are not acceptable. In such a case, though, talking about this with the parent involved is impossible, and so a split can easily arise in the family. The child with a yod or unaspected planet receives "protection" from one of the parents and may even be favored (I have seen this a couple of times). This will lead to problems with the other children in the family who will vent on the child involved. The split can build major tension in the entire family, which can sometimes lead to divorce. You cannot go and blame the child for this, although the parent's projections on the child may well be the catalyst of the crisis.

This doesn't make things any easier for the child with a yod or unaspected planet. The child experiences a conflict because people react to the child. On the one hand the child is rejected or plays the role of the black sheep. On the other, the child is praised to the skies and seen as exceptional. No wonder that yods and unaspected planets are often coupled with identity problems! Just try to put together an image of yourself from all these experiences! So it isn't so much that the yod or unaspected planet produces these identity problems, it's the experiences we accumulate in an environment with people who are part of the family dynamic that will continually be a source of suffering. In some cases, children who were entangled in these situations have an extra problem— that of a growing sense of guilt. This is connected with the fact that the widely differing views of family members about this child can oftentimes give rise to further contention, so that repressed material, fears, and problems that various family members have sometimes even surface outright.

The young child with the yod or unaspected planet won't understand a lot of this. The child will only notice that the talk about him or her is somehow connected with quarreling and contention, and in some cases unleashes an outright family fight. This is not the child's fault. The fact that he or she entered this world by a twist of fate, and possesses a number of traits that are an inescapable mirror for the family is something the child will not be able to put into perspective or comprehend early on. Discussions about the child only make the child feel the accompanying tensions.

If you have repressed something that you encounter in the outside world, you will have an emotional response when you see your repressed contents in someone else. This, too, is a hallmark of the shadow. This means, for example, that if you're always working hard and don't humor yourself in any way, you may have relegated everything that has to do with rest and relaxation to your unconscious. You then run the risk of being annoyed by people who live a more relaxed lifestyle, and you will tend to judge them out of hand in terms of laziness and irresponsibility. What you don't see is that because you, yourself, can't relax, you get overly worked up when you see that suppressed part of yourself being lived in someone else. Those who know how to relax hold a mirror up for you. I think it is fair to say that the power or intensity of your emotion betrays how significant the repression or problem is. So if you have a definite problem or are mightily suppressing something, your projection will be even more intense and the emotion will be stronger. Now if we think of this psychic mechanism in the context of children with yods or unaspected planets, it will be clear that family members who carry the most repression will have the most significant reaction to the child. The power of this emotion is great. And because of this powerful emotion, they will keep wanting to talk about it, but will do so in loaded terms. So time and time again, the child will hear the same things—things that seem to be about her or him, but which in essence are really the family member's own problem. The child will take the endlessly repeated negative remarks and warnings personally, and because of this, the child may become troubled by feelings of guilt, fear of failure, feelings of inferiority, and the like—even though it is really only a kind of repeat alarm for the adult. The more such adults raise the issue, the more they should realize that they have a problem themselves.

A last difficult issue that I have encountered at various times in people with a yod or unaspected planet is that a parent might initially sing the praises of the child, but, often for some trivial reason, turn around and start rejecting the child. However, this consistently only concerns parents who are very unaware of themselves and whose emotional development has been limited in some way. For example, a woman was truly adored by her mother in her childhood years. However, when the woman reached puberty, she made a remark about her mother one day that didn't suit her mother at all because it hit her at the heart of her weak spot. The mother flipped around like a leaf on a tree, and rejected her daughter overnight. The mother expressed her attitude in no uncertain terms: her daughter simply didn't *exist* for her anymore. If a parent is wholeheartedly projecting, and is completely unaware of this, such a parent will be very sensitive when a complex is touched. You can expect truly "primal reactions" that are not in proportion to what happened or to what was said. But talking about it is not easy, for, as long as that unawareness continues, the outside world is blamed and you run the risk of once again touching a sensitive nerve—with all the consequences.

A turnaround in the attitude of an emotionally immature or unaware parent can also have other causes. The birth of another child can be such a reason. All of a sudden all this parent's attention goes out to the new child and the previous one doesn't count anymore. This is connected with the following psychic dynamic.

In by far the most cases, if we dream of a baby, this little child will symbolize an ability, a talent, a potential, or a new attitude toward life that is dormant inside us, wanting to be born. In other words: there is an important piece in ourselves that wants to become conscious and that is demanding development. If we go in search of which piece that might be, we can also in actuality undergo rapid psychological growth. When something like this is at the point of breaking through, but we keep suppressing and repressing it, then we may all of a sudden be *gripped* simply by the sight of a real baby. The tangible baby becomes a symbol and in projection takes on the entire load of our own unconscious longing. If a parent has severely suppressed his or her potential, and another child is born to the family, this child can gain a symbolic meaning for the parent, one that overshadows everything else. The other children won't count anymore. And the child with a yod or an unaspected planet may end up dealing with the consequences of the emotionally immature behavior of this parent.

Fortunately there are also cases where parents become aware of what is at play and manage to channel upcoming tensions elsewhere in the family to protect their child. It is good to be aware that when a particular pattern has been in play for generations, it can also be worked out over several generations. We can help and support a child tremendously in doing this, even though, as we saw in the chapter on unaspected planets, it will take quite some doing.

Understanding for what is going on inside the child, guiding the child, and letting the child feel that you understand are very important conditions to give the child more of a chance to redirect the yod or unaspected planet in a positive way and to get to know it. This is not an easy thing for parents though, because even in situations of warmth and understanding, the child with the yod or unaspected planet will make very typical mistakes, overstep the bounds, suddenly clam up, and so forth. And time and time again, it will turn out that the child is usually very capable, but somehow is also living an inner life with which parents have little or no contact, and which doesn't work very well with everyday reality. This can lead to all kinds of errors in judgment, for instance, varying from irregular eating habits and continually underestimating how much homework there is to do, to not meeting obligations when they should be met. The child has a knack—just when he or she has done something good that deserves a compliment—for doing something to undermine the pleasant situation and create tension. Or else something will happen, that is not his or her fault, so that the compliment never materializes. Just as if something were to "hitch" the very moment the child might receive confirmation. For parents it is good to try to keep an eye out for this, and when the child is ready, also to explain what's going on, so that the child won't feel too rejected.

Still another issue regarding the child with a yod or unaspected planet, is whether or not the child is in the process of developing, unnoticed (the child often won't realize this, either!), a talent or ability. It may be that this hasn't come out yet, or whenever it does, it may seem like a nuisance or useless. With Neptune as an unaspected planet, a child may daydream endlessly, and only later will it turn out that this child has great poetic skill. By dreaming, the child was able to stay in touch with a natural inner shaping force.

Parents of a yod child, or a child with an unaspected planet, will be confronted by the necessity of having to adjust, not only in connection with the child, but also in connection with themselves. They will keep having to resort to their own devices. If they are able to listen to the message they will then receive, they will undergo a good deal of psychic growth.

We can help children like this in many ways. Let them feel around and search in safety and security, but do make them aware of the limits they need to know. Help these children establish contact with that troublesome subject matter inside, particularly at a later stage, when this can really be discussed. Don't take it personally that this child perpetually feels "different," both at home as well as at school. This is part and parcel of the theme.

If these children receive love and security, they will be much better equipped to live with the insecurity inherent in their themes. In such cases, we will see that they can also intensely enjoy things related to their yod or unaspected planet. At an early age, already very specific avenues that the child absolutely has to take may become discernible. A child with an unaspected Moon may, for instance, at a very early age, if parents provide stimulation and help, gain great pleasure from cooking and working with food, both for its tastiness as well as for the company, and be very happy doing this. In later life, this might develop into the ability to feed and take care of other people, not only literally, but also in the figurative sense, in the form of offering spiritual food, prepared with love, for one other person or for many others.

Or, children with Uranus in a yod configuration, who at first like nothing better than tearing gadgets apart and twiddling knobs, later discover how exciting computers are. These children turn out to have a latent talent that they develop in play and with much joy. As adults, these children may well have meteoric careers in this area.

Children born with a yod or an unaspected planet stand at a crossroads concerning a family dynamic over several generations. In society as well, these children will experience that they are wherever changes, crossroads, choices, and renewal are in the air.

CHAPTER FOUR

Effects of Yods and Unaspected Planets

Although both yods and unaspected planets mark turning-points in family dynamics, and both are connected with themes that have been at play and looking to be worked out for several generations, there are still considerable differences in the way a yod and an unaspected planet work in the chart. It is true that the two horoscope factors do share a number of basic hallmarks, even though they are different.

An unaspected planet is not influenced by other planets. This is why its hallmark is being singularly single-mindedly. It is obvious, recognizable, and can be easily described. Even though we, ourselves, may not recognize that we have one, those around us experience its effect very obviously. The domains of the unaspected planet are distinct, and as we have already seen, they hold an attraction for us. We are drawn toward them and can also perform great achievements through them. Unnoticed, we may be very concentrated on these domains and put a lot of energy into them. All of this in spite of the insecurity, doubt, and fear of failure in that area that we feel inside. The planet is and will remain clear, obvious, and itself.

That obviousness and clarity are lacking with a yod. Here we have three or more planets (or the MC or ASC, and two planets) that aspect and influence one another. We saw in chapter 1 that this influence is occasioned from such differing backgrounds that all kinds of tensions and ambiguities arise as a result. If one planet is active from its background (element, mode, and polarity), a second one wants to intervene immediately, from a totally different background combination. Planet Number 1 will lose quite some energy in standing up to Planet Number 2. And as if that weren't enough, a third one also joins in with a set of basic assumptions that are different once again, wanting to influence Numbers 1 and 2. The result is an ambiguous ball of emotions and feelings, fishtailing, turbulence, and a feeling of incapacity, because it's not even clear *what* is wrong, *what* the cause is, and what we can do about it. It's just as if a kind of diffuse chain reaction erupts as soon as one of the yod partners gets going. Because of this, there can be no question of a direction, or of single-mindedness, or of concentration. Initially no domain to which we are drawn will distinguish itself, as it does with an unaspected planet, and life will run in zigzags a lot more. There is a big chance that we will first start doing a number of very different, very diverse things before we reach the point where all of a sudden all the threads seem to come together. In retrospect it turns out that we have definitely benefited from all the experience we have accumulated. This is usually the case later in life. Only when children with a yod have received safe guidance can a form of orientation, and even a feeling of purpose, develop early on, but even then, getting there is more chaotic and troublesome than it is with an unaspected planet.

Unaspected planets and yod configurations have a number of similar expressions, and a number of divergent ones. We will first look at the general similarities, and then take a closer look at the differences in interpretation. In later chapters, I will work out a couple of examples.

1. We are not really aware of how yods and unaspected planets express themselves.

In explaining the background of the yod and the effect of unaspected planets, we already saw that a major hallmark is that we aren't really in contact with those parts of ourselves. With an unaspected planet we have no perspective on this at all and need to get to know that piece of ourselves by trial and error, and gain an eye for it. The lack of perspective on a yod is the result of the constant confusion that arises among the planets involved, causing wishes, longings, motivations, and actions in those areas to remain ambiguous and uncertain for a long time. Here, too, we can get to know them by developing an eye for them, being attentive, using trial and error, but this is more troublesome than with unaspected planets. Realize that when a yod involves three planets, this incorporates almost one-third of the planets in a horoscope. So roughly one-third of our entire psychic economy is involved in ambiguity, and that's a lot. This is the reason that yods are more of a problem than unaspected planets regarding things being unrecognizable and ambiguous.

2. We elicit particular responses we don't understand.

When planets work normally (even if we don't see or realize this), we will act from this basis, allowing wishes and longings to show up, and doing things we don't really think about twice. With an unaspected planet, there is a great proclivity for exaggeration, which we don't see ourselves, but which is, in fact, felt by those around. They will most certainly react to this. For instance, people with an unaspected Moon will have a great need for warmth and nurturing, and to their feeling will barely dare to ask for this. There is a longing inside. However, other people around them may be bothered by this "undemanded demand," by "something" that is radiated, that is not mentioned or articulated, but somehow seems to "suck." One mother who had a little boy with an unaspected Moon even nicknamed him "little suction cup"! This is one of the possible expressions of an unaspected Moon, and it will be obvious that the responses from people around who are bothered by it will not agree with our own feelings about the situation. If they say, "Don't stick to me like that," or, "You're suffocating me," or "You're always demanding so much of me," then the unaspected Moon can rightfully say that it doesn't understand, doesn't want anything like that, and doesn't mean it that way. To our feelings, the other is exaggerating, but in the eyes of the other, *we* are the ones who are exaggerating. A situation like this very quickly reduces to an "are so, am not" situation. In fact, both are right, depending on the point of view.

With yods, such exaggerations can also occur, but with yods yet another factor is at play. Parents have trouble really comprehending a child with a yod configuration. It's as if a part of that child's essence escapes us and we have a hard time getting close to it, as if it resisted discovery, in fact. The child is equally bothered by this, which often surfaces in the form of an insecure feeling about himself or herself, possibly also in the feeling of running aground on himself or herself. Such children don't know what they want and *what* they're running aground on, and then on top of this, thus ask for help in such an ambiguous way. This can come into play even in situations where everything is absolutely fine. The child will often meet with incomprehension and even irritation from those around. The child "shouldn't whine" and exaggerate so, and for once finally stop being difficult—as if the child were intentionally doing this! The child's insecurity makes visible the suppressed feelings of insecurity that people in the child's environment have, and this, too, can elicit rejecting or difficult responses. Moreover, the yod child, in a manner that is hard to describe, tends to continue on the track he or she happens to be on, even though the child doesn't really know that he or she is doing this. Result—parents and others have the idea that the child simply doesn't *want* to be cooperative, that the child is headstrong, and doesn't want to listen. In reality, this is decidedly not the case, although this impression does arise. And this will elicit other responses that the child will not understand at all.

Whether the issue is yods or unaspected planets, in both cases we're caught between a rock and a hard place: whatever we feel inside seems to be at cross-purposes to responses from the outside world. This does not promote self-confidence, and makes composing a balanced identity more difficult. We tend not to trust ourselves or the environment, or both, very much anymore. If this distrust continues though, we will, in fact, not have anything to hang on to anymore.

For parents, it is of the greatest importance to listen to what children with a yod or an unaspected planet have to say about themselves. It is serious business for them. Let them talk about how they feel, and don't jump on them about the fact that their behaviors don't correspond with what they think about themselves. So, help them, carefully, by making it clear that there is a difference, without talking them into feeling guilty or feeling inferior. Take the time for this; sometimes it can take years before the message really gets through. However, it is very important to give children (and adults as well) who run a higher chance of eliciting conflicting responses a feeling of safety, understanding, and unconditional acceptance.

Even as adults, these people will still have a conflict between inner experience and external response, although over time it will decrease as they gain more perspective on the unconscious problem, and manage to integrate and accept things.

3. We maneuver in incomprehensible circumstances.

If there is a conflict between "inside" and "outside," we will also run the risk of ending up in situations we absolutely don't want, or situations that turn out very differently from what was expected, or whose consequences are very different from what we could ever have foreseen. So it cannot simply be said that this is our "own fault." With yods and unaspected planets, we need more time than others to understand particular things about ourselves and be able to judge them in proper context. In the meantime we *are* living and doing, so we can get into all kinds of sticky situations.

This seems to affect romance. People fall in love with a partner who turns out to be very different than we anticipated in our wildest imaginings, or a partner who drags us into a world that is very problematic. The outer planets (Uranus, Neptune, and Pluto), in particular, may end up adding to the mix. One of my clients (with Venus in a yod with Neptune and Pluto) was thrown into constant agitation by her husband's unpredictable behavior. Not only did she psychically "get to see every corner of the room," but he literally dragged her all over the world and made sure that she couldn't settle down anywhere, so she would remain dependent on him. This was a long-term stalemate that lasted a long time because the woman's insecurity was exploited, as it were, by her husband, so he could have her for himself. She didn't see this for a long time. It was only after years of stress and falling ill more and more frequently that this started dawning on her. Or take the woman with Saturn, Uranus, and Neptune in a yod. She was looking for a stable partner who could be a fundamental support for her. With Saturn in her yod, she fell in love with a strong man. Later, however, he turned out to be an underworld figure, due to which the woman lived year in year out with the sword of Damocles over her head because her husband's enemies tried to avenge themselves on their children.

These are two examples of situations that nobody wishes for themselves, but which can be stirred up in some way by a yod or an unaspected planet—although a bit more by yods. These situations can be accompanied by a feeling of uprootedness and they make us resort to our own devices in every respect. It seems as if once yods and unaspected planets come into play, you have to start from zero in many respects—as if we first had to burn a bunch of bridges before we could really move. Those bridges don't contain just our own issues. They hold a lot of "old business" that has to do with the generation that went before. How we can make a good start, though, is significantly connected with the extent to which we have known understanding and safety, and the extent to which we have gained insight into ourselves and our projections.

Although I have seen uncomfortable, and even very extreme, situations regularly with yods and unaspected planets, I want to emphasize that we can also lead a good, normal life with them, although the risk of some stalemate or other is bigger than "normal."

4. We experience things "out of the blue" as we feel they have no connection with us. These events and happenings seem to come from the outside, and involve consequences for us.

This point is related to the previous one. The things that happen seem to come from the outside world—out of the blue, as with the woman who married a man who initially was very sweet to her, but who ended up dragging her into the underworld. This, for her, came from outside. She could see no connection at all with the life she had been living until then, but somehow she was now in it up to her ears. Without involving herself, and having nothing to do with it at all, she was constantly confronted by the dangerous consequences of this life.

Psychologically, we could say that she fell in love with a man who had all of this inside himself. The fact that she didn't feel or see this reflects an inner problem. Although there is certainly some truth to this, we should not forget that the yod or unaspected planet is a family dynamic. The woman is the carrier of a quantity of stored psychic energy that comes out in this way, usually in a troublesome manner. This is why the whole of her predicament cannot be shifted only onto her shoulders, because it is connected to a much bigger "picture," and is also closely related to the following points.

5. What crosses our path often involves a scare, a shock, insecurity, or some other uncomfortable situation. We feel we cannot exercise any influence over this. It is simply happening.

The case I mentioned is already an example of this, but we can still add that in most cases there will be a shock to cope with, or we'll get involved in something that scares us, or that elicits a lot of tension. It will quickly elicit, "Now why does this have to happen to *me* of all people?" This is not the same thing as the proverbial "pulling ourselves up by our own bootstraps," because it usually has nothing to do with stupid mistakes. It relates much more to the complexity of situations we can't get out of just like that, or to an event that will upset a plan in one fell swoop so we can't get any farther.

With a yod or an unaspected planet our life can take sudden and unexpected turns due to specific events. They can be events of any kind, but they are often pretty confrontational, as in the case of a very gifted ballet student who had Venus and Pluto involved in a yod. She was capable of tremendous expression, and had almost finished the ballet academy, with the offer of a job already in her pocket. Then she had an accident and broke her back. She was not allowed to dance again. Her entire life had revolved around ballet, and her parents had always helped her and encouraged her in this. Her family dynamic was one with a lot of relationship issues in previous generations, and some had reached a pretty critical point. A number of family members in previous generations had been very artistic, but because of the unbending opinion "that this was done only by women of dubious morals," the inclination had been quashed and a succession of women had to satisfy themselves with "simply being a housewife and mother." This girl's yod, containing Venus and Pluto, reflected all those themes, both the art as well as the relationship issues. And there she was, a truly gifted dancer with great artistic expression and a very promising future. With a single blow her world was shattered. For a year she despaired deeply, but then managed to get hold of herself and climb out of the pit. She began studying psychology (a Pluto theme) and noticed she was enjoying it more and more. She has now reached the point where she says she is happier with her new direction than she was before with ballet. She still loves ballet, but feels she has become more balanced. With ballet, she said, you can never be yourself. You are not allowed to eat much of anything because you always have to pay attention to your body. A serious ballet career does not allow for a husband and children, and you can be very lonesome in fact. She has a sweet partner and is determined to make something of her relationship, and she would love to have children. In her study of psychology, she has gotten to know facets of herself she had not seen before. And at the moment she is concentrating on forms of therapy that involve play, music, and art—once again the substance of Venus and Pluto.

What initially seemed like the total collapse of her life turned out, in retrospect, to be the rigorous beginning of a new, definitely happy phase. I have seen these kinds of turns many times. The problem, however, is that with a yod or unaspected planet we can also remain stuck in the sorrow and the initial shock, and in an attitude of self-pity, so we don't see what is wanting to reveal itself. This is why there are also counterexamples where no new road was taken. What I have seen, though, is that somehow there is always a new beginning ready and waiting. We see this, however, only after some time, and only if we want to.

6. We often feel like we're in a stalemate and have been wronged.

As in the previous example of the ballet dancer who had a serious accident, many people will get the feeling after a significant event that they are stalemated, and it is not unusual for them to have the additional feeling of having been wronged. If something significant and difficult like this happens, when for the rest we are really trying to do our best in life, are honest, and have a clean slate, it is difficult to swallow that something so serious would happen. This causes feelings of despair that keep making us ask, "Now, why me? What on earth did I do wrong to have to go through something like this? I didn't deserve this, did I?" and so on. No one can answer these questions, and it is, to be sure, very harsh. It is precisely in this feeling that the risk inherent in yods and unaspected planets of getting stuck at this point and of feeling rejected by everyone and everything lies.

7. If something has to go wrong, it will happen without our being able to do anything about it. We often encounter situations that are exceptions to the rule, and we may receive negative responses to this when, in fact, there is nothing to feel guilty about.

People with a yod or unaspected planet often stand at a crossroads, not only as far as they and their birth family are concerned, but they will also notice this at their place of work or in their community. Very often we see someone with a yod or unaspected planet join a company at a critical point when that company is being faced with change, restructuring, or a makeover. Whether and how that change takes shape is another question. What is at issue is that yod people, and people with unaspected planets, also show up on stage when there is a turning point or where one has to be effected. Princess Diana, with her yod configurations, entered the British royal family and introduced a time that was confrontational for that royal house. The distance between the royal house and the people came increasingly into focus, and the people began to demand change, absolutely after Diana's premature death. No matter what we think of her, or of the Windsors, it is a fact that because of all the turbulence surrounding Diana, the role of the monarchy and its function was debated once again. Whether a new form will definitely come about, we can never deduce from a yod pattern. However, Queen Elizabeth II has an unaspected Sun. And with her Sun also functioning as a royal, sooner or later the theme of honor and respect crosses her path by means of a stalemate. Fate sent her Diana as a daughter-in-law, and the wheel began to turn.

The story initially arouses the impression that it all went wrong, both for Elizabeth and for Diana. We should look at this in a different way though. The result of the fact that people and events come together at a juncture in time is that precisely because of the stagnation, the grinding to a halt, or running up against problems, we are able to clear the decks and move on. When we are in the middle of the turbulence, this is hard to grasp and understand.

We can also see that "crossroads function" in another light. For instance, a medication that everybody was raving about had just been patented and put on the market. Unfortunately at one clinic, though (where the doctor had a yod and two unaspected planets), things went wrong with a patient who took the medication. He stuck to all the guidelines and took all the side effects into account, but in some incomprehensible way, things still went wrong. Subsequent research then showed that in *very* special cases, under rare physical circumstances, there are risks affiliated with the use of this medication. And such a case hardly ever arises, but did by chance in this doctor's clinic. In fact, this is a very important event, because the experience provides an important contribution to the continued research of this medication, and also improves insight into when we should prescribe this medication and when we should not. However, the manufacturer of the medication did not respond very politely. The manufacturer was angry because the bad publicity would affect sales. Instead of dealing with the problem constructively, the manufacturer took it out on the doctor, who wasn't to blame at all, and who also couldn't have done anything. All he had was a yod and two unaspected planets in his horoscope! And so he runs a bigger risk of experiencing precisely those things that are the exception to the rule, or that tiny deviation that "never occurs from a statistical point of view." No wonder you sigh, "That's what *I* have?"

8. Often we have to make impossible choices, or even choose between two evils.

Particularly if we are involved with a progression or transit (or if a progression or transit forms a temporary yod) situations can take place when we cannot move on and we *must* make a choice, but we *can't* choose. No matter how we weigh and study the matter, any way we look at it, it feels like choosing between evils. None of the options is what we want, and there are a lot of objections, ifs, ands, and buts in connection with all the options. We feel like we are standing with our backs to the wall and have no place to turn. Often the resolution happens of its own accord, when the aspect by progression or transit is past, but we have no perspective on this during the stalemate. Even the question of whether we have to choose or let things run their course is a problem. In short, yods and unaspected planets may bring "impossible" situations several times in life. This can occur on a great variety of levels, even though the occurrence will be linked to the themes of the yod or to those of the unaspected planet.

An example of this happened to the former Dutch Minister of Defense, Joris Voorhoeve (Chart 1, page 57). He has a duet between the Sun and Mars in his horoscope. His Sun is located at the beginning of Capricorn, Mars at the beginning of Leo. They inconjunct each other and neither forms a major aspect with any other planet. In a duet, both participants behave like unaspected planets. Voorhoeve, with his unaspected duet-Sun, was the leader of his political party, the People's Party for Freedom and Democracy (VVD), and with his unaspected duet-Mars, was the Minister of Defense! During the period of time that he headed the VVD, this party was going through a difficult time. When Voorhoeve was Minister of Defense, he became involved with Srebrenica, one of the most traumatic experiences for this ministry since World War II. Neither of these situations were "Voorhoeve's fault." In the light of yods and unaspected planets we can place this in a larger perspective: whenever an organization or an institution has reached a critical stage, or is facing a turning point, or has to change direction, or whatever, there is a big chance that it will get a leader with a yod or an unaspected planet. This leader, in fact, stands outside the process in which the institution finds itself, in the sense that the leader may be totally irreproachable and be of absolute integrity, but during the term of leadership will become involved with all kinds of "sleazy" things, with intrigues, ambiguity, accusations, and other unpleasant matters often connected with a time of ambiguity and chaos for an institution in transition. Or else this leader will go through an unexpected, sudden, and drastic crisis, and have to trim all the sails in order to steer a middle course. In such a crisis, this leader will be backed against the wall. There will be several times when this leader will have to choose from alternatives that are all equally undesirable. So, choosing from among evils.

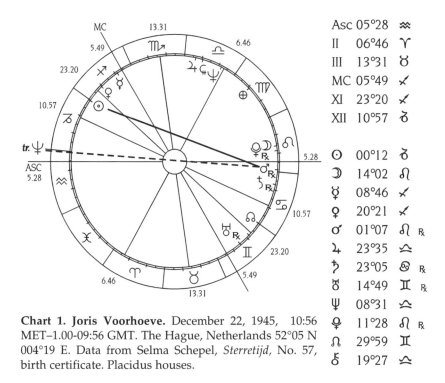

Asc	05°28 ♒
II	06°46 ♈
III	13°31 ♉
MC	05°49 ♐
XI	23°20 ♐
XII	10°57 ♑

☉	00°12 ♑
☽	14°02 ♌
☿	08°46 ♐
♀	20°21 ♐
♂	01°07 ♌ ℞
♃	23°35 ♎
♄	23°05 ♋ ℞
♅	14°49 ♊ ℞
♆	08°31 ♎
♇	11°28 ♌ ℞
☊	29°59 ♊
⚷	19°27 ♎

Chart 1. Joris Voorhoeve. December 22, 1945, 10:56 MET–1.00-09:56 GMT. The Hague, Netherlands 52°05 N 004°19 E. Data from Selma Schepel, *Sterretijd*, No. 57, birth certificate. Placidus houses.

In all respects, this is what Srebrenica was for Voorhoeve. His unaspected Mars "sucked" him toward the Ministry of Defense; he was asked to accept the position of minister and he agreed, obviously ignorant of the imminent disaster. This is the "classic" pattern: a situation from outside that stands in direct connection with your unaspected planet or yod (Mars and defense are "by the book"!), and consequently under these circumstances, we go through all the stalemates and crises that can belong to a yod or unaspected planet. Of course this doesn't happen nonstop, and we also go through a lot of fun things with this unaspected Mars. But stalemates and impossible choices just happen to lie in wait with an unaspected planet or a yod. And what was Voorhoeve supposed to do? A lightly armed Dutch unit in a serious set of circumstances, without a good mandate to be really able to act, had to deal with a Serbian raid after months of hard times, with no assistance forthcoming. This by itself is already a crisis situation, but the unit had to face this while they had no gasoline, had been eating only emergency rations for months, and were having a very hard time, as a few former members had made known in radio broadcasts. So the Dutch unit's choice of options was already a stalemate.

Another troublesome side of yods and unaspected planets is the feeling of being wronged. This applies to the situation we end up in, a situation we really didn't deserve and which is not our fault. However, it also applies to everything around such a situation, particularly misconceptions about matters, accusations, and such. We run the risk of being blamed for things we haven't done. In fact, out-and-out lies may come out. In short, we run a bigger risk of being dealt the Joker. This risk is the biggest when the unaspected planet, the duet, or the yod is activated by progression or transit.

With Voorhoeve, this happened during the summer of 1998, when Neptune became stationary at the beginning of Aquarius, and formed an opposition with his unaspected Mars. (Pluto by transit, by the way, also came to a standstill over Voorhoeve's MC, which made him extremely vulnerable to being handed the Joker.) All of a sudden, Srebrenica was in the spotlight again, and along with it, Voorhoeve's role as minister. Richard Holbrooke, the American negotiator, had written a book in which the Netherlands was placed in a very bad light, and in which, according to insiders, he painted a totally erroneous picture of matters. Voorhoeve wrote Holbrooke a pointed letter about this. However, the book is out on the market, and making history. So, the deception of Neptune. When the new cabinet took over, the new Minister of Defense immediately had to deal with the stories and rumors about Srebrenica. Accusations were uttered by a former general, as if Voorhoeve had intentionally withheld the truth.

Voorhoeve was stabbed in the back and reacted with dismay and bewilderment. With Neptune afflicting Mars, it is, however, imaginable (not inevitable, but within the realm of possibilities), that deception and betrayal, or withheld facts (Neptune) on the part of his former staff or colleagues at the ministry might surface or have played a part—matters he can do nothing about; a minister depends on staff. But the blame will fall on him. This is the type of stalemate where action or decision-making is a big problem. It is difficult for an outsider to judge such a situation, because we don't know what was happening behind the scenes. However, if we know the effect unaspected planets and yod configurations can have, we can see that what Voorhoeve went through is a textbook case, and this demands caution in judging the situation. With yods and unaspected planets we can make mistakes, even major mistakes. It is, however, from the standpoint of astrology, not possible to say whether Voorhoeve made any mistakes. I only want to use this example to illustrate that a person who has integrity, is upstanding, and has clear-cut qualities, can become entangled by a duet (in this case) in a nightmare and be made accountable for it in the bargain, even though it crossed his path "from outside" and left him only a choice among evils.

9. Our lives are characterized by a perpetual "searching" quality.

One of the things I always say to clients and students when explaining yods and unaspected planets is that life in this regard signifies "searching with a capital S." It may sound strange, but we were really not meant to find definite answers—once they are there. As soon as we receive an answer to a question, we seek further. It's as if nothing can wholly satisfy us, and there is always that sensation in the back of our minds that there must be *more* to it, and the question, "So is *this* all there is?" These questions have nothing to do with dissatisfaction, but there is always a little voice somewhere in the background that keeps intruding, in all kinds of ways. It can give a feeling that when we get the job of a lifetime, we may think, "It's only temporary, because this *can't* be everything"—as if there were important experiences still awaiting; experiences we are afraid we might overlook. On the other hand, we have absolutely no idea what we seek and what we would really like to find. There is only that vague feeling. . . .

This can be troublesome in relationships as well, because this feeling has nothing to do with the relationship as such, but belongs to the basic hallmarks of a yod or an unaspected planet. This is why it is good to realize we don't need to stare at *finding* something until we're seeing double, we only need to learn to enjoy the fact that we are *on the road*. Enjoying the process of seeking, of the quest, instead of directing ourselves at finding something is, in itself, a giant step forward in learning to live with this vague feeling. Regardless of what we find, no matter how important it may be, we will keep feeling, "Is that all?" And the road goes on. Even on our deathbeds we may pose this question!

The flip side is that if we don't become aware of this quality, we may have ongoing trouble with feelings of dissatisfaction and restlessness. It can influence our moods and give us a negative approach to life. Something along the lines of, "It's never any good anyhow," or, "It'll all go wrong again anyway." Don't end up in this kind of spiral, because it is one of the pitfalls of yods and unaspected planets.

On the other hand, there is a very positive dimension to that seeking. Those who learn to live with it well and who don't let themselves be bothered by this feeling occasionally eating at them, will never doze at the wheel of life. Even as they get older, they will fall into a lethargic pattern less easily because their spirits will keep moving and looking for something that cannot be named. This provides the capacity to remain flexible in spirit well into old age and to gather a deep wisdom in the domains of the planets involved. This provides a wealth in which others can also share.

Don't be tempted to describe what you seek. You won't be able to do it. If those around you ask, explain that you simply derive pleasure by being busy with all kinds of things. Help children with yods and unaspected planets particularly to find that pleasure in seeking and discovering. This will be very useful to them. And don't be surprised if you find extremes here as well: many children with yods and unaspected planets, while seeking, may change their course of studies, several times even, before they're on track. There are, however, children who suddenly know from within what direction they want to take in life. The seeking doesn't end here, though; it can also transfer itself to an attitude that the child develops *within* the theme that is fascinating, so that a lot of knowledge can be built up in play. Thus, children with an unaspected Uranus, or Uranus in a yod, may suddenly discover that the world of computers is theirs. If a computer is made available, they go in search, from technique to use, from playing to programming—with a considerable phone bill as a result of all that searching for patch routines or information on the Internet. This searching is not to be stopped. However, should you ask, "What are you looking for?" they would be hard put to reply. "Surfing the Net" may dovetail perfectly with that searching quality. Children can get stuck in a particular behavior with this, too, though, and then it can turn against them.

This searching quality enables people with a yod to survive hard times. Security and a smoothly running society and economy are not part of their experience anyway. They have no internal equipment for these things. They are at their best in times of change and at turning points, and *this* is where yods and unaspected planets can also play a significant and creative role.

Unfortunately the customary education system and school financing are not particularly helpful to children with unaspected planets or yods. Stringent requirements and the lack of space for inner seeking make it hard for these students. They are capable of excellent study habits, but what they hold inside will not tolerate a clear-cut pattern, as the following point reveals.

10. Our lives don't allow for planning; and yods and unaspected planets do not allow direct guidance.

As an almost logical consequence of the initial ambiguity, lack of a grasp of the subject matter, insecurity, and all kinds of unexpected situations, is the fact that people with yod configurations and unaspected planets are able to plan their lives only with difficulty. Of course you can make plans and a certain number will be realized. Just keep in mind that things often won't work out the way you had foreseen or the way you might want. This may have to do with adversity, or with sudden shifts in situations (as well as changes in yourself). This doesn't have to be unpleasant all the time by a long shot though. Yod configurations and unaspected planets tend to bring you to your destination after all, but along byways and inexplicable paths you would not have dreamed up yourself, by means of both saddening experiences and hilariously funny ones you will greatly enjoy.

It will very often be the case that you line things up for yourself, only to have all kinds of things intervene—down to your plan for the day. This has nothing to do with unwillingness, and it also doesn't mean that you couldn't get anything done. What yods and unaspected planets need is time and space. If you give people with these horoscope factors an assignment that has to be done in an hour, there is a chance that the pressure will have an adverse effect. The yod will start doubting hugely and the unaspected planets that are needed for the assignment will just then momentarily seem to withdraw entirely from the situation. So never place pressure on a plan and don't get yourself all worked up. Something that works excellently, for instance, is making a little list of goals and tasks, with a particular period of time to be able to work on them. It is better to write down five tasks and to say that they have to be done by the end of the week, than allotting one task per day. This last increases the pressure and doesn't work as well. By giving yourself breathing room, you allow the needed unaspected planets to surface in their own time, so you can, in fact, really enjoy working on the assignment! Therefore, never crack the whip over people with yods and unaspected planets! (Unaspected planets have the most trouble with this. They won't function well anymore, and will snap shut or get too stressed. And this is a shame, because that very unaspected planet is an ability, but it wants to be put into play in its own time and will be able to perform exceptionally well then!)

Too much pressure can work adversely. However, forcing yods and unaspected planets to make choices on the spot is not productive. The stress that accompanies this only increases feelings of insecurity. Pressure results in these people snapping shut and not functioning anymore, which reinforces insecurity, and also creates feelings of powerlessness and ignorance, when in fact there are no grounds for this. Yods and unaspected planets *force* us, by their sensitivity to pressure, to approach things in an easy and relaxed manner, and to stand more in the here and now, since plans need to be constantly adjusted anyway. This is a tendency that runs counter to our Western culture of *now*, where speed, constant pursuit, efficient time management, goals, and efficiency are supposed to carry the day in order to keep up. People with yods and unaspected planets are the shadow of this, as it were. Not that they don't want to participate, that isn't the issue. They are simply *different* and don't have the flashy equipment that keeps our society running, maybe even making it run amok. Yods and unaspected planets might well be the key to another way of being, whereby happiness is achievable, even *without* constantly pursuing and chasing after things. Another case of a turning-point, perhaps?

11. Sometimes the unexpected turns into the best experiences.

What has come out particularly in this chapter are the problems and troublesome points of yods and unaspected planets. These simply cannot be avoided. However, they also have other things up their sleeve, although a lot depends on the way we learn to handle these things. I have noticed that sometimes, in the natal chart, a yod or unaspected planet was activated by progression or transit, or that a temporary yod was formed at an important, positive turning-point in someone's life, or at a very important step in the life, as if this were indicating something in no uncertain terms. Now the yod can be described as "the hand of God" and can offer very special experiences that will have repercussions in the psyche for a long time.

When Jupiter entered Pisces by transit and formed an exact yod with my natal Saturn and Neptune on one hand and Pluto on the other, I received the Regulus Award for Education, in Atlanta, at the UAC convention. This was a distinction I had not at all expected, even though I knew I had been nominated. Needless to say, I felt most honored by this.

12. Exceptional experiences.

Whenever an unaspected planet or yod is temporarily activated by progression or transit, or a temporary yod is formed, pay particular attention to subtle things. Premonitions, dreams, and little signals will occur more frequently under this activation, and can lead to breakthroughs you had not thought possible! It isn't beyond imagining that on the one hand you are caught in a kind of stalemate in the external world, and on the other hand, a whole new road is unfolding in your dream life, or new insights break through as the first tentative signs of a turning point. Listen to them, work with them, because this may be the beginning of a new phase. I have met people who had a yod involving Pluto and Neptune. When these yods were activated, abilities broke through in the area of magnetism, alternative healing, seeing auras, and the like, particularly in the area of the "unseen world," to state it broadly. Before this time they had had no inkling of this, some had never before even entertained interest in this field. They were confronted by these new interests in very diverse ways—through illness, through being able to see things all of a sudden, through dreams, through an out-of-body experience, and so on.

With yods and unaspected planets, experiences can be *very* exceptional in the positive sense. The only risk is that you may be so overwhelmed, that you start doing radical things. This can suck you out of reality, as I have seen a number of times unfortunately. As with a sweet, warm woman, who had been happily married for years and run a business with her husband. She had a series of progressions and transits of Pluto and Neptune that formed yods in her horoscope. Suddenly the capacity to heal people through magnetism broke through for her, and she experienced moments of automatic writing. It was an entirely new world for her, and she wanted very much to continue with healing work. Considering there were still a number of yods in the process of forming and the theme was spread out over the coming years, I warned her not to do anything radical, and above all to keep her feet on the ground. After all, this wasn't the first time sweet homemakers had come to me, always at the ready for others, and often also handing in pieces of themselves, and overnight packing their bags and disappearing, or going tilt in extreme attitudes and opinions. Due to the overwhelming experiences with yods, you can very easily lose your orientation and then burn the bridges behind you too quickly. She reacted warmly and wholeheartedly to my warning and was definitely not planning to do anything crazy. She wanted to keep both feet on the ground, even though her development was going at a fast pace. And she told me she had a good spiritual guide.

Some months later I spoke with her husband. He told me that his wife told him a couple of weeks after our conversation that she needed the house for her healing work, and that it would be best if he left. Her new life calling left no room for him. He felt as if he had "simply been tossed out." "I don't recognize my wife anymore," he said, "she has completely changed." I didn't speak with his wife again and so cannot report her view. However, it is not unlikely that she was gripped by an idea or ideal, and turned off onto an escape route with it. Such a person may, however, feel happy on this escape route for a time.

Taking an escape route can plunge you into an unreal situation, as it were, that leads you away from balanced development, which is always a risk inherent in yods and unaspected planets. However, the ways of yods and unaspected planets are inexplicable and it is equally possible that such a radical act or escape route is part of a change of track inside you, so that after some time you "wake up" and know better what you want and can do, and how you are going to approach things. It is true that there will often be a lot of sorting out to do.

13. We feel different from everybody else, but we also travel a unique road in life.

People with yod configurations or unaspected planets often experience the second half of their lives as totally different from the first. Most people undergo a turn-around in some way or other that is very important. In many cases we see this reflected in their profession; in other cases, it is more of an internal process reflected in their attitude toward life, in opinions (societal or otherwise), and philosophical or religious views. We could hardly have had any notion of these new paths when we were young. Sometimes the directions may be ones for which we never had any sympathy, or which we even detested. Yet, in looking back, we are able to see the thread running through life that brought us to the point where we are now.

I have seen countless examples of this, from the tax consultant who became fascinated by aura reading, to the dissident Václav Havel who became a president (see below). It will not be unusual for our unique, very own road in life to be one that deviates from the pattern into which we were born, meaning the family dynamic. Sometimes it will also deviate from the customary patterns of the society or the culture in which we live. With yods and unaspected planets, it turns out that we have great creative potential to be in close touch with ourselves and to express something unique.

To people with yods and unaspected planets this may often sound strange because one of the things I invariably hear from them is that they aren't really aware of any such talents. There is almost an incredulity that they might actually have those talents. Their response then runs, "I'm always an exception to the rule, so that will surely be the case again this time." This somewhat stand-offish and sometimes even negative approach is related to insecurity and feeling *different* from other people.

Many people with a yod or unaspected planet have had this feeling from early on, sometimes only slightly, sometimes in a more extreme way, in the sense that they feel like they don't belong, were born in the wrong family, etc. This being "different" is

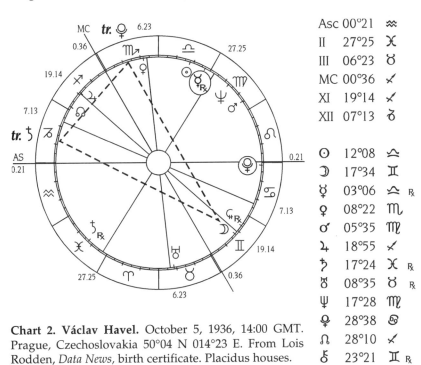

Asc	00°21	♒
II	27°25	♓
III	06°23	♉
MC	00°36	♐
XI	19°14	♐
XII	07°13	♑

☉	12°08	♎	
☽	17°34	♊	
☿	03°06	♎	℞
♀	08°22	♏	
♂	05°35	♍	
♃	18°55	♐	
♄	17°24	♓	℞
♅	08°35	♉	℞
♆	17°28	♍	
♇	28°38	♋	
☊	28°10	♐	
⚷	23°21	♊	℞

Chart 2. Václav Havel. October 5, 1936, 14:00 GMT. Prague, Czechoslovakia 50°04 N 014°23 E. From Lois Rodden, *Data News*, birth certificate. Placidus houses.

something they can't precisely define. It's more a vague feeling in the background.

If they do indeed dare to shape their later lives *differently*, they run the risk of remaining stuck in the idea of still not being part of things, resulting in a feeling that even this new direction in life isn't one that really fits them, although they do seem to have a talent for it. So the lack of identification with the theme involved in yods or an unaspected planet avenges itself here, although things don't have to get to this point. I can also give you countless examples of people who, after an internal or external turn-around in their lives started intensely enjoying and learning to live with this feeling of searching and insecurity—a feeling that even became the driving force behind their development! Jung's horoscope is a nice example of this; see chapter 14.

An Example: *Václav Havel*

Havel has an unintegrated Mercury in his 8th house, and Mercury is also the ruler of his 8th house. (See Chart 2, page 65.) The following themes will therefore step into the foreground in an all-or-nothing attitude or situation, and at the same time also in pure form as in an ability and in the possible concealing of this ability through insecurity:

Mercury: Communication, analysis, writing, thinking, and speaking.

Ruler 8: The world of power, what is hidden, resistance, depths, understanding of human nature, Life and Death, just to name a few of the many domains.

Pluto, too, is an unaspected planet in Havel's horoscope, which only emphasizes the unaspected ruler of his 8th house.

Havel became known as a writer (unaspected Mercury as talent!) and as a dissident (Ruler 8 *and* unaspected Pluto). For years he resisted the stringent communist regime in the former Czechoslovakia, and despite countless arrests, prison sentences, house arrest, and other punitive measures to control him, he did not allow himself to be subdued. Remember that an unaspected Ruler 8, as well as an unaspected Pluto, have an unlikely amount of fighting strength and resilience once they identify with something! In the West, Havel became *the* face of the dissident movement in his country. Even though there were other important dissidents, the fact is that someone with a yod or unaspected planet will have more visibility.

Something else that keeps striking me about yods and un-aspected planets is that you are often already unconsciously involved in building on your future activities without being aware of this, and even without wanting to. The same is true of Havel. Because of his unrelenting criticism of the communist government and the determined attitude with which he endured in his role of dissident, there was for the entire nation but one man who could lead the country after the revolution, and that was Havel. So it appears, even though he had always firmly declared that he would absolutely never want to take on an administrational function. Such a position seemed awful to him and he didn't aspire to it at all. However, due to his years of activism, he had gained a lot of trust, and had also shown evidence of balanced managerial and organizational qualities, while maintaining a human and personal approach. This is what he had built up over all those years, without being aware of it himself. At the so-called velvet revolution (the revolts took place without any bloodshed), Havel was confronted by an ability he wasn't even aware of yet himself, but which he had shown in recent years. And so he was immediately named to the country's highest office.

On taking office as the first president of Czechoslovakia after the fall of the communist regime, we see in his natal chart the transit of Pluto from Scorpio in an exact inconjunct to his Moon in Gemini, while Saturn is also in the process of entering an inconjunct with his Moon from Capricorn. The sextile between Pluto and Saturn in the sky at the time of Havel's taking office thus forms a yod with the Moon in his natal chart. As an unaspected planet in a temporary transit, Pluto can really get things rolling!

Havel did not take on the presidency wholeheartedly though. He realized that he was the only one who could help get the country back on track due to the people's trust in him, but he actually didn't feel like it. Here is the inner stalemate and the choice between evils—by refusing the presidency he destroys his goodwill, and he knows that his country would end up in trouble. Becoming president was not something he wanted, but something toward which his unconscious had, in fact, driven him in the previous years because of the activities of his unaspected Mercury/Ruler 8 and unaspected Pluto. The yod is very clear: his Moon is the ruler of his 6th house, the house of work and service, among other things. Work (6th house) and service (6th house) were demanded of him on an administrational level (Saturn) with power (Pluto).

The yod brought him into office, but Havel knew how difficult it would all become. Not only because of the fresh aversion he felt, but also because he was very very aware of the problems coming down the road, such as Slovakia wanting to secede.

The only way to face up to such a yod situation is not to let the fact that you are *truly* successful socially go to your head. Try not to idealize yourself, remain modest and calm, and try to deal with things that cross your path creatively and without pushing the envelope. Havel indeed began in a quiet, honest, and modest way with his new lot in life.

CHAPTER FIVE

Interpreting Yod Configurations

Now that we have seen what the general hallmarks of yods and unaspected planets are and what you can generally expect to experience with them, we can now shift to interpretation. What does a particular unaspected planet do, and what can you say about the yod planets themselves?

There is a big difference in approach between interpreting an unaspected planet and interpreting a yod. It is as easy to describe and interpret an unaspected planet as it is hard and complicated to approach a yod. Here we are not only involved with the various planets in the yod, but these planets are each also additionally the ruler of a house, or even several houses. If the ruler of a house is located in a yod, the affairs of that house will become involved with the theme of the yod, or you will have "yod-like" experiences with or relating to matters pertaining to that house. If Mercury and Venus both take part in a yod, it may well be that half the horoscope is involved in the dynamics of the yod. The picture that comes out then is almost not to be untangled; one thing works against a second and the second contradicts the first. And yet there is a latent ability in the air that wants to break through. The idea of the yod is in conflict with any clarity or system, and even talking or writing about yods is more complicated than you'd like it to be!

If you want to explain to a client with a yod how it works and everything that is related to it, it's good to begin with the general backgrounds and tendencies that we discussed in chapter 4. Even if you don't know how to interpret the yod any more specifically, the general story will already be very recognizable in practice and may promote acceptance. Later we will also start looking at how you can best live with yods. Considering that the feelings of a yod can so often be overpowering in someone's life, it is good to talk about this at the very beginning of your interpretation; doing so will also provide starting points for the rest of the interpretation.

The planets that participate and form a yod are a good place to start in building your interpretation of the yod. My experience is that in general the personal planets (the Sun through Mars) seem more tangible than the rest. In my view, this is mostly related to the fact that the personal planets generally happen to be more recognizable and therefore play a clearer role in everyday life. The slow planets are much more difficult to recognize in the individual, but in a yod they play as important a role as that played by the personal planets.

Because the participating planets in a yod are constantly influencing and making things difficult for one another, you will need to keep pointing out, in discussing any of these planets individually, that each particular interpretation you offer will again be influenced or even undermined by the other participants. As soon as you are engaged in the domain of one of the planets, another yod planet will get mixed up in it and seem to try to take over the helm, as it were, through emotions and restlessness. The result is a fishtailing back and forth between emotions and/or activities. As soon as a calm seems to have arrived, number three will get involved and the upheaval is complete. In a yod, you will never be able to isolate and distinguish the wishes, longings, and activities of one planet (something you can do with all the usual major aspects and aspect configurations). It will seem as if a kind of veil were covering the participating planets. It also seems that this simply will not be *allowed*, whether because your own feelings, restlessness, or emotions intervene, or because of troublesome events or developments outside you. Just as if it had to keep being proven to you that the very thing you achieved or combated in the area of the participating planets was *real*.

Because of all of this, none of the planets in a yod can be described well in isolation. They'll slip through your fingers like a piece of soap. This is unfortunate because you would love to be able to offer your client security and clarity in this area, but it seems even interpretation and clarification fall under the yod effect. This also means that I have to keep my options open in the discussion below and point out other factors. This is why I will illustrate various things as extensively as possible with anecdotes and work out my interpretation primarily based on examples. A number of steps follow below, but a different order is also possible.

1. Take each yod planet separately and explain that each represents an energy that will be accompanied by restlessness and searching.

This stage of the interpretation will seem very much like that of unaspected planets (see chapter 6), where this is also one of the steps in the interpretation. You can simply take the basic meaning of the planet concerned and describe it in terms of a latent power that is covered up by restlessness, insecurity, and searching. This goes for all the planets, both the personal ones as well as the collective ones. If we use the Moon as an example, we first need to look at what the Moon means for everyone, what its general dynamics are. In order not to turn everything upside down right away, it's best if you leave the background signs out for now and introduce them in a next step as an interpretational factor.

The Moon is subject matter that becomes active when we feel unsure or unsafe. The Moon in a sign indicates how we try to get back on our feet and feel good again, and lunar aspects are possible tools for this. The Moon also provides information about how we care for others and are able to accept care, how we can give and receive nurturing, and how we want to shape atmosphere, domesticity, and congeniality. If the Moon is located in a yod (or if it is an unaspected planet) we are more vulnerable and insecure regarding these points. We are thrown off balance more readily. This has nothing to do with instability, but we more readily have inner doubts and we have more trouble calming down again right away. We have a great need for warmth and congeniality, and show this in an exaggerated fashion at one moment, while at another moment we crawl all the way back into our shell. Experiences of rejection cut deep and make us more readily vulnerable than is the case with others.

In the area of the Moon we are restless and searching. Even if you get all the nurturing in the world, there will still be a "But . . .," as if it were hard to grasp that everything is fine. Somehow, under the surface there is still a longing, although at the same time you don't know why or what's wrong. This makes itself known particularly in a gnawing, restless feeling that can make you unsure when care-giving and nurturing, or creating a mood, or substantiating your role as a parent are concerned.

With regard to this last point: the Moon is relevant for both the father and the mother in parenting. After all, it represents nurturing and care-giving, and both father as well as mother can shape this. The Moon therefore does not indicate the mother, but much more your own sensitivity to atmosphere, domesticity, and care, which you can easily project onto both parents. The Moon in a yod can make you very sensitive to tension at home, to emotional pressure and problems. These may actually have existed, in fact, but they don't always have to by a long shot! So even if they didn't exist, there would still be an emotional vulnerability to any tension around. A Moon in a yod often has a hard time feeling at home, understood, and accepted, and parents will have to pay particular attention, because a fear of attachment can easily arise. Paradoxically enough, this is also frequently accompanied by an (often obsessive) urge for attachment, and both extremes can come out in behavior.

Most adults with an unaspected Moon or yod Moon who have children go through a phase in which they have to seek and feel around for what it means, exactly, to be a father or a mother. It is not unusual for this to be associated with the feeling of not being good, not being able, and a lack of self-confidence on this point, and at the same time a fascination for family, extended family, and children, and feeling yourself very attracted to these things. It can't be predicted whether balance will be established, or whether you'll remain at one of the two poles. At the one extreme you will do everything to avoid starting a family, and in the other case your whole life may even revolve exclusively around your children.

Doubts about care-giving, nurturing, atmosphere, domesticity, home life, etc, can keep raising their heads, create uneasiness at the craziest moments, and make you wonder if you're doing things right, or whether what is here now is in fact what you want, and so forth. Meanwhile you may radiate something that *asks* for nurturing and security, which those around you are supposed to give you, and oftentimes this may—unintentionally—come across as possessiveness. At the same time this Moon is an ability, a theme through which you can express something exceptional, in a small way or in a large way. For the internal world of the psyche it doesn't matter whether you are a tremendous support for many people and children in and around your home, and can help them very well, or that you set up grand projects on a governmental level to help children in the third world. In both cases you see a great strength in the area of the themes of the Moon.

☆　☆　☆

You can also approach the collective planets in this way, considering each planet is linked to its own domain and has its own dynamics. Pluto, for instance, gives us the urge to dredge up stones from the bottom, to undergo and live through things intensely, and leads us through processes of transformation. At the same time, it is the energy that confronts us with the dark sides of ourselves and life. It is the urge to grow and gain depth, and at the same time the fear of anything connected with these things.

In a yod configuration, this energy is already difficult to grasp and not to be guided, which normally causes us to be restless, and makes us even a bit more uneasy. It seems as if it were brewing and simmering deep down inside us. It is not unusual with Pluto in a yod configuration to have a spot hidden deep inside you that always hurts. You don't know what it is or why, but it's as if there were some kind of deep sorrow or deep pain inside, often accompanied by a feeling of fear. The dynamic of this same Pluto is, however, one that wants to hide this as much as possible from the outside world, so that nobody really knows you. Sometimes this pain literally has something to do with experiences in your past, although even as a baby you had this as a factor in the way you reacted to things. Here, too, nothing has to have happened in reality to give you that "wounded feeling." It can result in the arising of a distrust of life, which can be projected onto particular people, sometimes onto people in general. The dark side with which Pluto confronts us is also a side to which you are not only *more* sensitive, it also seems to cross your path in the form of experiences with people who are not trustworthy or who are psychically not well balanced.

Here the searching nature of a planet in a yod configuration turns Pluto into a motivation that wants to go deeper than deep in both a positive as well as a negative sense. The deepest still isn't deep enough, because the question, "So is this it?" will always be in the background. This entails a tremendous potential for renewal and transformation, but at the same time a big chance to go through a significant crisis. With a Pluto like this, if you cannot achieve one, you will strive with singular intensity to achieve the other. An example of this is Pluto in the yod of Diana, Princess of Wales. If she couldn't become a queen anymore, then she would be the Queen of Hearts in the hearts of the people. The crises in Diana's life are probably familiar to most people. Another example is Pluto in the yod of C. G. Jung, who, after a severe crisis and great internal desperation, was able to provide enormous depth to psychology, and who kept searching up to the moment he was lying on his deathbed. He also absolutely did not want to be identified with a school of thought or a movement; he didn't even want to be a "Jungian," because he couldn't stand being pinned down in any way whatsoever. That would limit his space to seek and only hamper throwing old baggage overboard.

In the positive sense, people with Pluto in a yod can become gentle from the depth of the values they have stumbled across. Again, this can be in little things or big things. However, there is an equal risk of succumbing to an ever-deepening distrust. The yod itself cannot indicate which way things will go; this will have to do both with circumstance as well as a person's own choices.

In this way you can delve into all the planets of a yod. The Moon was an example of a personal planet and Pluto of a collective one. The crux in any case is that you take the basic meaning of that planet and combine it with restlessness, insecurity, seeking, *and* strength.

2. Take the backgrounds of the signs into consideration to further fine-tune the effect of the planets.

The collective planets (Uranus, Neptune, and Pluto) remain in a sign for so long that they present something more akin to generational data. This is why they will need less explanation regarding sign background; they come into play more in the picture of the times. The planets Jupiter and Saturn are half personal and half collective. Although they, too, remain in a sign for a long time, they move significantly faster than the outer planets. Jupiter takes almost twelve years to move through the zodiac, Saturn takes almost thirty years. So Jupiter remains in a sign one year on average, and Saturn two-and-a-half years, although there are great variations due to the retrograde movements of both. Nevertheless, we do need to weigh the sign background of these two planets. It will become clear that Saturn in its own sign of Capricorn can have a lot more impact in a yod than when it is in Aries, for instance. The most important thing, though, is to interpret the personal planets from their background sign. It makes a big difference in a yod whether you have the Sun in Leo, or in Cancer. Sun in Leo has a greater urge to manifest itself than the Sun in Cancer, and could therefore show greater extremes of expression than a Sun in Cancer. Thus the background sign helps you to fine-tune things.

Imagine that you have Mercury in a yod. The theme of communication then gains all the aforementioned hallmarks. We should take communication in a broad sense: the way in which you organize knowledge and facts, and line things up, the way in which you talk, read, learn, and write, are all part of this concept. In a yod, Mercury becomes insecure and restless in these areas, and is vulnerable.

If Mercury in Gemini is located in the yod, there is always a big chance that such a person will speak and respond with ease anyway, because Mercury in Gemini is capable of a glib chat and a rapid response. A yod will change little in this as such, even though the yod will insure that at unpredictable moments this person will feel unsure and so may make mistakes. Making mistakes is not so much a hallmark of a planet in a yod, but may be the result of the restlessness and nervousness of the yod.

Mercury in Cancer by nature has a lot less of that ability to chat glibly. This background for Mercury demands emotional safety and a congenial mood; only then can Mercury in Cancer express itself well. If the mood's not there, Mercury's capacity for contact will also be placed under pressure. Not that Mercury in Cancer is incapable. Far from it, these people may be gifted speakers! On one condition, though, and that is a feeling of belonging, a congenial atmosphere or "feeling at home" with people. As it happens, Mercury in Cancer is in a good position to create these conditions in order to be able to feel good.

Now, if you have Mercury in Cancer in a yod, you are confronted by the problem that you have with yods in general regarding the theme of "belonging." You feel different than other people, and are very vulnerable where atmosphere, security, and congeniality are concerned. These are precisely circumstances that are important to you in order to be able to come into your own in word and deed. This means that in a yod configuration, Mercury in Cancer will still be confronted by different problems than Mercury in Gemini! Even though Mercury in Gemini will seem to have it easier because, due to its background, Mercury is not dependent on a feeling of security, its problems play out on a different level, such as being preoccupied by facts that haven't quite been accepted yet. Mercury in a yod is often interested in *precisely* those things that are less accepted, or that are rejected by others around, and the like. The issue in this example is therefore not a question of which sign background would be better for Mercury. What is most important is to show that a planet functions from a sign, and that this important facet counts in the interpretation of a yod.

3. Show that the planets in a yod constantly influence one another and that they will cause a lot of restlessness and movement.

An example from practice: A yod involved the Sun, Saturn, and Uranus. The woman who has this yod has been practicing astrology for years. She says it took a long time before she was able to develop a feeling of identity. Through her orientation toward personal growth and psychological insight, she managed to gain more perspective on who she is and what she wants (Sun). From time to time, however, she was confronted by the feeling she couldn't hold on to that perspective. Just when things are nice, a feeling of distrust (Saturn) crops up, just like that, out of the blue. This might be a distrust of herself, and also a distrust of life in general. Or else sudden events (Uranus) and circumstances will make sure that she starts doubting herself again. Or just when she really feels like doing some astrology (Uranus), she'll get saddled with circumstantial obligations, inhibiting circumstances, with adversity, and so forth (Saturn), or a defensiveness will crop up inside that gives her the feeling she first has to check whether she did in fact fulfill all her obligations. Unwillingly she has to change course, and is unable to get to herself (Sun). It would seem as if her hobby, astrology, cannot be free of problems that place her on the spot and force her to make choices, and then she often has to "choose" things she would rather do at some other time. Family life and obligations may also easily undermine her identity and sense of self. Still, she derives a lot of pleasure from astrology and psychology, and manages in cheery fashion to face tensions. If we look at this example, it seems her Sun (identity) is very vulnerable as soon as she activates this subject matter. In other words: as soon as she chooses for herself, wants to show who she is, feels good in her skin, has confidence in herself, and vitally steps toward life from this standpoint, the doubts of Saturn come, as if Saturn were standing by, waiting to bring the Sun down a notch as soon as it manifests itself. So the Sun cannot come out without Saturn starting some undermining action, an action filled with doubt and distrust.

This can also be the case, of course, in a simple square between the Sun and Saturn, but in the normal major aspects you are capable of gaining perspective a lot sooner on what you are doing and what is wrong, so that a square or opposition between the Sun and Saturn may symbolize not only a troublesome aspect, but also a good and reliable tool for you. This is different with a yod. The undermining is more insidious, more invasive, less comprehensible, and harder to shake off, at least in the first part of your life. It usually takes longer before you really learn to deal with this. It seems as if the contents involved are much more interwoven. So you can't talk about the Sun without also taking into account the vulnerability, doubt, and distrust of Saturn. This isn't all though. Uranus is also participating. This means that as soon as this woman wants to be herself or wants to choose for herself, sudden tensions, inner restlessness, irritation, and such, crop up. Often I also notice in a yod configuration with Uranus that the person in question just cannot find the peace of mind to start doing something. You *want* to do something, but in one way or another fritter away your energy (or allow this to happen) by simply allowing a thousand and one things to intervene. Before you know it, the time you had to spend is gone, and you are left with that feeling of dissatisfaction and restlessness.

The yod is thus a remarkable and conflicting mixture of all these factors, and initially none of them succeed in gaining the upper hand or any elbow room. As I have already mentioned, it often takes *years* to find out about this, so the second half of life for people with a yod is often more pleasant that the first half (if they are aware of their dynamic and are prepared to tackle it).

In this example we studied the yod primarily from the Sun. This is a tendency you can easily have as an astrologer, because the personal planets offer an easy leg up for interpretation.

Now, take Saturn, for instance, as a starting point. It is the planet of durability, responsibility, method, and resoluteness, on the one hand, and of fear, distrust, and melancholy on the other (I am restricting myself here to just a couple of buzz words; it has infinitely more nuance, of course). The minute the woman responsibly wants to do the things she has to do (Saturn), all kinds of things can intervene (Uranus), or she might feel strong resistance from the Sun, and have the feeling that life is setting traps for her and not giving her any space. This is when the Sun would like to go its own way most and choose to do what she enjoys, which gets in the way of her meeting her obligations. Uranus seems to help the Sun just a little bit by demanding space and freedom, but the minute she makes room for herself, the Sun peeks around the corner again with a question like, "Do I really want this?" and Saturn meanwhile holds an onslaught of guilty feelings in store. Thus the entire process seems to consist of a nonstop shoving and tugging among the three subject matters involved, so that none of the three can just function in peace. Right away the other two intrude and thwart the first somehow. This is also why it is so difficult, as I mentioned earlier, to describe a planet in a yod: as soon as you try, your client will say that none of it is recognizable. That would be true, too, since the picture simply cannot be clarified due to the constant interference. Astrologers will have the problem of wanting to describe and interpret the subject matter, but continually having to say that the situation is always different from what they are now pointing out.

4. Explain how what has been discussed leads to insecurity for each of the participating planets, and how that insecurity may express itself.

It is good to take a longer look at the insecurity that this dynamic brings about with your client. In fact, you are dealing with two sources of insecurity. Because of the fact that yods and unaspected planets are usually connected with a generational dynamic, its inherent restlessness will play a role in your existence, and along with it the troublesome projections you can get from it. Added to this is the insecurity deriving from planets in the yod configuration that exhibit a dynamic where they cannot develop and nonstop have to fight all kinds of resistance, possibly coming from the outside but primarily internal much of the time. Your lack of comprehension, due to the background of the three different elements, the three different modes, and the two polarities, accentuates this once again.

However, it is also important to emphasize that this insecurity can have a particular function. In the areas of the participating planets you will find no rest, and this also means that you can't play hide-and-seek in those domains. You cannot escape the urge to do something with them and find a form for them. Due to the fact that these contents prevent you from sticking to a "sluggish" and customary pattern, and force you always to keep on searching, a capacity for deep wisdom and great power lies hidden here. If you are capable of accepting insecurity as the price for this ability, and to see that it is not meant to undermine you but to keep you searching, a lot will already have been gained. I will always repeat this, because it is crucial point for dealing with yods and unaspected planets—let the insecurity be for what it is, knowing that you just happen to feel it, but that the real situation is not "your fault." Flip the channel and continue on your way! Only when people keep identifying with their insecurity will they in fact be constantly busy suggesting (hypnotically) to themselves that they can't do anything This is unfortunate because you can do incredibly much *precisely* because of your yod or unaspected planet. You can take the basic meaning of each of the three planets, supplemented by the sign in which each is located, and the hallmarks of that planet described as you always do, but supplemented with the distinguishing feature of a larger doubt, insecurity, and restlessness this time. Don't forget to talk about the positive side though!

5. Indicate how people seem to get hopelessly entangled in situations of fate.

Yod configurations are unmannerly enough to get you caught up in troublesome situations, and often very unpleasant or impossible circumstances at that. Painful situations that elicit feelings of a stalemate are often associated with yod configurations. These may be situations in which you rightfully ask yourself, "Why did I deserve *this*?" In the previous chapter I already presented a couple of general examples of this. In this chapter my concern will be a more specific interpretation. The stalemate, the painful and troublesome situations, happen to be very strongly linked to the planets participating in the yod, and with the houses that these planets rule. It is hard to deduce from the yod itself which of the yod planets will step into the foreground most, so around which planet the stalemate will occur. Although I have often heard the opinion that the apex planet is supposed to be the most important (the planet at the top; the base being the sextile), in my experience that has never been true. Precisely due to the constant turbulence and mutual influence of the participating planets, there is no single planet that comes to stand at the forefront. Sometimes, though, the painful situation or stalemate will exhibit itself most clearly around one of the yod planets, and this might be the apex or any other planet (or planets) in the yod. I have often seen that at other times other planets within the yod would drive people into a corner as well.

Regarding their tendencies, they can all three symbolize a specific situation, and if more planets are participating in a yod, then that also applies to them. It is, however, messy to indicate beforehand whether problems will occur primarily around one, two, or all three of the participants. On top of this, the issue may also be a planet as ruler of a house, so that the crisis has less to do with the theme of the planet than with the theme of the house that the planet rules. I have found that when people tell me about their life and experiences, they recognize the personal planets within a yod much more easily than the trans-Saturnal ones. I will provide a couple of examples of experiences you can have with yod configurations, focusing on the participating planets. In later chapters even more extensive examples will be discussed.

Examples of the Venus–Pluto–Neptune Yod

A well-known example of this yod is Prince William, the oldest son of Prince Charles and Princess Diana. Venus is the apex, and Pluto is in sextile with Neptune, the base. William's childhood was long subject to his parents' marital problems, which were carried too far by the media in an almost unbearable way for a child, both through the books his parents authored as well as by the paparazzi and tabloids in England and abroad. He was born already burdened by a generational theme, and Venus is certainly indicative of the many relational problems in previous generations, on his father's side of the family as well as in his mother's line. This makes him extra-vulnerable when he experiences this dynamic up close. Together with his younger brother he was audience to this ever-intensifying drama, and it must have been frankly awful to have to see the contents of his parents' bugged intimate phone conversations and arguments in the media. After the divorce, things seemed to be better between his parents, but due to the premature death of his mother, things can no longer be talked out to closure. His mother's last love brought him once again to a stalemate: it is known that he did not advocate her marrying Dodi. What goes through a child when he sees his mother become happy with a controversial man, in a relationship that will result in a lot of problems for everyone involved?

Venus in his horoscope is Ruler 4, and Pluto, Ruler 10. The pivotal point that symbolizes both parents emphasizes the dynamic in William's childhood even a bit more.

Pluto in the yod might have to do with the intense manner in which the dramas in his childhood developed. Jung also has Pluto in a yod (but not Neptune or Venus) and Jung was inwardly confronted by intense issues and certain irrational fears. The ability inherent in the yod of understanding the human psyche and fathoming it is often the result of that inner Plutonian confrontation (Jung), possibly coupled with intense events in the outside world (William), so that the theme of Life and Death may also play a role. For William, this theme will be expressed by, among other things, the death of his mother. For Jung, the theme of Life and Death came into play, among other things, through his fascination and fear of the corpses that washed ashore around the Schaffhausen waterfall, close to where he lived for a time, and through ominous dream images when he was a child.

☆   ☆   ☆

Other difficult life situations I have seen with a Venus–Pluto–Neptune yod are also linked to the themes of Love and Marriage, clearly a Venus theme. A few examples. A woman with this yod was born into a family she experienced as being pleasant. Her grandparents (on both sides) had been dead set against the marriage of her parents, and had never brushed this under the rug in the presence of their grandchildren. There was no direct problem with the parents, or in their marriage, or affecting the children, but there was a very tense family atmosphere surrounding the parents' marriage. Her grandparents on both sides turned out to have marriages that were held together for the sake of appearances (money played a significant role here), but marriages whose contents didn't amount to much, according to this woman. When this woman moved into a rooming house and began to develop herself independently, she fell in love a number of times, and finally married. Every single one of the men with whom she fell in love turned out to be unable to handle a relationship. Once she fell for a very rich man (with whom she felt very sure of herself), until she noticed that he was having her secretly followed everywhere, and that he was throwing her increasingly off balance through manipulation and subtle "twists" until she no longer knew who she was. Another boyfriend turned out to have the traits of a pathological liar. The man whom she married at first also seemed to be the real McCoy, but she hadn't been aware initially that the man had a multiple personality disorder, even though she thought he acted strange now and then. Their marriage was exceptionally complicated for years, until she couldn't stand it anymore, and asked for a divorce.

Manipulation (Pluto) or undermining (Neptune) linked to the theme of relationship (Venus) is an expression of this yod that occurs with regularity. We just saw an example in which experiences cross your path from the outside. Pluto in the yod, however, can also affect your own behavior, and likewise mean that the demands and expectations you have of the relationship are exceptionally high because you feel unsafe and insecure. Then you, yourself, are unconsciously and unintentionally the manipulating factor in the relationship, so you may elicit very unpleasant responses. Or else you idealize everything to escape from reality (Neptune) and land with a jolt face to face with yourself again. With such a yod, you could thus unconsciously and unnoticeably be the crux of the problem yourself, or go through life with somebody who has a lot of problematic sides. If, however, you are aware early on of this situation, it is definitely possible to have a good, longstanding, and happy marriage, a marriage that may even be exceptional, and in which the two of you may form a deep unity. A significant coping process and inner confrontations often do come first though.

Venus also often literally has to do with security. It's not for nothing that Venus indicates the kind of money or paper currency in the horoscope of a country! Venus yod situations may also entail a confrontation with a choice regarding concrete security. I have seen this work out more than once in the sense of keeping a marriage together and remaining in a financially comfortable situation that is, however, an emotional drama; or stepping out of that marriage, to be consequently completely bled dry by the partner, financially or emotionally. I met one woman with a Venus–Pluto–Neptune yod whose ex-husband transformed into a stalker and didn't give her a moment's peace. This only happened after she had started a new relationship.

One man with the Venus–Pluto–Neptune yod experienced as a child that his father used him as a "cover" for his extramarital affairs. He would often go off supposedly to do something with the boy, and then take him to his girlfriend's. The boy was bribed with candy and toys so he wouldn't tattle, and at the same received subtle, but unmistakable threats as to what would happen if he did say anything. His father had many girlfriends, one after the other, all of whom started following him. The father also had children with some of these women. They started making financial claims on him, so then his father saw only one way out with his family, and that was emigrating to Australia. The son had just started elementary school and felt totally uprooted. In Australia his father didn't have a permanent job right away, and this meant that sometimes they would live in the same place for a year, and then move again to live somewhere else for a couple of months. Sometimes things went well for the family for a while, materially speaking, and then in the next months they would be poor again. Finally the family returned to the Netherlands, but couldn't really settle down there anymore. The man has a lot of trouble building up a feeling of attachment because there is a deep fear that it will be broken again. And as it would happen, *he* was to experience that the first girl he fell in love with in the Netherlands had to go abroad because her father's company was sending her father out for a number of years, and he was taking the whole family along. He literally said, "Why did that have to happen *precisely* to *me*!" For this man, Neptune is the ruler of his 4th house, so there is also an indication of domesticity and domestic circumstances, childhood, and parents involved in the theme—very appropriate for what the man experienced. Although Venus, the female planet (besides the Moon, of course), is oftentimes brought into connection with one's mother, the active problems in the yod of this man can clearly be traced back to his father. So this makes it difficult to make any statements about which parent is actually causing the problem. Often there are also all kinds of psychic problems that are hidden from the eyes of the outside world, but that determine a lot, as the following example will show.

A woman with a yod including the Moon, Venus, and Pluto grew up in a family where the mood was often very oppressive.

Her mother suffered from bouts of depression, something that is obviously emotionally stifling for any child. The relationship between her parents wasn't good, either. The woman described their situation as difficult, having an undercurrent she could describe no better than as "threatening." Although the Moon and Pluto in her yod may well indicate her mother's depression, there was more. The woman noticed, as she got older, that her mother's depressions very often coincided with her father's behavior. She became aware of how he always managed to break her mother down in a very two-faced way. So, for instance, if he gave the mother a compliment for something she had done, he would relativize or negate it afterward, or would make a sly dig, often suggesting that you simply have to cheer up a depressive woman. She and her brothers and sisters did not see either this or any other undermining behavior on the father's part. The little compliments were considered real, so the children had the impression that their father was, in fact, being good to their mother. Gradually, however, they discovered the great unspoken tension in the marriage, and their father's morbid mindset to keep his wife so controlled and to treat her like a patient, so that the outside world would say how good he was not to run out on a wife like that, but to keep taking care of her. The woman discovered this during her high-school years, but wasn't able to talk about it with anyone. It was just as if she were seeing things wrong; she felt as if she were trapped in tremendous isolation. It turned out later that she was right, but only after years of falling out with various family members.

In this example, we see that, with the Moon in the yod, it seems at first that the issue is the mother, but later that the deeper cause lies with the father. Of course it lies with both, because neither of the two turned out to be emotionally adult enough to break through the pattern. The daughter with the yod, however, felt the "whispering of the walls" and became trapped, even though she was the only one to distinguish the truth. But then, a child who is still living at home, going to school, and who is a minor has no options.

I have heard countless stories of this nature, dramatic ones as well, of parents who ran away, of abuse, of very serious illnesses, and more. So many that during the first years of my yod research I started with a very negative picture. This adjusted later on when I had met more people with yods who had found a way to deal with them and clearly seemed to be happy. How you can deal with a yod is something I will talk about in the following chapters. Here, for a moment, the emphasis will be on the unpleasant experiences and the feeling of "Why *me*?"

6. Give examples of how people can keep ending up in exceptional situations, or how a yod gives rise to misunderstandings.

With a yod configuration you often get into situations where change is needed on a small or a large scale, or where it is at the point of taking place—turning-points. Again it is the planets in the yod that indicate which domains will be involved, both in their meaning as planet as well as in that of house ruler. An example is a woman who has Mercury in a yod with the Moon and Neptune. She told me that in her childhood she had often had problems with teachers. Mercury in a yod will have its repercussions in education in the broadest possible sense, and a yod with Mercury can present problems in the area of learning. This may be a learning problem, although not always by any means. It can also be a problem around teachers. I have met various children with Mercury in a yod (or as an unaspected planet) who had to change schools one or more times, and when they were finally at a school where they were starting to feel at home and had a really good instructor, the instructor would become ill, and the substitute would turn out to be a problem. However, what I see just as often (a lot of times even when Neptune participates in the yod) is that the child will innocently ask a question about the one thing the teacher doesn't know. Or, if in an instance the teacher "rattles on," not knowing the exact answer to a question concerning a slightly obscure topic, it will be precisely the yod child who happens to know the answer. This child is then caught in a dilemma. For, if the child *says* what he or she knows, the teacher will look like a fool and it will be obvious that the latter was beating around the bush. If the child says *nothing*, then the truth will have been violated. These kinds of moral dilemmas belong with yod configurations and force the child to face a major problem.

With Mercury in a yod, the issue is often facts, knowledge, subject matter, or conversations. The woman in this example with Mercury, Moon, and Neptune in her yod, experienced both sides: "catching" teachers on misinformation, but if she said anything about it, *she* would be blamed for something. She also had many unfortunate changes of instructors. Furthermore, she sees a lot of things most people don't see, like soft colors around people—their aura—and moving shapes in that aura. If she responds to this, she also often receives all kinds of negative responses, and has learned that she can oftentimes see things in their aura even before the party involved has become aware of the emotions, moods, and problems that go along with them. In other words, she sees in the figures inside the aura and the movements of the aura what is coming down the road, and sometimes also which direction somebody's thoughts are taking. As a child she often reacted to what she observed in this way and was considered "fanciful," and "lacking manners," because you're not supposed to say those kinds of things about adults. Thus she learned to distrust not only her capacity to observe the unseen world (and later on the ability to see what goes along with it), she also lost any trust in her capacity to observe everyday reality and to transmit this. She didn't know anymore where one thing ended and another began, and what was real and what was not. It took a very long time before she was able to unravel that problem.

Neptune gives her the ability to see through a fixed form, but immediately meddles with Mercury as soon as she is engaged in learning, reading, thinking, etc. Since it is in a yod, this intervention will be troublesome and chaotic, or strange (in "normal" eyes), but this doesn't have to mean that she is seeing things incorrectly, or that she is wrong! With a yod, you seem to have a nose for bringing something of yourself out in the wrong situation! The woman in question might be able to sense, as it were (Neptune), what someone else needs or what's wrong, and then want to take care of it (Moon). However, when she wants to put this into words (Mercury), she happens to be too vague, or suddenly becomes unsure of herself, or starts to show caring before she has explained various things, or suddenly starts feeling very unsure emotionally, and on and on. It seems as if the wheel starts turning and she has trouble shaping and expressing what she is experiencing or observing on another level. If this happens to you as a child, you can easily get an inferiority complex, of course.

Often, though, I see the communicative skills of children (and adults) who have Mercury and Neptune in a yod develop a great deal when they develop a hobby in the area of music or art—I have seen music work particularly well. As if this can somehow make the tension ebb away. This may even cause a great inspiration to break through which can express itself, for instance, in the way in which a musical piece is interpreted. With Mercury in a yod, technique somehow cannot become completely polished, although this is more than compensated for by the exceptional expression and power that can come out in the interpretation, whether this concerns professional musicians or people who play music for pleasure. Thus with yod configurations we see more opportunity for misunderstanding because of the yod, and there is also more chance of ending up precisely in that position in which you hit the exception to the rule, or where you are the only one who knows the answer, although that answer brings you to a stalemate. Often a yod pops up where a piece of Shadow needs to be coped with, and certainly not always just by the person who has the yod. In this person's surroundings, that other person—with his or her yod —pops up exactly at those moments when those themes are coming into play.

7. Point out the risks of the yod planets involved.

In light of the above, you might conclude that each planet in a yod entails a particular risk that can run out of hand, from the previously mentioned insecurity and ambiguity, the lack of understanding, and erroneous projections, down to the unpleasant events and stalemates. The extent to which such a risk will occur is, however, not to be specified. I do want to emphasize here that in the many cases I have investigated I have noticed that you cannot say that whatever happens to the person who has a yod is her or his own fault. We should rigorously dispel the idea that it is a "punishment for a mistake or sin," because you do more harm than good with such comments.

I know a woman, for instance, with a yod configuration that also includes the Moon. As a toddler during World War II she was placed on a transport to a concentration camp and lost her mother there. After the war she went from one foster family to another and had severe emotional problems—small wonder. She really wanted to have children and give them everything in order to offer them the opportunities for development in life of which she had had to deprive herself. She married and is happy with her husband. Her first child was a daughter born with Down's Syndrome, a significant and serious form at that, in addition to a severe motor disability, causing the child to keep flailing and rolling and screaming day and night. The woman cared for this little girl night and day, until she died a natural death at age 19.

I have come across other cases in which the Moon in a yod goes together with a child who needed a lot of extra attention, or with a child who was in some other kind of trouble. Here, too, this is not by any means always due to dysfunctional domestic circumstances. On the contrary, one can often say it in fact entailed parents who dealt with their children consciously and with concern.

In addition I should mention in reassurance that there are many people with the Moon in a yod who do not experience these problems, and with whom the yod takes shape in another way. So you can't flatly say that the Moon in a yod will cause problems with parents or children. However, the possibility of this, it is true, is greater.

8. The MC or the ASC with two planets: a yod and a duet

Whenever two planets form a sextile with each other, and neither forms an aspect with any other *planet*, we have, in fact, a duet, and the two planets in it have an unintegrated effect. Now, should the two planets form an inconjunct with either the MC or the Ascendant, then there is both a yod—two inconjuncts with a sextile at the base—as well as a duet—the "unaspected" sextile. The criterion for being unaspected is, after all, the absence of aspects to planets; and the MC and the ASC aren't planets. The same thing of course goes for an inconjunct both of whose planets form no aspects to other planets, but one of which forms a sextile with and the other an inconjunct with the MC or the Ascendant. Here, too, one can speak of a duet and a yod at the same time. The interpretation remains simply that of a yod, but the effect, in terms of tension, lies somewhere between that of a yod and a duet. After all there is no third *planet* to increase the turbulence. The fact that the MC or the Ascendant is involved, means primarily that we experience the field of tension in finding an attitude to maintain outwardly. The constant action of *three* planets is missing though. There are two here, so this is easier to get a perspective on and easier to handle, even though the whole will, of course, still have a lot of the troublesome attributes and fall under the interpretation of unaspected planets.

9. Analyze the possible ability of the yod.

Both the astrologer, as well as the client, will have to make peace with the thought that with a yod you are not in any position to articulate the latent and dormant ability of the yod in question. It can encompass so much, and *so* differently from how it first showed itself, that it is simply the safest thing not to burn your fingers on the subject. Often the second half of the life of someone with a yod is totally different than the first. This is usually not the result of a conscious choice, but mostly of a combination of circumstances in which all kinds of unforeseen events and situations contribute to a chain reaction, as it were, and cause the second half of life to bring forth a totally different life situation. It is very possible that along with this you really find or have found your rhythm. Many people with a yod who have actively wrestled with the aforementioned problems and have found their way through, will even point out that they have found a haven that is difficult to describe in the middle of what is otherwise a turbulent life. They will also point out that they have figured out that because of the searching and insecurity during the first half of life—which in-cluded doing the most diverse things, holding very different jobs, starting various programs of study (without completing them all), and the like—they have ended up during the second half in a situation where, to their surprise, they need, can use, and can in-tegrate the experiences they accumulated through all those falter-ingly undertaken activities. As if there were an invisible thread running through all their fishtailing back and forth that uncon-sciously pointed out the way for them. However, to get to this point, the person with the yod has to watch out not to end up in the negative side of the yod, the side of self-pity and inactivity—because then things will start getting really difficult.

A yod can make a person incredibly creative, precisely be-cause of that urge to be searching all the time. This is why people with a yod can be very refreshing and ahead of their time in many respects. They will always notice that those around them can't muster much understanding for this though—during the first half of their lives, at any rate. The second half of life is different in this respect, as well. I have met a variety of people with yods who, during the course of their lives, changed their circle of friends rad-ically, ended relations with a number of family members, and fi-nally had a whole new group of people around them among whom they felt very much at home. In this case, you will see that those with a yod can finally arrive at a situation in which they are understood and in which their qualities are recognized, but which they will themselves have cooperated actively to create. A yod gets nothing for nothing, and so it forces you to shape your life.

If we look at the horoscopes of well-known people with yods, we will see that the themes that made them famous always had to do with the themes of their yod (or unaspected planet). Jung is a good example of this: Jupiter, Pluto, and Mars in a yod, where Jupi-ter represents the doctor (and religion) and Pluto psychology. Mars can indicate unbridled effort and energy. The enormous conceit that goes along with a yod-Jupiter combined with Pluto and Mars got him into trouble: he simply *couldn't* adapt himself to the teachings of another, in this case Freud, and therefore he abandoned his pros-pects of a safe job and a position of honor and prestige.

Pluto is Ruler 10 and Mars Co-Ruler 2 in the yod; here we see in a yod the theme of social profiling (10th house) and that of the need for concrete security (2nd house) also involved in the situa-tion of the stalemate. On the one hand, the connection between the two rulers indicates that he is seeking security (2) and career possibilities (10). On the other hand these two houses, if only be-cause of the fact that they are involved in a yod, brought him once or more times in his life into a stalemate, so that he had to choose between "evils" as it were. In his situation it was Jupiter as Ruler 11, the house of friendship, which completed the stalemate: he was a friend of Freud's (11) and had good prospects because he was Freud's designated follower (10), which would offer him security (2). However, he *couldn't* commit to a compromise between his own insights and those of Freud (Jupiter) in the area of psychology (Pluto) and was thus faced with an impossible choice. He could go his own way and break off the friendship, with all the insecurity this would entail, or keep going along the same road as Freud and retain security, but continue to feel nothing but resistance inside. Neither option was a pleasant one for Jung, but he was driven from inside to choose his own way.

The crisis followed, but after that he was able to follow his own path and become an innovator and a pioneer in the area of depth psychology. And, as is customary with a yod, he presented themes that caused him to be far ahead of his time, and so not well understood by the "mainstream." He proposed synchronicity, openly showed his interest in astrology and the I Ching, presented an impressive analysis of The Book of Job that kicked the shins of quite a few clerics, without doing this intentionally, as it happened. He took alchemy seriously, which until then had been considered by scientists as the first step toward the science of chemistry, and then began to study the subject, eventually breaking the code.[1] Jung's talent revealed itself precisely because he was preoccupied with these sidetracks, because he looked at and approached things differently. If you had tried to describe Jung's ability during his day, you probably wouldn't have thought of the combination of alchemy, I Ching, astrology, and old Chinese thought, because there was hardly anything known about these themes.

It may be the case now, too, that there are people with yods who are preoccupied with a vision, a view, an insight, or a theme you simply can't come up with, precisely because they will lie beyond our circle of thought. Years ago I spoke with a man with a yod horoscope. He had found his own way and founded a unique school in the Netherlands—a school to train clowns.

So it is very tricky to try to name the abilities and talents of a yod, since you, yourself, can't arrive at the ideas inherent in the direction that these people will take. It is therefore best to simply describe the hallmarks of the yod planets, as we encounter them generally in the books, and to say that the abilities and talents lie

---

[1] C. G. Jung, *Memories, Dreams, Reflections* (New York: Pantheon, 1961; New York: Vintage, 1989), p. 204.

on the level of one or possibly more of these planets, and very likely on the level of a unique combination of all the planets, so that the houses they rule are also involved. Considering the very diverse development of these talents, I have become very careful with regard to attempting to describe them concretely. A yod—as I mentioned before—is just like that piece of soap that keeps slipping away. By describing the planets and the rulers of the houses though, you can create a picture of the energies that will have something to do with the abilities and talents.

10. Show how the houses are connected by their rulers.

We saw in the example using C. G. Jung what part planets play as rulers. (For an extensive explanation of house rulers, see my book *The House Connection: How to Read the Houses in an Astrological Chart*.) If the ruler or co-ruler (the ruler of an intercepted sign) is located in a yod, the distinguishing features of the yod will extend to the matters of this house.

A house is generally considered "a set of circumstances," with which I am only partially in agreement. For, a planet in a house says that with that specific energy (planet) you have the need to manifest yourself in that particular domain (house). To a certain extent houses do, in fact, have to do with patterns of inner needs, even though these might be different from those of the planets. A house represents an area that draws our attention, or one we want to engage in if we have planets in that house, or if the ruler of the house forms the necessary aspects.

A house that is involved in a yod by means of its ruler indicates the area where at least once you will have the feeling of standing with your back to the wall, having to make impossible choices, or being confronted by an in-some-respect-ungraspable, or at-first-glance-unsolvable problem, like Jung with the co-ruler of his 2nd house in a yod (and the ruler of his 2nd house in a duet). He had to make a choice in which his financial position was literally on the line and figuratively, the idea of firm ground was under his feet. After all, going one's own way in the developing field of psychology, *away* from the mainstream of that moment, is an uncertain prospect for one's wallet. On top of this, it elicits questions like, "Where *do* I stand, anyway?" and, "How much inner security and motivation do I have, anyhow?"

In the meantime I have plenty of examples of people with Ruler 2 in a yod who at a particular moment in their lives had to make a drastic choice that entailed considerable consequences for their income. A woman, for instance, with Ruler 2 in a yod that also involved Pluto, could no longer find a niche in the company where she was working, particularly because of the tough, macho atmosphere. She landed in a crisis and decided to quit and wait to see if she could earn an income with other projects. Because she was quitting, she would not receive unemployment compensation. She knew that beforehand, but she *couldn't*, from inside, wait any more for possible resignation proceedings or for particular arrangements, and she could also not tolerate the idea of otherwise taking sick leave for a while. She felt an unavoidable and forceful need to leave the company—and this precisely at the moment when there was a considerable promotion in store for her.

So there she was—at the point of getting a much better position with an extremely comfortable salary and a confirmation of her qualities—a situation of which many were jealous, the more so as this was happening at the beginning of the 1980s when there was very high unemployment—and on the other hand that enormous inner restlessness and the feeling of not being able to work any longer in that corporate culture. Her friends advised her just to take a vacation and by all means accept the promotion. She'd be crazy to let that go for such an indescribable feeling. When she raised the matter at the company, management even offered her a vacation to relax for a little while. She was no doubt tired from all that hard work. After the vacation she could start in her new function.

What do you do in a case like this? There are all kinds of "good reasons" to keep moving up in that company and only one vague reason not to do so, that "feeling" that just kept insisting. This woman all of a sudden, in a burst of strength, decided to leave the company immediately and submitted her notice, leaving behind her a bewildered human resources director and similarly shocked management. There she was, without an income, only some savings, and the big question, "What now?" She knew it felt good though, and stood by her decision. Since then, she has built up her own company with very different norms and standards and a way of working that do fit with her. She now looks back with great satisfaction on the step she took back then. At that time, it was a step into the dark, but it turned out to be a new beginning. In another domain she did pay for that step: friends and acquaintances and even a couple of family members abandoned her. She was no longer interesting socially. I have seen these kinds of emotional events before with Pluto in a yod.

This course of events regarding the 2nd house shows a couple of things that are so typical of a house involved in a yod: first of all the stalemate, the "impossible" choice, the inner restlessness, and a situation in which the whole world is telling you that you're making the wrong choice, but then it turns out that that "wrong choice" finally gives your life the kind of turn where your talents and abilities can develop. It may happen that you have to choose several times with regard to a particular house before you arrive at such development. How many times, however, cannot be predicted.

With Ruler 11 in a yod, I have seen the following often take place: a stalemate concerning the theme of friendship, possibly of one's own making, but often as a result of a complex situation in which the psyches of both parties were so interwoven that you could hardly speak of fault; and often a total renewal of one's circle of friends, after one or more intervening events. It also often happens that within your circle of friends there is someone who, on the one hand, means a lot to you, but on the other is a very problematic figure from whom you have to tolerate a lot or who elicits a lot of inner uneasiness in you. With such a person you can go through a crisis, or undergo something together, so that the friendship grows deeper or else leads to problems. However, in a crisis, precisely when you feel abandoned by everything and everybody, someone will cross your path with whom you can build a very sincere friendship. Or else it turns out that there has been somebody nearby for a very long time whom you now start to see with different eyes and from whom you receive a lot of help and friendship, and to whom you can also return this in kind. Oftentimes this person will also be a "loner," or someone who in society opted for his or her own colors and way. Thus Ruler 11 in a yod can go together both with a crisis situation regarding friendship, as well as offer a very exceptional friendship that arises at a strange moment or through a remarkable combination of circumstances.

Houses that are involved in a yod by their ruler are thus often the domains where troublesome and unusual developments present themselves, but in which there also lies exceptional potential. The horoscopes used as examples in later chapters will be extensively devoted to this.

Yods are turning points, and people with a yod are point persons in the process of change, on a large or small scale, regardless of the form in which this takes place. Yods can make you feel very unsure, as we saw before, so that you cannot come into your own, but remain stuck in defensiveness, self-pity, or fear. However, this is definitely not necessary, and yods hold an exceptional amount of promise! By understanding what the dynamics are, and what role yods play in a larger context, we can make a lot of our lives. We will start looking at how you can deal with yods in a positive way in chapter 9.

CHAPTER SIX

Interpreting Unaspected Planets and Duets

In the previous chapter we saw how complicated the interpretation of the yod configuration is. With unaspected planets and duets, the approach is slightly easier because we have fewer "participants," and also because the diversity of elements, modes, and polarities does not come into play here. With an unaspected planet there is exclusively one energy that finds expression without being influenced, and which can exhibit itself in extremes. In a duet, two planets that aspect each other exclusively where neither forms an aspect with a third planet, there are two energies. Experience teaches that they may each work independently, as if the other didn't exist, although they may also manifest themselves in combination. In this last case, they retain the hallmarks of an unaspected planet. This is why the emphasis in what follows will be on these planets functioning on their own. Where necessary, extra space has been devoted to the interpretation of a duet.

1. Use the basic meaning of the planet and emphasize its extremes.

Every planet has its own, distinct meaning. As a psychic energy, it represents a particular pattern of needs, particular motivations, and their resulting actions. As a theme, it also represents a lot of other things. Thus, Mercury represents the motivation for our need for contact with others, for communication, and for indicating, arranging, and transmitting facts. As a theme, Mercury has to do with a variety of things, such as hands, lungs, pens and pencils, arterial roads, books, etc.

An unaspected planet tends to manifest starkly the extremes in which, driven by its motivations, it can show itself, so that on the one hand it brings out its own identity very clearly, but on the other, suddenly can't find that identity anymore. In both of these cases, the possessor of the unaspected planet initially has no notion of this effect; those around only notice it all the more. So, use the original meaning of the planet, emphasize the power of expression it has, and emphasize the chance of extremes.

Matters that have to do with the planet involved may also occur intensely, or in extremes, or suddenly lead to problems in the life of the person involved. I provided the example before of an unaspected Mars and a huge wasps' nest in the attic. However, with an unaspected Mars, people may also experience problems with household appliances that get hot, like ovens and toasters. It would seem that this will cross your path in some way. Once I learned from a little boy with an unaspected Mars that he thought tiger balm (a very pungent, tingly, strongly scented Asian balm) smelled so good that he decided to rub it all over himself. The results are left to the imagination.

So, be a little more alert regarding the themes that belong to an unaspected planet, but don't let them scare you off, because they really don't have to lead to any dramas. Also, remember that an unaspected planet is also an ability and may contain positive surprises in its domain as well (about which more later).

2. Point out that the unaspected planet will elicit a feeling of "searching" and an inexplicable uneasiness, which is, however, inherent to it. This searching also involves feelings of insecurity.

Due to the fact that the unaspected planet is not connected with any other planets, you will feel an inner urge to go looking for it. Therefore it will give you feelings of "hunger," of "searching" regarding the themes that concern it. Since you do vaguely feel the energy, although you initially can't quite catch hold of it, you will also experience insecurity expressing it. An unintegrated Sun, for instance, will have a tremendous need for recognition and will intensely seek its own identity. "Who am I? What do I want?" are frequently posed questions. Should there be confirmation from the outside, it may not be picked up in the right way. Not that that person isn't happy about it; it's more as if the person doesn't really catch on to what exactly is going on, can't quite place the compliment, or doesn't know what to do with it, denies the situation, etc. It's as if there were no peg to hang it on. The unaspected Sun will therefore keep searching for identity and confirmation, even in situations where there's no need to do so, or confirmation already exists. This also produces a kind of "demanding" quality sometimes experienced by others as a burden, but not understood by those with the unaspected Sun. People like this may require a lot of attention at first, and are seen in the outside world as dominating, while they feel very unsure of themselves. After all, they still haven't experienced that Sun at all yet, and they are still searching and feeling around for themselves.

Also, themes that have to do with the Sun may unexpectedly lead to problems. Difficulties with higher-ups, meaning conflicts with power and authority, will come up quite a lot. There is an obvious paradox here. On the one hand, the unaspected Sun would like to be an authority, and on the other, it becomes doubtful and unsure whenever it has to take on that role, which makes it tend to scramble back as soon as it gets a chance to prove itself. At the same time, the Sun, thus the theme of authority, represents a true power and ability in these people (see later), which they will unconsciously recognize in those around them in a position of authority. Such people will simultaneously attract and repel them. It seems as if those in authority express the shadow, as it were, of people with an unaspected Sun, but then the shadow's light side: a still undiscovered talent. This does not take away from the fact that projecting the shadow can lead to all kinds of problems, such as idolizing one person or being greatly annoyed by another. Projections usually lead to irregular behavior because they come out of the unconscious, and contents of the unconscious may either come across as syrup or seem like loose projectiles, with all the consequences of such.

3. Unaspected planets are accompanied by tricky circumstances and a feeling of getting entangled in problem situations, sometimes with the feeling that fate has a hand in this.

This resembles planets in a yod that are also involved in an unpleasant or, to your feeling, "impossible" circumstances. For an unaspected planet, this involves its own energy and meaning purely. This kind of situation sometimes combines with an unaspected planet exhibiting itself in exaggerated behavior, or in the lack of an adequate response at a moment when you should be able to call on that energy, but it seems to be inaccessible. In other cases, the factors will sooner come from outside and be deposited on your plate as raw material.

An example of this concerns a man with an unaspected Saturn, who is expected to follow in his father's footsteps in a successful family business. The business is in good standing and enjoys a long tradition. Initially the man hesitated and wondered whether he wanted to do that or not. Dealing with the restrictions and the responsibility that go along with a managerial position, in particular, felt threatening—precisely Saturn's theme. He had enormous doubts and felt awful because of them. In the end, rational motivation caused him to choose to continue the family business and he joined the management. His motives involved security: it is a business that is running well and has a well-organized structure, and he thought that by pursuing this he would in any case be assured of work and an income without running too many risks. A sense of tradition also came into play: you couldn't just dismiss such an old business. In fact, we see all kinds of Saturn themes come up here, from restrictions and responsibility, to security and tradition. For years he worked himself into the company in a way that for an outsider seems almost overly conscientious and dutiful (the extreme side of Saturn). He is now in fact already prepared to take over his father's role, although his father doesn't want to retire yet, and they will continue working together for a few more years.

Once the son had finally decided to follow in his father's footsteps, he exerted himself 100 percent and everything went well. Until he fell in love. The girl is energetic and dynamic, does a lot of sports, and has a modern, carefree demeanor. This wasn't the classic girl the young man's parents had in mind. So, they rejected the girl, even though in a legal sense he no longer needs their permission to marry. They gave him an ultimatum: if he chose her, he would lose his position in the company and not be allowed to succeed his father.

That's quite a stalemate, and choice is extremely difficult for him: he totally adores the girl, but, with no less devotion and sense of duty, for a number of years already, he has invested himself in carrying on the business. Thus this is clearly a choice between evils. Neither choice appeals to him. He keeps asking himself, as so many people who have a yod or an unaspected planet do, why this had to happen to him.

I have also encountered diverse cases where things were resolved, but also cases where a painful wound remained, as in the case of a woman who has a duet between Saturn and Venus (she also has a yod that includes the Sun). Both planets are unaspected, and both may arrive at a stalemate individually or together. In the previous example we saw the pressure of the parents as the background for the Saturn problem. With this woman, something similar came into play. She fell in love with a man she described as enthusiastic, carefree and open, and very warm and kind. This man didn't mince words and pointed out to her how dominating her mother was. The mother didn't feel this man was right for her daughter and when the man entered the military, the mother intercepted all his letters to her daughter, so her daughter received no answers to her letters. In fact, many of the letters the daughter had written never reached the soldier because the mother would promise to mail them, but never did. After some time, things fell silent and the letters on both sides stopped. This caused the daughter no end of grief and for the rest of her life she kept longing for this man. She married another man, with whom she had a decent marriage as such, but she always considered her husband to be her second choice. Her heart remained with the first man.

Very accidentally I heard about another situation, also a woman with a Venus–Saturn duet and the Sun in a yod configuration who experienced the very same thing! This woman also kept longing for the man she never saw again. Only when her mother became elderly and had to move, did she find a little packet of letters while helping her do so: the intercepted letters from her former boyfriend that revealed how much he loved her. She set out to find him after all, but it turned out he had passed away in the meantime. His family told her that he never married because he had never been able to forget his love.

These are tragic situations where those involved get the feeling that life punishes you more than you deserve. I must also mention here that frankly not everybody with a duet is going to live through this type of experience, even though I do hear this kind of story, particularly about people with yods, unaspected planets, or duets.

Another example of the way you can get caught in a sticky situation with a Venus-Saturn duet is the Monica Lewinsky case. In her unawareness about this part of her nature, she succeeded in destabilizing a president and being part of a situation that even influenced the stock exchange when insecurity about the president's fate made the markets fall!

4. Unaspected planets have tremendous power and form pure talents.

Precisely because we are searching for the substance of an unaspected planet we are very preoccupied with it, and will unnoticeably develop the talents that it provides. Thus, a great power, which is extremely positive, can radiate from an unaspected planet. However, this actually only applies to those who have already done a good bit of coping and who have learned to accept themselves, or found ways to give the manner of expression unique to the unaspected planet a place in their life. Then we see that an unaspected planet will often even indicate profession, or plays an important role in the work life, or represents an important hobby or interest. The urge to live out and find a form for this planet remains, and the searching will keep coming into play in the background as well, but will no longer be dominant.

The same applies to the insecurity—we may finally realize that it is simply there, but that in fact it really says nothing about the question of whether we can do something or not. Then we can separate the insecurity from what we want to do with the energy of the planet. As a result, we see that precisely those who have undergone some amount of maturation in this process become very happy with their unaspected planet.

There is another phenomenon that comes up here. The planet involved may express itself not only powerfully and positively, but it may also significantly remain itself, since it is not being influenced by other planets. We also see with a duet a great capacity of both planets to remain themselves, they really don't always combine.

The power of an unaspected planet is also very pure and easy to describe. Go to the crux of the meaning of this planet and there lies the ability, there lies the power. This energy can be cultivated, developed, and expressed in all kinds of domains appropriate to that planet. We may even get rich by it! Jimmy Carter has an unaspected Saturn. He got rich off the peanut, which grows underground, and by virtue of this belongs to Saturn. Beethoven became famous through the grandeur of his compositions. He once said that even if he had many more orchestras at his disposal, they would still not suffice to express what he wanted to express. Beethoven had an unaspected Jupiter.

I have met various people, both men as well as women, who learned to live with an unaspected Sun. What remained in the background was the feeling that the life they were leading couldn't be everything life had to offer. However, they were aware that this feeling didn't fit with the actual situation. One man stated it as follows:

Something in me is a kind of wanderer who is at home everywhere and nowhere, is on his way to something he doesn't know what. I just let him go and wait and see where he ends up. Meanwhile I live as normally as possible in the here and now. Even though I keep having the feeling that the wanderer is once again going to bring me onto the track of something very new. . . .

This is a wonderful rendition of an unaspected Sun, and a wise attitude on this man's part. He lives his life in the here and now, but holds open a little door just in case a new challenge crosses his path. With an unaspected planet, this will oftentimes happen!

The people who learned to live with the restlessness, the insecurity, and the searching of their unaspected Sun clearly had fun in life and were enabled to enjoy it. They did not allow themselves to be pushed off the playing field by the still regularly surfacing insecurity and uneasiness. Several of them have leadership functions and a lot of responsibility, which they can handle very well and which has also brought them recognition. In fact, they have a marked talent and know how to deal with troublesome situations, providing good guidance and leadership there. What you notice about them is that they have a powerful personality, and a demeanor that focuses attention on them, as it were. This is a form of dominance and centrality (an emphatic side of the Sun) that they may use well in some of their professional situations, but it will get them in trouble on a regular basis in personal relationships—from partners, friends, and family. For, unintentionally and without being aware of it, they are palpably there and this is something that is not always appreciated by those around them. This may already have played a role when they were children. I have seen extremes in people with an unintegrated Sun (or unintegrated Moon). Either there was a very close bond with one or both parents, perhaps even a bond that was too close, with strong mutual identification, or the relationship with one or both parents was a big problem. Here, too, it is difficult to equate the Sun with the father and the Moon with the mother. I have encountered a couple of cases where children with an unaspected Moon had a psychologically unhealthy relationship with the mother, in the sense that they were playing the role of mother, in a way, to their mother. One boy already early on played the role of husband to some extent, without the sexual aspect, but more in the form of caring behavior and a feeling of responsibility toward his mother. In these cases the children took strong positions against their father.

However, I have run into as many cases where an unaspected Sun indicated an obsessive bond with the mother, or where an unaspected Moon totally rejected the mother in favor of the father. Again, therefore, experiences that cause me to prefer to talk about the *theme* of parents, and not to name one of the parents specifically.

However, the people who have in the past had such experiences with an unaspected Sun or Moon, and who were enabled to cope with these experiences and to give them a place, can function very well in the domains of their unaspected planet. A man, for instance, with an unaspected Sun, who went through a very restrictive childhood with a forceful mother and a strict, often absent father, was concerned as an adult about the fate of underprivileged youth in the ghettos. By himself, in his free time, he organized sports sessions and contests, as well as other group activities, where children could express themselves in an enjoyable and sensible way. His motivation is in line with the theme of the Sun: in this way the children were able to gain more self-confidence! Those youngsters really loved him.

Or the woman with an unaspected Moon who, economically speaking, belongs to the lowest stratum of society. She adores children and does absolutely everything with her own children as well as others' children. She manages even with the most limited means to turn anything into a festive occasion. She helps at the children's school, is one of the mothers who reads aloud, among other things, and she is one of the organizers of school trips, parties, and creative afternoons. She enjoys it thoroughly, and has an absolutely pure talent for transplanting herself into the world of the young, and dealing with them creatively.

5. Unaspected planets also rule houses.

The houses ruled by an unaspected planet are included in its dynamics. So the domains they reflect will also be involved in all-or-nothing kinds of expressions, risks and challenges, with lack of understanding, entanglements of fate, and not in the least again—great talent and great power of expression.

Often, in the domain of the house that contains an unaspected house ruler, on the one hand you will have the feeling of being sucked toward activities and themes that belong to it, but on the other, you won't always be able to access them when you want to, by any means. One man with an unaspected ruler of his 8th house described his feelings once as follows:

> *I do sense my problems are there, but when I want to put my finger on them, it's just as if I get bounced back by an invisible rubber wall the minute I think I can touch them. Then if I go at it with the expectation that I will encounter that wall again, there will be the one time that the wall won't be there at all. In that case, I sail into a low point in no time, sometimes approaching depression, and suddenly find myself surrounded by problems.*

I have heard others talk along the same lines about the unaspected ruler of their 8th house. It turned out time and again that somewhere in the background they sensed something was wrong, but weren't able to put their finger on it. If they then suddenly did get a sense of what it was all really about, this immediately entailed a kind of crisis as well, as if they were getting everything on their plate all at once. This might be in the form of emotions, strong feelings, and the like, thus from inside, but also in the form of a rapid succession of difficult situations in the outside world with which they became inescapably involved. Ruler 8, unaspected or in a duet, can cope with and solve such problems, but it has its own unpredictable rhythm. Even when people with an unaspected Ruler 8 go into therapy, the image of the progress can be very unpredictable, and sometimes seem like three steps forward, two steps back, and another three steps forward—like a kind of zigzag or hippety-hop pattern. If you look at it over a period of time though, you will see that people like this who have been stuck for a while, suddenly make a lot of progress, and finally get themselves back on track as others do.

If you play hide-and-seek with yourself in the area of the unaspected ruler of a house, you will inadvertently maneuver yourself in the craziest ways into all kinds of impossible situations, where you will often encounter the mirror image of your inner self in the outside world, and not infrequently magnified, or in a more extreme form than necessary. To stick with the example of the unaspected Ruler 8: your need for attention and power will become greater than is good for you, your manipulative capacity will increase, but you will have no perspective on that, and at the same time you will run a greater risk of being manipulated yourself, and of becoming entangled in the dynamic of power. The chance that you will end up in a kind of double role in a particular area of life will also become greater, and no matter how, this combines with plenty of emotion. You will seem to be aware, but the things you do will be riddled with unconscious behavior, of which someone who wants to manipulate you can make ready use. Monica Lewinsky is an example of this, as well. Her Venus duet is also the ruler of her 8th house, and in the press we were able to see to what extent she became a pawn in a much larger power game (see chapter 12).

With Lewinsky things got terribly out of control, but variations of her problems can arise on a smaller scale in the daily lives of people who repress the dynamic of an unaspected ruler of the 8th house and unconsciously live this out.

Something we need to keep in mind both with yods, as well as unaspected planets, is that both the planet's theme as such, as well as the planet in its capacity as house ruler, may relate to issues that have been coming into play for several generations. For instance, when we see to what extent people with an unaspected house ruler can unconsciously get themselves into fixes, we shouldn't just say that it's *their* fault and *their* choice, or *their* own lack of awareness. Although these factors may come into play, and although it is possible to have tremendously positive experiences in the domain of planets and house rulers in yods (as well as in the domain of unaspected planets and unaspected house rulers), it seems as if the person who has such a theme is revealing to the world the dynamics that were repressed (or that have been a problem over several generations), which want to become visible so that he or she can work out the problem. It's as if there were a dynamic at play that incorporates more than just what belongs to that one person. This is why I first want to take a look at a more inclusive background in which we can study the themes of yods and unaspected planets, and then indicate the best way to deal with these dynamics.

CHAPTER SEVEN

The Shadow and Evil

In the previous chapters we saw that yods and unaspected planets occur primarily where a particular problem is being ignored or remains unsolved, or there is repression of a particular theme, and this is happening in a family over several generations. In Jungian terms, we are clearly involved here with a *family shadow*. It is also responsible for the fact that the child with a yod or an unaspected planet will run a greater risk than the average child of encountering more extreme projections and attitudes from particular family members, because this child will hold up a mirror to these family members of their unlived but active, unconscious patterns, simply by being there. In order to understand how this family dynamic can influence a child with a yod, we'll take a close look at the mechanism of the shadow, first.

The Shadow

We encounter words like ego, consciousness, and others in all kinds of reading material, but they're not always understood in the same way, by any means. The basic assumption behind this discussion will be meanings as used in Jungian psychology. C. G. Jung distinguished a *consciousness* and an *unconsciousness* in the psyche, and the unconscious was divided into a *personal* and a *collective* unconscious. The words already say it: the personal unconscious belongs to our own psyche, the collective unconscious is universally human and we share it with everyone. The core of our nature, which Jung called the *Self,* resides in the unconscious. He described it as both the center as well as the outer confines of the psyche. With this he meant that we have a knowing inside that encompasses much, much more than we are able to grasp with our consciousness. From this deep knowing about ourselves come impulses to grow. There seems to be an unmistakable motivation coming from this Self that urges us to realize ourselves and to become who we are inside. The process of (self-)realization Jung calls the *process of individuation*. (See figure 4, page 105.)

This process begins immediately at birth. The consciousness is barely there yet, much is still in a latent state. As the total psyche has the Self at its center, our consciousness has the ego as its center. We are born with an ego that still has to develop and flower, or, as Erich Neumann puts it so nicely: The Self is born, the ego is made.[1] The ego forms itself over the course of years on the basis of our aptitude, on the one hand, and our experiences and choices on the other. The ego has an exceptionally important function, and we could actually describe it as the "central reporting and regulation unit" of the consciousness. Everything that comes into play in the field of our consciousness is seen and judged by the ego, and on these grounds the ego makes decisions. Just as air traffic control at an airport keeps an eye on and directs the busy incoming and outgoing air traffic, making decisions when there are problems, our ego works the same way regarding all the oncoming impulses it senses from inside (meaning from the unconscious), and all the impulses, demands, and circumstances that it encounters in the outside world. Thus, the ego must constantly make choices, every minute. We do this automatically in the great majority of cases, and a good portion of our choices are inspired by what was taught us within our cultural pattern.

Try for a day to stop and think about all the things you do. In fact, this means an equal number of choices to do those things. At the same time, this entails an equal number of choices *not* to do *other* things! The things we don't do receive a place in the personal unconscious, and if we keep making one-sided choices and so repress similar actions, we will build up an enormous load in the unconscious around that theme, which will break through sooner or later.

In Western culture, for instance, with its increasing emphasis on pursuit and achievement, we learn early on already that we have to do things, have to learn them, and be able to do them. Lounging around and fantasizing are judged in many cases to be bad or undesirable, "because you don't get anywhere that way." Children learn early which values are rewarded and which are rejected. If they go along with this, you will see that they will automatically make the choices that get rewarded, and in doing so consequently not make certain other choices. Once adult, they will continue this pattern just as automatically.

---

[1] Erich Neumann, *The Origins and History of Consciousness* (Princeton: Princeton University Press, 1954), p. 252.

Figure 4. The Psyche.
Drawing after Jolande Jacobi

Now imagine that you learned that you are supposed to work and that lounging around is bad. As an adult you will unconsciously be inclined, even in relaxed situations, to look around for something to do because you have rejected sitting quietly and doing nothing. In the meantime, however, every time you "make the choice" to start doing something, you are likewise making a choice to repress sitting quietly and being good and lazy for a moment. If you do this long enough, the repressed part will become so strong that it will start getting in your way. The symptoms of this can already be recognized at an early stage, in dreams and in your projections, among other things.

The fact is that everything you repress will be "seen" in a distorted way in your environment. So, if you have continually repressed "just sitting quietly for a moment," you will keep being annoyed by people who are just relaxing and doing nothing for a minute. You will tend to see these people as being "lazy," or think they are being irresponsible, not meeting their obligations, and all the rest. If your child is dreamily staring off for a while, you will also tend to make remarks or criticize this, and without noticing it, you are cracking the whip on the basis of your own repression. In short, you are annoyed by things in your environment that you have repressed in yourself and you aren't seeing them in proper perspective. This is what we call projection.

If a projection is significant, you will tend to get involved with this theme in the outside world, mostly in a way that isn't very nice, because a projection is compulsive and does not have a sense of humor. After all, you are standing face to face with your own repression! This is what we call *the shadow*.

We have two kinds of shadow—the personal and the collective one. In a culture there are particular values and opinions that are commonly shared, and this means that other values, attitudes, and opinions are dismissed as undesirable or invalid. These last then belong to a culture's shadow. The same goes for personal life: the choices you make with your ego—whether they are well thought out or not—will determine at the same time which values you do not wish, and the unmade choices vanish in the direction of the unconscious.

Everybody has a shadow. Even the hippie or alternative person who doesn't wish to conform to the societal pattern has made choices: for these people the choice is to live the values their culture has repressed, and so their shadow will be aligned with the values of the culture in which they live. The result, then, is that the majority of the members of the society in which they live will reject them, because they are living a life according to values that are the shadow of the collective. This rejection should, as a rule, be seen as a kind of self-defense on the part of the psyche, because the issue is a confrontation with your own repression, your own shadow. You would prefer not to see it, so you will reject the person outside you who bears the distinguishing features of your shadow.

You can learn to recognize the shadow by looking around you for a moment and to thinking about who and what annoys you. Okay, it's true this isn't such an uplifting game, but you do learn to see which traits can be found in your unconscious that are evidently disturbing enough to elicit irritation when you see symptoms in the outside world. Now does this mean that you are precisely the same as the person who annoys you? No, this isn't how you should look at it. If you are annoyed by a thief, this doesn't mean that you are unconsciously one yourself. What it does mean is that you have problems recognizing that situations may come up in your life where you will overstep the bounds, and that you would prefer not to be reminded of the fact that as a child you took cookies or sugar cubes on the sly, or that you snitched some things from your brother or sister. Or else that, if you receive too much change at a store, you "forget" to mention it. Nobody is completely blameless. Your annoyance at the thief outside you is only a summons to become aware that you, too, are capable of not always being so scrupulous. For most people this stays on a trivial level, and doesn't mean that you're doing it to the same degree as the thief who annoys you. Your annoyance is an emotion that belongs to a projection arising in yourself. This projection tells you there is something else in your personal unconscious that you have to face, or, in other words, something has to connect with your central reporting and regulation unit, your ego.

As paradoxical as this may sound, an ego that has a perspective on your "nasty traits" and knows what you are capable of, is a more powerful and better equipped ego than an ego that lives in a world of pretense where you are only "good." Just as air traffic control at an airport is better able to intervene and prevent accidents when it is up to date on the limitations of the system and other disturbing factors, so too it is with our ego. The more aware we are of our shadow, the more capable we are of making choices that really fit us. We will also react less emotionally and therefore live more balanced lives.

Your shadow may also have a very light side. If you have particular abilities and still undeveloped talents that are still dormant in you, these also belong to the shadow in your personal unconscious. Many people who lack self-confidence will have a quantity of inner strength comprising their shadow! This will also be projected outwardly and coupled with emotion. But now we see that the expression of this is that you start to extol and worship someone else who shows a particular strength or self-confidence. At this point you are not capable of seeing that this other person is also simply human and has doubts; for you the person is a guru, a leader, an ideal that seems unachievable to you. However, nothing could be further from the truth. The fact that you are touched by that person is precisely the sign that there is a similar strength in *you* that would be only too happy to be "woken up," meaning to make a connection with your ego! This doesn't mean that you should become exactly like this other person. This person reflects something that you also have inside, but that you need to develop in your own way.

A shadow can thus be dark as well as light, but it will always have to do with our own unlived side, with the choices we did *not* make, with the talents and abilities we have not developed, but that do belong to us, and with the unpleasant little characteristics we have that we don't want to see.

Yods, Unaspected Planets, and the Shadow

If the same themes are repressed over several generations in a family, or were expressed in an overcompensating way and so are an unbalanced, then we can in fact speak in terms of a collective shadow in that family. If many family members have the same problems and repress the same things, they will consequently all feel negative emotions when they encounter in projection what they repress. This is exactly where the rub is regarding yods and unaspected planets, because the child born with a yod or an unaspected planet is, in fact, bound to make the problem, which most family members will have tried to repress for several generations, visible within that family. This alone is enough for this child to elicit emotions and reactions automatically, without even having done anything!

Such reactions may exhibit extremes. Family members who are still busy vigorously repressing their own problems will not be able to tolerate the child's seeking and groping, the insecurity that he or she displays in the area of their repression, because they have come face-to-face with their own problem. They don't even have to be aware of this, it may be very deeply repressed, but the child elicits annoyance and, in their eyes, can do no good. If the projection is intense (correlating to the depth of the problem in that family member), the child will have all kinds of negativity dumped on her or him and will be dealing with an attitude of rejection. The child may even be blamed for things with which he or she has nothing to do. By burdening the child with these emotions, the family member in question can momentarily "vent" his or her own inner tension. After all, it's always easier to blame someone else for your own inner unrest, rather than look at yourself.

On the other hand there may be family members who themselves have already gotten involved with that theme. They may not yet have dared to take the steps they should to become themselves, but at least they are aware of the problem and the inner processes, even if it can't be talked about in the family. These people will see the child who has the yod or unaspected planet wrestle with the problem and will be touched in a different way by

what the child lets them see. There is a chance that they will idol-
ize and maybe even worship and overrate the child, because "this
child is going to do what we didn't dare to do. . . ."

The child with a yod or unaspected planet thus runs the risk of
being the object of one party's negative shadow projection and another's positive shadow projection. There are an equal number of
judgments and attitudes inherent in this, and the child will notice
that on the one hand, he or she can do no good and is adamantly
rejected, and on the other, is praised to the skies and seen as exceptional. These aren't particularly the rudiments for gaining a balanced view of yourself and building a stable ego. This is also one of
the reasons that yods and unaspected planets are accompanied by
so much insecurity. In such cases, it is almost literally a life-saver
for such children when their parents understand what's going on
and are themselves busy coping with the family dynamic. It is possible, as I indicated earlier, that the parents themselves may have
pretty much come to terms with this family repression and still
have a child with a yod or unaspected planet. This has nothing to
do with the question of whether they were successful or not. There
are larger forces at work. It's as if there were a more inclusive family dynamic that is aiming at a definitive and irrevocable change in
the pattern. Children born with a yod or unaspected planet will
mark the turning point and may even play a unique and positive
role in it. However, if these children receive the message in a negative way, they may also succumb to it psychically.

If parents understand what's going on, they can give these
children a safe shield of understanding and help, so that they will
learn to deal with the extremes in the projections they encounter.
Such children can definitely have a very happy childhood and feel
safe. However, this does not take away from the fact that they carry the "turning-point idea" as a personal theme in their lives, and
will tend throughout their lives to end up in situations where restructuring or turning-points are in the air. This is so dormant and
still so undeveloped though, that nobody will have caught sight
of it, and if such people then enter a company, group, or another
family, they will become part of a process that has much larger
consequences than anyone can oversee. The turbulence that arises
will bring to light a lot of shadow projections on the part of most
of the participants in the process, both dark ones as well as light
ones, and as a rule what comes into play will be pretty complicated and sticky. However, precisely this coming to the surface of the
shadow means that it can be integrated, which makes a clean, positive, new beginning possible.

In most cases this plays itself out on a small scale, but we can also see such processes on a large one. In that case, people with a yod, an unaspected planet, or a duet will play a role in bringing a collective shadow to the surface, with all the inherent turbulence. The entanglements in the Bill Clinton-Monica Lewinsky affair form a textbook example of this. Monica Lewinsky's Venus-Saturn duet became a pivotal point in bringing to the surface the shadow around the theme of sexuality in America.

The shadow has a personal side, as we just saw. It goes deeper than this though. The shadow is also an archetype. This means it is a general human dynamic, a primal motivation with a tremendous power. Each person, regardless of the development of that person's consciousness, has, by virtue of the sheer fact of being human, the archetype of the shadow in the depths of his or her (collective) un-conscious. This gives people the capacity to do evil and to do all those things that they and/or their culture reject. Yet this doesn't mean that they *will* go and do these things! Jung, however, did keep emphasizing that you can stay out of the hands of archetypal evil only by confrontation with your own shadow. For, if you exclusive-ly and singularly identify with what is "proper" and "good" and pay no attention to the evil traits in yourself, and the evil of which you are capable, you will be very susceptible to the archetypal shadow breaking through. You will plant quite a few evil seeds in yourself and in your environment, and may even do the most atro-cious things in the name of what is "good." The shadow will belea-guer you and try to pull you off balance, something to which the countless stories about saints bear witness: were they not torment-ed time and again by the most awful spectacles and visions, or con-stantly tempted? On account of their powerful striving for purity, a choice on the part of their ego, the shadow-of-impurity was also activated in their unconscious, and they had to confront it.

Whenever people lose touch with the personal shadow, they are also in greater danger of identifying with an ideology that has claims to an absolute validity or truth. Here, too, this entails a re-markable lack of humor; nothing at all is relative. It doesn't mat-ter what area this ideology belongs to; it might be of a religious nature, but could also be political, or other. The issue is that there is an invasion of "absolute" forces that take possession of the ego, so that these people lose their human measure. They lose their in-dividuality and become the mouthpiece for an idea or ideal, and time and time again will be driven to decide to attack everything that conflicts with that ideal, and possibly get rid of it. They cause much suffering by doing this, but will themselves suffer as well, because their unconscious will make them feel that they are on the wrong track and will make them restless, unsure, and fearful. If they don't understand what the connection is, they will project the cause of this onto opponents to their ideal, and so become even harder. Under the guise of what is "good," they will act as hard as nails and precipitate evil. This process can play itself out on a small scale in a family where, for instance, one or both parents avoid confronting their own shadow and fall into the hands of an absolutist ideal, so that they deny themselves, their children, and others around them even an inch of space. And they will do this in the name of what is good! On a large scale this can play out at the level of a nation or of a religious movement.

Whenever processes like these play themselves out on a large scale, it will be oppressive and painful for those people who are unable to conform to them—meaning people who are seeking their own way and whose individuality insistently looks for another channel. Such people will get the collective shadow stuck on them, and will become the dissidents of a nation, or the sinners in the eyes of a particular movement.

Of course, there will also be more than enough people without a yod, duet, or unaspected planet who may be dissidents and bear the brunt of a nation's or a group's projections, but this is not the crux of the issue. What is going on with yods, unaspected planets, and duets on a deeper level is that when these people show up on the scene of such a struggle, many things will happen around their person, whether they want it to or not. They will become part of a social process that is much larger and more invasive than what they can oversee or realize, and in some way or other they will play the role of catalyst. The chance that they will make history because of this is therefore also greater. Examples of this are, for instance, Ayatollah Rubolla Khomeini (Mercury-Venus-Uranus yod, see Chart 3, page 112), Václav Havel (unaspected Mercury = Ruler 8 and unaspected Pluto, see chapter 4, Chart 2, page 65), Mahatma Gandhi (unaspected Mercury = Ruler 8, see Chart 4, page 113),[2] Alexander Solzhenitsyn (Mercury-Pluto duet, unaspected Jupiter and Neptune, see Chart 5, page 114). What is also striking are the reversals they experienced during their lives, as for instance from dissident to president! Just because people with yods and unaspected planets feel an inner urge to go their own way and find their own answers to questions from deep down, it is very difficult for them

---

[2] There are a number of differences in data offered for Gandhi's birth time. Jan Kampherbeek, *Cirkels* also uses this time (No. 618). Other times mentioned are 7:12, 7:58, 7:09, and 7:45 (Taeger's choice in *Internationales Horoskope Lexikon*) and 23:00 (all LMT) and a 2:30 A.M. GMT.

to conform to trends and isms. The paradox, though, is that in negative development they may turn into an ism themselves! Rudimentary for the role of catalyst, in the positive sense, is the courage to remain consciously close to your own inner voice. Otherwise you risk becoming a pawn in a grotesque game where you are victimized far more easily for your lack of awareness, both through your own actions as well as those of others, as we will see with Princess Diana (Chart 8, page 162), Prince Charles (Chart 9, page 171), and Monica Lewinsky (Chart 13, page 187).

If you possess a yod or duet, and you get involved with the collective shadow, you will have judgments typical of it dumped on you that aren't easy to swallow. The way in which people look at you and the propaganda created against you are often too grotesque and exaggerated to be justified in any way. You may rightfully ask what made you deserve it. A larger evil seems to be brought down on your head than is reasonable. Still, you have to manage to deal with it, one way or another—it's simply a part of your life. It does call up philosophical questions, though, about what good and evil actually are and why it all happens the way it does.

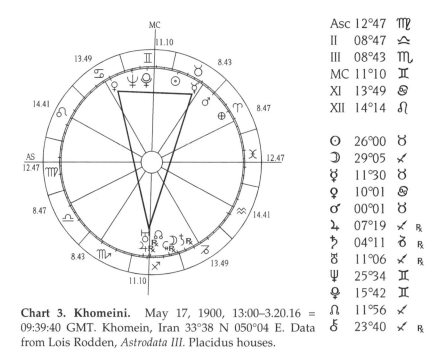

Chart 3. Khomeini. May 17, 1900, 13:00–3.20.16 = 09:39:40 GMT. Khomein, Iran 33°38 N 050°04 E. Data from Lois Rodden, *Astrodata III*. Placidus houses.

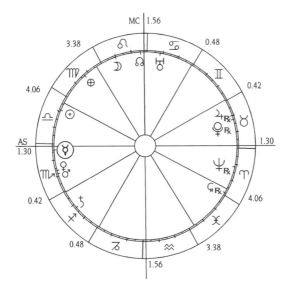

Asc 01°30 ♏

II 00°42 ♐

III 00°48 ♑

MC 01°56 ♌

XI 03°38 ♍

XII 04°06 ♎

☉ 08°57 ♎

☽ 20°11 ♌

☿ 03°47 ♏

♀ 16°27 ♏

♂ 18°25 ♏

♃ 20°10 ♉ ℞

♄ 12°22 ♐

♅ 21°41 ♋

♆ 18°25 ♈ ℞

♇ 17°39 ♉ ℞

☊ 04°11 ♌

⚷ 01°23 ♈ ℞

Chart 4. Mahatma Gandhi. October 2, 1869, 07:33–
4.38.24 = 02:54:36 GMT. Portbandar, India 21°40 N
069°40 E. Data from Marc H. Penfield, *The Penfield Collection*, 2001 data, No. 696; and Jan Kampherbeek, *Cirkels*, No. 618. Other times sourced are all A.M. (7:12, 7:58,
7:09, 7:45). Taeger's choice in *Internationales Horoskope
Lexikon* is 7:45. Also mentioned are an 11:00 P.M. and a
2:30 A.M. GMT. Placidus houses.

In all those problems we can easily overlook the fact that the
collective shadow's breaking through also entails significant positive sides. Every culture and every society have traits that are seen
as desirable or as undesirable. The undesirable character-compo-
nents are repressed by most people in the culture and are relegated
to the unconscious. However, all people have their own character
and so they also have their own shadow. If we were to live without
a shadow, this would mean living completely in harmony with the
wishes and judgments of society, and that would come down to the
death of our individuality. Now, the light and positive meaning of
the shadow is that it helps us find a way out of automaton-like or
diminishing situations. We do turn into automatons if we function
in a merely adaptive capacity—aside from having trouble because
we're not really like that inside. There is then the danger, at the
same time, of people ending up in high social positions who fully
adhere to society's ideology, completely identify with it, but who

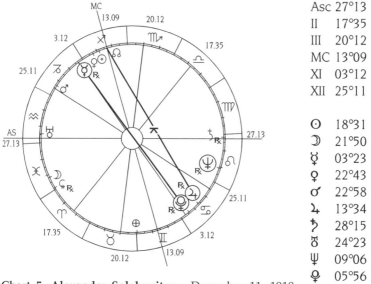

Asc 27°13	♒
II 17°35	♈
III 20°12	♉
MC 13°09	♐
XI 03°12	♑
XII 25°11	♑

☉ 18°31	♐	
☽ 21°50	♓	
☿ 03°23	♑	℞
♀ 22°43	♐	
♂ 22°58	♑	
♃ 13°34	♋	℞
♄ 28°15	♌	℞
♅ 24°23	♒	
♆ 09°06	♌	℞
♇ 05°56	♋	℞
☊ 12°48	♐	
⚷ 28°57	♓	℞

Chart 5. Alexander Solzhenitsyn. December 11, 1918, 08:39 GMT. Kislovodsk, U.S.S.R. 44°01 N 042°44 E. Data from Marc Penfield, *The Penfield Collection*, 2001 data, No. 1724 and Lois Rodden, *Astrodata II* (who also mentions 11:00 A.M.).

are blind to the shadow sides of it, or who deny the faults of this ideology as much as possible. Otherwise they would risk losing their identity and position, after all.

Such people are no longer capable of moral action. They will follow the law to the letter and are capable of inhuman acts in order to keep feeding the ideology. They will have become dependent on gaining confirmation of their person from outside and are nothing more than the role they are playing on this stage. They will not be in touch with their own shadow, the place where unlived content resides, after all, and may have increasing trouble with invasions of "absolute forces" from their unconscious. Further talk or discussion is impossible with these people, or living with them, for that matter. All that is individual will have disappeared.

It is precisely our shadow that protects us from this kind of a scenario. The function of the shadow, no matter how troublesome it may be, is simply to preserve life, to preserve individuality. After you have confronted it, and are in the process of integrating the shadow, you will, in fact, see people become more human and balanced and respond in a more adjusted manner. So this is not indiscriminate adaptation, but adaptation through the conscious choices you make, without repression.

It will be the shadow that rebels against particular laws and rules, against restrictions, codes, taboos, and so on. No society will remain the same, because if values surface in enough individuals who until then belonged to society's shadow, that society will have to face them and change.

Just as young children have to go through phases where they react against their parents in order to find their own individuality, individuals will at a certain moment have to break the rules on a large scale, precisely to keep that society alive. Real renewal and change often demand overstepping limits that were considered sacred until then, and sometimes laws have to be violated in order to bring about renewal or to cultivate new creative initiatives.

You will no longer need to make the shadow reprehensible. On the contrary, integrating your shadow can give you the courage to become yourself and to *stand* for what you think is important. This will enable you to catch the signals of social developments that are going the wrong way, and you will be able to decide consciously to what extent you want to go along, or that you are going to resist. If you resist, you will no longer be well adapted, but you will be paving the way for something very new in society, on a small scale or a large one.

Precisely on these points we often find unaspected planets and yod configurations. In the process of becoming themselves, these people wrestle with issues of an ethical and moral nature a lot more than the average person. Yods and unaspected planets do not, however, provide real support or answers; they are only part of the "turning-point situation." The actions you perform—or consciously refrain from performing—can have major consequences in the long run though. Those with the yod or unaspected planets don't always get thanked for that, by any means, and they run the risk of not being very well understood. This was the case, for instance, with Willy Brandt (mayor of West Berlin after the Cold War and afterward chancellor of what was then West Germany). In the end he decided to flee to Sweden because he could no longer identify with the social developments in Hitler's Germany. His unaspected Pluto and Ruler 8, as well, made him exceptionally sensitive to the unarticulated, dark sides and the dynamic of power, and he ran into an internal moral dilemma. (See Chart 6, page 116.)

People who didn't understand him, condemned him and thought that he was running away from problems. This is not how things were on a deeper level though. Just as in fairy tales, one time the hero has to fight and another time had in fact better run away, this is also the case with yods and unaspected planets. One can say that this entails an ongoing feeling of being with one's back to the wall and then being able to choose only from among evils. Staying is bad and running away also doesn't seem good, but what should you do in a situation that offers no way out? Sitting tight and waiting is the best remedy, as we will see later.

We'll go back now to these processes on a small scale, because similar scenes play out on this level. Jung emphasized that it is of the greatest importance for all people to develop themselves in a way that fits with their inner self and to give their abilities and talents a place of their own, and not push them away, even if they don't altogether fit in with the environment in which these people grew up, or in which they have to function as adults. Artistic children in intellectual families should get every chance to develop their artistic ability, because if that talent remains undeveloped, it will commit mutiny from the dark depths of the unconscious. If you leave your abilities and talents within reach of the shadow, they will become malignant seeds both for yourself as well as for your environment. It is evident when a particular talent or a particular character trait has had to be dormant for several generations, that we can inevitably expect some negativity. It will be the

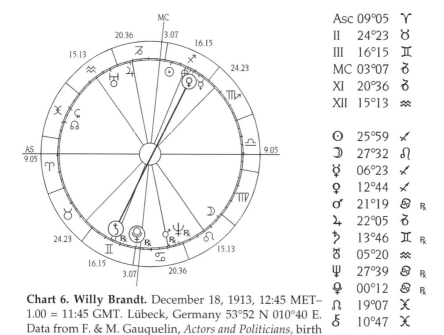

Asc	09°05	♈
II	24°23	♉
III	16°15	♊
MC	03°07	♉
XI	20°36	♉
XII	15°13	♒
☉	25°59	♐
☽	27°32	♌
☿	06°23	♐
♀	12°44	♐
♂	21°19	♋ R
♃	22°05	♉
♄	13°46	♊ R
♅	05°20	♒
♆	27°39	♋ R
♇	00°12	♋ R
☊	19°07	♓
⚷	10°47	♓

Chart 6. Willy Brandt. December 18, 1913, 12:45 MET–1.00 = 11:45 GMT. Lübeck, Germany 53°52 N 010°40 E. Data from F. & M. Gauquelin, *Actors and Politicians*, birth certificate. Placidus houses.

child with the yod configuration or the unaspected planet who will lift the lid off the pit or have it lifted off, as it were, unconsciously and unintentionally.

We see moral dilemmas, ethical issues, and stalemates arise in small circles, too. The urge you feel inside and the insights that well up inside turn out, as with so many people, not to go together at all with the morality and views of the collective. However, it seems as if yods and unaspected planets have something like a patent for seeing or feeling things just a little bit differently. So you may end up in situations in which you have to do things that are considered normal in the family setting in which you grow up, or that are deemed proper by the collective morality. Except, for you doing them doesn't feel right, you can't get behind it. So what do you do? Do you follow the voice of the group or your inner voice? If you do follow your inner voice, how do you know it's holding the right end of the stick? And won't you be inviting all kinds of trouble because of your deviating attitude?

These are typical questions whenever we get caught in such a conflict. There isn't a single guideline, not a single certainty, no handle whatsoever for us. We may strongly feel another vision inside, but we feel the doubt or uneasiness and insecurity just as much. So there is a conflict, a pure moral or ethical conflict over something about which outer and inner worlds think so differently that you get stuck in a stalemate. No clear answer is possible. However, as Jung determined, among people who have undergone the torments of their conflict long enough, a hidden development comes to light that offers them sufficient security to continue on the road taken, so that they are in fact accepting the risk that they may be making a mistake. Total security doesn't exist, of course, but it is in the spirit of Jung to keep fostering a certain doubt about your own behavior. To put it in other words, do your level best, but never exclude the possibility of a mistake. It is important, though, that you do what you feel you have to do with all your heart and from inside. This is when exceptional and creative qualities can break through.

If we look in fairy tales, for instance, to see how evil is approached, we see that there is always a paradox concerning evil. In one instance, the evil can be combated only by actively opposing it and battling it out; in another instance, it turns out that only total passivity or running away is the way to go. In my practice I keep seeing that with "normal" conflicting aspects in progression and transit, openly approaching evil and taking it on is an effective stance. However, with yods and unaspected planets this is absolutely not the case! With both, but particularly with yods, the strategy is to wait and we will benefit the most by just allowing fate to wash over us. This is an obviously passive form of waiting—not undertaking any counteraction, not actively taking things on. In our present culture this is already quickly misinterpreted—this would be cowardice, bear witness to little courage, and so forth. However, this kind of judgment evinces lack of understanding for the yod situation. There are situations in which action can worsen the business and elicit new problems, and where quietly waiting or temporarily withdrawing is the best thing to do. This has nothing to do with a lack of courage. On the contrary, it is a wise attitude.

So there are two possible attitudes for approaching evil in general—active in "normal" situations, and passive regarding yods and unaspected planets. Fairy tales do almost unanimously offer one attitude to get out of problems though: accept the help of an animal. You may never harm this animal, otherwise things will go badly with you. In dreams and fairy tales, animals psychologically represent the fundamentally instinctual side of our own nature. It is a piece of nature inside us, our bond with our primal instincts. These are what can help get us out of problems. However, in our culture we have gradually become very alienated from that little bit of nature—for generations already.

We already saw how people with yods and unaspected planets can end up in difficult situations, situations where they come face to face with evil, wrestle with moral dilemmas, and keep posing the question, "Now why does this have to be happening to me?" This is all the more distressing in situations where a child with a yod who is still very young experiences all kinds of things, such as a serious illness, or some other situation that a logically reasoning brain simply can't correlate with "what that child deserves." There are people who see this as a punishment for misdeeds in a former life, and thereby draw it into the realm of "one's own fault." However, for those who do not believe in reincarnation or who approach the concept in a different way, this is not an answer.

These children seem to have been selected by "Nature" or Fate to make the evil side of life (or of nature) visible without the children necessarily being bad themselves or showing "black" character traits. We arrive at a border here beyond which we cannot pose any more questions, but come face to face with God, with Life, with Nature, with the Tao, or whatever you want to call it. Face to face with *everything* and the all-encompassing, with Good *and* Evil, which belong together like day and night. For a culture where death is taboo, a child dying is barely imaginable. It runs counter to all sense of justice. And yet, I have seen impressive examples of children who were dying, and who, in dreams or drawings, showed a maturity that was extraordinary even before they became ill. In the professional literature, as well, we encounter many examples where, in the unconscious of these children, there is already a preparation for the nearing end taking place, even before anybody has even the slightest clue as to what is about to happen. Likewise you will see with many children a very open approach to death, as the Dutch book *Morten Age 11* stresses once again. It's as if these children's Self had knowledge of their life span and were unconsciously preparing the children for the dying process so they are "ready," and won't have problems coming to terms with approaching death. At a time when nothing seems to be wrong yet, some children make drawings in which they draw people with distortions of those parts of the body that later turn out to play a major part in their illness. (See, among others, Gregg M. Furth, *The Secret World of Drawings: Healing through Art*.)

This forces us to judge these situations differently. Evidently there is another order or power at work, one that goes beyond consciousness. I think that it is mistaken to try and come up with some "human justification" for this. It occurs in nature; it is part of life, and we should accept it. Larry Dossey, in an analysis of the question why illness occurs, has this to say:

> *The customary answer Western religions give is that suffering is a punishment from God for misdeeds. However, when Jesus stood in front of a blind man, he himself denied this association between physical imperfection and sin: "It was not that this man sinned, or his parents, but that the works of God might be made manifest in him."*[3]

However, there are countless matters we can accept only with great difficulty and that we can't validate from the Western view, either. How do you stand regarding children who are beaten, abused, or psychically pushed aside? Children whose legs have

---

[3] Larry Dossey, *Recovering the Soul* (New York: Bantam, 1989), p. 247)

been torn off by cheaply produced and randomly hidden land-mines? Or people in former Yugoslavia who were brutally driven from home and hearth, or who perished or were wounded in a raid? The evil we see happening here is also much more serious than the victims "deserve." As people, we are standing face to face with archetypal Evil that is enacted, as it were, by people who are obsessed or affected by it and are living it in their projection—"seeing" this great evil in someone else rather than in themselves. Those who are innocent are often the victims here. It is comforting to come up with still more judgments about the victims, or to say that something like this makes sense and that the victims will surely be able to learn something from it. These are frequently mental constructions made in an attempt to grasp the event and place it. We should realize, however, that we are doing this from a conscious perspective firmly rooted in our culture and therefore not objective. Moreover, it is horrifying to stand face to face with these awful expressions of evil, and this produces the need to categorize and label it as quickly as possible so that we can give it a place. The risk inherent in this is that we can deny or repress the real depth and intensity of this evil by building a theory around it. Then we are involved more with the theory than with the phenomenon itself.

These kinds of discussions always elicit lots of emotion because they involve confrontations with yourself and with the way you are trying to live with the distressing incidents you hear about and that may happen to you. I only want to point out here which dynamics are at play; there is no definitive answer to be given to the how and why of that great archetypal Evil. All cultures and religious schools of thought have their own opinions about it and live with it in their own way. I just want to call to mind that this force is simply a part of life, as awful as it is. It is a pure statement of fact and not something to be validated. A second statement of fact is that all individuals, whether influenced by religion or culture, have their own judgment and opinions about it, and also specific areas of repression accordingly.

The reason I am broaching the subject of this greater evil is that what I have seen with a number of people who have yods or unaspected planets is that they fell victim to an evil that was somehow greater than they deserved, and they really had to wrestle with it. Rightfully a kind of "Job" situation: having a sincere attitude toward life and still to be given a nasty, often even a very nasty blow by fate. Incomprehensible and not to be imagined. And yet, this is what happened to them.

In addition, I want to state very clearly that of course not all people with yods and unaspected planets will experience this. It does seem, though, that they are still somewhat more susceptible to ending up in situations like this, situations that can no longer be made sense of by our normal opinions about Good and Evil, and that are in total conflict with our normal sense of justice. The things that happen to these people make up the concrete form, as it were, of our deeper questions about Life and God and about Good and Evil, and these are issues that will touch us to the quick if we really dare to go into them.

I have seen that the serious things that came into play around somebody with a yod or an unaspected planet sometimes in the end turned out to be the catalyst for new developments in a group or a society, later on and in a different context. Sometimes the person was himself or herself still part of this; with others this wasn't the case, although in retrospect their situation had also set off a process whereby changes in a larger context were able to come about. As if that great evil that crystallizes and touches a particular person was, in the end, the beginning of new development. However, it often turns out that the one possessing the yod or unaspected planet can no longer reap the fruits. Here, too, such people appear to play a role in a "turning-point."

It has not been possible for me thus far, though, to see *whether* somebody who has a yod or an unaspected planet will experience such a situation, and if so, its intensity or depth. I have seen that there is a bigger chance of such a situation with yods and unaspected planets, and these people will in some way mark a turning-point on a larger scale or in a larger context. The dynamic that they put into operation is beyond their personal limits, and only by looking back will you be able to see what the scope of the events was.

CHAPTER EIGHT

Unaspected Planets and Temporary Yods by Progression and Transit

Whthen people have a yod in the natal chart, the yod will be activated by progression or transit from time to time. This will often be a time when many confrontations arise and the yod's themes step to the foreground. However, even if people have no yod in the horoscope, they may temporarily have one by progression or transit and will suddenly be confronted by a dynamic that they haven't encountered before and that may be very defining. This certainly doesn't always have to be negative, and in many cases has to do with turning-points and insights that are unexpected. However, these times are troublesome; they come as a surprise; and they are uncertain. In a later chapter we will see some examples of this.

Activating Yods that Already Exist

The yod in a natal chart consists of a number of themes that represent both a sticky interaction among themselves as well as a kind of ability or talent when combined together. If an important transit, notably of the slow planets (from Saturn out), occurs over one of the three yod planets, the inner turbulence of the yod will be boosted and the talent will be activated as well. It is up to people with yods to be on their guard not to identify with the restlessness of the activated yod, and also to watch out for signals that point in the direction of their desires, talent, or ability. Often those signals are not direct and not clearly "readable," but they trickle in throughout the entire process. When a yod is activated we can expect extremes. On the one hand, we may feel we are not understood, and feel at loose ends, "really not knowing what to do anymore." On the other, things may happen that set people on the path to self-realization without being aware of it at the time. It may happen by means of small things, such as reading a book that somebody recommended. The subject matter of that book may, in retrospect, have provided a change in direction. Except, as long as the yod is activated, we won't see it.

An example from practice: a high school boy's natal yod was activated by Pluto. He felt he had ended up in an inner vacuum. He had absolutely no idea about what he wanted to do and wasn't motivated, either. Pluto, of course, swings back and forth around particular degrees in the zodiac for a longer time as a result of its lengthy retrograde motion, and all year the boy had been bothered by inner tension and restlessness. At school, he had to repeat a grade and it seemed as if he couldn't learn very well. He was unable to indicate what was wrong and didn't grasp it himself. There were no clues for this lack of motivation and the dynamic to be found in his life circumstances at that time, and the boy realized this. He was also badly confused by being so at loggerheads with himself without any detectable reason.

Pluto has to do with coping, and from conversations with his parents, it turned out that he had, in fact, been badly teased in elementary school, and this past experience was still having an effect in some way, and was asking to be coped with. His parents decided to have him undergo special therapy, and in the months that followed it began to have an effect. His parents also discussed the question of what he wanted to do in life. Did he have any dreams of what he wanted to be? How did he look at things? Everything remained very vague; the boy just really didn't know. For a time he had also not been able to work up any interest in his hobbies and seemed to be unmotivated in every way. Considering he had in the past always been interested in gadgets, his parents asked him if he would like to have a computer. Not just for games, but to make real use of it. In the back of their minds they were thinking that these days a computer is a useful tool for children anyway with regard to their future. The idea appealed to the boy and so a computer was purchased. In retrospect this seemed to be right on the mark. Not only did the boy's motivation and his pleasure in life return, through the therapy and the computer, but it turned out he even showed talent in the area of computers. Now he is absolutely certain of what he wants to be later on!

From this example we can clearly see the ambivalence inherent in the activation of the yod: unpleasant situations or feelings accompany the beginning of new development. Except: this last you still can't see, even though it's already there. I have seen this so many times: if a yod is producing problems by progression or transit, the germ of the solution is already there, but you don't see it yet. Once the period of the progression or transit's effectiveness has passed, the solution will unfold itself without your having to do anything special for it. The only thing required of you is that you keep your eyes and ears open so that you may also observe it in actuality. For, if you remain too fixated on "misery," you won't see the beginning of what is new, so it will be unable to develop any further. Precisely because the solution presents itself so naturally it is all the more reason not to undertake any drastic countermeasures in response to the adversity and problems that may come up. This doesn't mean that you have to remain passive and do absolutely nothing. In the example of the boy, we saw after all that he also went into therapy and got a computer. It was a situation where he and his parents "gave" with the situation. They didn't deny the problems, tried not to find any parties to blame, tried not to fight what presented itself, and simply used whatever presented itself as raw material and looked for a way to deal with it, without wanting to force results. The computer did not come into the picture to "push" the boy in a future direction, but was bought in the hope that he would get involved with something again, even if only temporarily. So: no grand expectations and no pressure to bend life into a particular form. There was space to feel around, to experiment and try things out, also space to wait for what life had to offer. This is precisely what it's all about with activated yods: you may temporarily step into something important to you at that time, but expect nothing more. It may be that what you do at that time is the help you need to get out, but you won't continue with it later. (At an even later stage you may suddenly reach back, however, to what you were doing then and will get a lot out of it!) Sometimes with an activated yod, however, you can see your future take shape directly—in retrospect, of course, because during the activated yod, you won't have any perspective on this yet.

Thus, living with what presents itself and working free of pressure and grand expectations with the raw material you now have at your disposal is the best way to deal with a yod. So *don't* fight! Offer no resistance, but try to respond to what you feel *now* and think is good or fun to do now. This attitude also applies, moreover, to temporary yods by progression and transit, if you have no yod in your natal chart.

The planet that activates the yod also provides necessary information. Where Pluto was going back and forth in transit in the example of the boy, one could also say that a Pluto theme lay at the bottom of the dynamic—problems coping with unpleasant experiences. Of course Pluto will produce this in all its aspects, and numerous children without yods may also have the feeling of having missed the boat if they cannot cope with their experiences easily. With a yod, though, a more elusive feeling comes into play; everything is less clear and harder to grasp. This is the negative side. At the same time you will see with yod configurations precisely a bigger chance of having something cross your path that entails a turning point in your life! This is the positive side. This turning-point may be triggered by a fun experience (like getting a computer, in the example of the boy) or else by a negative experience—for instance getting entangled in relationship issues in a nasty or confrontational way—that prompts a new insight into life or allows a new attitude toward life.

Forming New Yods

Every sextile in a horoscope is a potential yod! That is, if a planet is temporarily located "on the other side," forming an inconjunct with each of the other two, you will have a temporary yod configuration. The progressed Moon and the transit of Saturn will each, if you become old enough, make an entire cycle through the zodiac three times in your life. and so will temporarily make a yod three times in your life out of every sextile in your natal chart! Now, aspects of the progressed Moon don't last very long, and even a transiting Saturn, compared with the slower planets or with progressions, is over pretty quickly. However, transits of Saturn may mark months during which we may to a certain extent have a yod experience.

Also, if you have an inconjunct in your horoscope, this may easily become a yod if a planet by transit or progression becomes located at a point where it forms a sextile with one point and an inconjunct with another one. Of course both the MC as well as the ASC can also do this by progression.

A third point to consider is the temporary sextile formed by slower moving planets in the sky. In general, it is considered a pleasant factor that there has been a sextile between Neptune and Pluto since the middle of the 20th century. One thing we usually don't think twice about is that this "pleasant sextile" is forming one yod configuration after another in its passage through the zodiac. Take Neptune in Sagittarius, for instance, and Pluto in Libra. These two signs are both inconjunct Taurus. This means that when this sextile slowly moves up the zodiac, one Taurus after another will have a temporary inconjunct created with their radix, or natal, Sun by Neptune in transit on the one side, and by Pluto on the other. And considering that Mercury is usually located nearby, it will sooner or later have its turn as well. In other words, this sextile in the sky has had the following consequences:

Pluto in Leo, Neptune in Libra: All Pisceans will have coped with a yod;
Pluto in Virgo, Neptune in Scorpio: All Arians had a yod to the Sun;
Pluto in Libra, Neptune in Sagittarius: The Taureans had their turn;
Pluto in Scorpio, Neptune in Capricorn: All Geminians had a yod;
Pluto in Sagittarius, Neptune in Aquarius: The Cancereans are having their turn.

In this last case, we see something else suddenly coming up: at the beginning of Aquarius, Uranus temporarily made a sextile with Pluto in Sagittarius, while Neptune was still back in Capricorn. The nature of the collective sextile changed and brought great accelerations. The temporary yod that people with a Sun (or other planet) at the beginning of Cancer were given to cope with was also a more active, dynamic, and fast-paced yod than if Neptune had taken part.

From the list above, we can see that it won't be long before half the zodiac has had to cope with a yod over the years because of this Pluto–Neptune sextile! And this of course includes not only those who have the Sun there, but also those who have other planets or points there.

This means that every person will go through a yod period several times in life—with the progressed Moon and the transit of Saturn, at any rate. Probably however, one or more planets or points will be involved in temporary yod configurations, for instance due to the sextile of the outer planets.

In practice, a temporary yod often turns out to have the same turbulence and dynamic as a natal yod—you can end up in the most complicated or unpleasant situations. However, if you have no yod in your natal chart, a temporary yod is still different. Since there is no question of a collective Family Shadow and the entire family theme doesn't come into play in the same way; there is no continuation of its effect in a temporary yod. If people have a natal yod and it is activated, the hidden family themes may also begin to come into play. This is, however, not the case with temporary yods.

This issue certainly demands further clarification, since in practice I see people who get a temporary yod and who often suddenly take all kinds of action and start taking things out on others. People often told me that in this period they wrote angry letters to family members, that there was some kind of falling-out with particular family members, and so forth. So it is possible that to some degree plenty of facets of a family dynamic and theme may surface, even when we don't have a yod in the natal chart and temporarily only "barely" get one. However, the difference between a temporary and a natal yod is that the latter is in a family dynamic that is already old and typically includes generations, whereas the temporary yod usually has more to do with battling out and coping with a "younger" dynamic.

A "sudden" new yod also demands a somewhat different interpretational approach than the activation of a preexisting yod. Activating a preexisting yod means that the ever-present dynamic will now come out more pointedly, but then through circumstances like those indicated for the activated planet, or by activities or situations that belong to this planet. For the interpretation of these yods, we should go back to the interpretation of the natal yod.

In studying a totally new yod, we are confronted by the same dynamic as for natal yods, such as the restless interaction of the three participating planets, so that there is no calm, no direction can crystallize, and we keep getting caught in dynamic or unpleasant situations. The turbulence, then, is similar to what we discussed regarding the yod in the natal chart. However, this turbulence disappears completely as soon as the yod by progression or transit is past and this may very well come down to "waking up from a bad dream." If there is no yod in the natal chart, it really is harder to deal with the themes of a yod, because the inexplicable feelings, the ambiguity, the feeling of having our back to the wall, and such, are new and so we have not yet been able to develop tools for these things. People who have a yod imperceptibly learn to live with these energies and dynamics through familiarization and another kind of attitude toward life, so that a new temporary yod may be tricky, but will not be such a great shock or produce so much confusion.

We should analyze a yod by progression or transit according to all its components. Look at the radix points that are included in the yod, an existing sextile, for example. Which planets are they? What do they represent? What have you done with them until now? What experiences do you have in the domains of these planets? And don't forget that these planets are each also the ruler of a house. What experiences do you have in the areas of life included in houses they rule? These themes may be woven separately or in combination into a temporarily very confusing pattern that tosses your life around. The planet forming the temporary yod by transit or progression indicates what that turbulence will stir up or "cause." It may concern the psychic pattern that belongs to that planet, but also a person or situation or activity that falls under this planet, or a circumstance that belongs to the house the planet rules.

If a sextile of the slow planets is the cause of a yod, the story is a little different. This is when there is one energy in the natal chart that suddenly gets involved with two different influences that will be on a tense footing with that planet in the natal chart. Considering this concerns a sextile of the slow planets as a rule, this entails causes or situations that effect a larger group or the entire society and in which you become involved with your planet. I have experienced more than once that activation from such a collective sextile brought the person in question into a situation about which at that moment there was much discussion in society, or which was a burning issue among particular subcultures. Unintentionally and unnoticeably they therefore became part of a process that was working itself out collectively.

The "Stretched-Out" Yod

If you have a sextile in your horoscope that is pretty exact, meaning well within orb, the planet forming the temporary yod and the inconjunct with both sextile partners will do this at just about the same time. Imagine, you have a sextile of a planet at 23° 15' Leo to a planet at 23° 55' Libra. Now, if a planet comes to be located at 23° Pisces, this planet simultaneously creates an inconjunct at 23° Libra and at 23° Leo. The orb in progression and transit within which we determine actual activation is 1°. (See figure 5, page 130.)

There are, however, numerous sextiles that are not as exact as in this example. Now imagine that you have a sextile from 20° Leo to 23° Libra. Now if a planet becomes located at 20° Pisces, it creates an inconjunct to the point in Leo, but not to the one in Libra. This planet at 20° Pisces may even be stationary and go retrograde, and only much later again aspect that point in Leo, and still much later the point in Libra. The question is whether one can still say this entails a yod. The answer is: yes. However, we do see that the effect grows less intense the longer the passage of time between the aspecting of the one point and that of the other. So this entails a "smeared out" or "stretched-out" yod. The entire period, meaning beginning from the time the first point is aspected until the aspecting of the second is out of orb, will acquire a kind of yod mood, which of course becomes most noticeable at the moments at which one of the two inconjuncts becomes exact. If slow planets are involved in this transit, or slower planets by secondary progression, the mood of the yod will come into play for many years, but will be dormant, or in the background, should there be no aspects within orb. If we take the case of 20° Leo and 23° Libra again, we will see an activating of this type of yod when a planet arrives between 19° and 21° Pisces (one degree before and one degree after the exact point of 20° Leo). Now things will quiet down a bit, until the planet arrives at 22° Pisces, because then it arrives within a 1° orb of forming an inconjunct with the next planet, and this effect will be noticeable as long as it is moving between 22° and 24° Pisces (or 1° before and 1° after the exact point of 23° Libra).

It is possible that when this planet is retrograde, it will make an aspect to only one of the two sextile planets, but not both. Practice reveals that the effect of the yod is really past when this last aspect is definitely out of orb, regardless of the question of whether both planets are aspected once again or not.

Every time a transit comes within orb, you will see the theme of the temporary yod played up again, and often every next or repeating creation of the aspect will be a continuation of what was already at play. Or else a new problem will appear regarding the already familiar themes, new light may be thrown on the matter, or a new development will appear regarding the familiar themes. It is

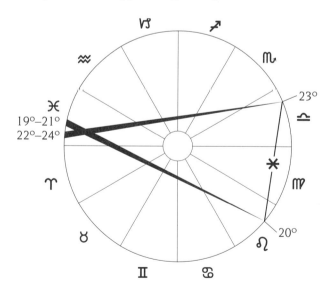

Figure 5.
The formation of a temporary yod.

a lot less likely that something completely different will suddenly present itself. In most cases the issue revolves around the by now familiar themes, even though very new points of approach may present themselves or problems concerning this come up.

Several Yods at Once by Progression or Transit

Imagine that you have a sextile between Mercury at 6° Cancer and Venus at 6° Virgo. If Uranus has arrived at 6° Aquarius, it will create an inconjunct to both Mercury and Venus, and this is a temporary yod. If Pluto is at 6° Sagittarius at the same time, it will create an inconjunct with Mercury, while Uranus is also creating an inconjunct with Mercury. So, another yod. Now this entails a double yod configuration (see figure 6) where the two yod configurations share a leg. The yods are:

Pluto–Uranus–Mercury;
and Uranus–Mercury–Venus.

If one of the points of a yod consists of a conjunction, this entails two yods. For example, the Sun and Mercury are conjunct in Cancer and create a sextile with Venus in Virgo. Now, if Uranus creates an inconjunct with the Sun-Mercury conjunction on the one hand, and Venus on the other, we have two yods:

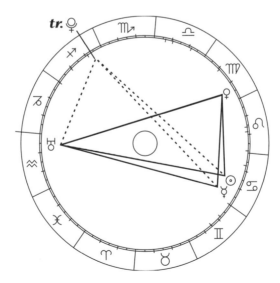

Figure 6.
A double-yod configuration by progression or transit.

Uranus–Mercury–Venus;
and Uranus–Sun–Venus.

If we use the transit of Pluto from the previous example along with this, two more yods are formed:

Pluto–Uranus–Mercury;
and Pluto–Uranus–Sun.

We can now see that because of the sextile between Uranus and Pluto in the sky, four different yods are formed with the friendly little sextile between the Sun and Mercury in Cancer, and Venus in Virgo. These four yods may come up in combination, but each may just as easily express a completely different theme. In this case, somebody may end up in four different tricky and complex situations all at once, but be on the way to encountering just as many exceptional renewals!

Unaspected Planets by Transit and Progression

If you have an unaspected planet in the horoscope, it will also create aspects by progression and transit, or start receiving them from other planets. If it is a fast-moving planet, like Mercury, the transits will last only briefly, usually a matter of days. This is insufficient to start up a larger process. Mercury by primary or secondary progression, though, can take its time to work itself out; it lasts a good while longer! If you have a slow planet that is unintegrated, like Pluto, for example, you will, of course, notice the inevitable when it transits.

One of the primary hallmarks of unaspected planets, as we saw, is that their content in some way is not yet connected to ourselves. So each time this unaspected planet by progression or transit forms a temporary aspect, or each time this planet is aspected by another planet, it just means that a particular piece of our psyche (the planet with which it forms a temporary aspect) suddenly comes into contact with that unaspected energy. So all of a sudden we can become a little more acquainted with our unaspected planet and see it at work. In principle, this also means that the older we get, the better we can get to know our unaspected planet or planets, and can learn to deal with them better and better. This needs time, but there is certainly a gradual growth taking place in the degree to which that planet's themes become familiar and recognizable.

Initially we will notice that when a temporary aspect involving such an unintegrated planet is formed, we will also be confronted by the extremes this planet can exhibit. I have seen the strangest things happen when this is the case, and I have gained the distinct impression that it doesn't much matter whether a harmonious or unharmonious temporary aspect is made by or with an unaspected planet. It seems to be the case that a temporary aspect will cause this planet to pop up suddenly like a devilish little jack-in-the-box and insure both scares as well as fun surprises. I have seen people with harmonious temporary aspects with an unaspected planet get into serious trouble through extremes in their own behavior or circumstances, but also people with their unaspected planet in temporarily conflicting aspects walk away with extremely energizing and positive experiences. So I therefore tend to say that the energy of an unaspected planet is stronger than the nature of the aspect in which it is temporarily involved.

This makes predicting future tendencies around an unaspected planet a guessing game. Of course we know which areas are going to be activated, but the result of this is very uncertain. To give you an example: I have seen people marry when the Sun was by secondary progression over their unaspected Venus, but have also seen people with precisely the same aspect file for divorce, without the rest of the horoscope offering any clear indications regarding this. One thing was certain: the issue was the relationship theme. However, the extremes you may see differ widely.

So be careful where interpretation is concerned. All the more so since extremes may present themselves in a way we cannot predict. I have seen various cases where transits of Pluto created aspects with an unaspected Sun or Moon—harmonious aspects as well!—which combined with an invasive illness. In some cases the answers lay in medical errors made during early childhood, in others genetic problems surfaced, and so on. In all cases, the person involved could do nothing about, was ignorant of, and couldn't adapt to the situation. Then it's a matter of undergoing, being flexible, and looking to see what would be the best thing to do about the illness. Moreover, this is only very rarely fatal. Here, too, it seems that living through this kind of confrontation is accompanied by an often radical change in attitude toward life, which was experienced as being a positive thing. Various people who went through this claimed years later that they had really found themselves because of this confrontation, and only then realized that they had hidden away a creative piece of themselves early on, or had not dared to live a particular part. After coming face-to-face with fear and darkness, it seemed as if their true Self had appeared out of that darkness.

Over the course of the years that I have been studying yods and unaspected planets, an image has gradually come out of how we can best deal with yods and unaspected planets by progression and transit. This is what the next chapter is about.

CHAPTER NINE

How Should We Deal with Yods and Unaspected Planets?

If an unaspected planet is temporarily aspected, or once a yod is active in the natal chart, whether this is a natal yod or a temporary yod created by progression or transit, the best way to deal with it is as follows:

1. Be sure to really live out and experience emotions, but don't be overpowered or swept away by them.

Unaspected planets and yods are associated with a lot of emotion. They may include extremes, as we saw above; from euphoria to deep sorrow, from sudden insights to unmotivated emptiness. It is the unpleasant emotions that we experience when we are in dynamic and difficult situations that we would usually prefer not to feel. It's hard enough already, so why hurt ourselves even more by feeling our grief deep down once again? With activated unaspected planets, and without a doubt with activated yods, we tend not to want to feel and experience it all anymore, we want to hide the emotions or relativize them mentally. One escape route, for instance, is to place what is happening in a theoretical framework in order to be able to understand it and then to stop and think about the theory more than about what is really happening.

It turns out to be very important, though, to stand in direct contact with our feelings and so also in direct contact with our emotions. Precisely then we will see a mechanism by which we suddenly break through the pain and something new is born, in the same way the pains of childbirth precede a new life. If we try to repress sorrow or rationalize it away, there is a danger that the new life won't be born, or it enters the world in crippled form.

We need courage to realize concretely during a period when we're standing with our backs to the wall that this is the case, and there is nowhere to go. And also to realize that it will be impossible to maneuver out of things without tearing our clothes. We may easily become scared, go into a panic, or get the feeling there are no prospects for us. Dare to feel this, but know that it is only temporary and that at a later point in time we will surely get out. If we do dare to feel at this time, we won't be repressing emotions. This means that we aren't giving the yod a chance to build or expand on complexes in our unconscious.

2. Retain integrity at all costs, and dare to become aware of who you are, in spite of your doubts.

For people who have yods and unaspected planets in their natal charts this would seem like somewhat strange advice. How can you know who you are and what you want when you are so involved with yods or unaspected planets? It seems unfeasible to dare to realize who you are. However, from another point of approach, you will be able to do this.

You have already lived a piece of life, experienced conflicts, made decisions, and you know the themes you must deal with and the ones with which you have not (yet) come to terms. This knowledge of yourself, this experience with yourself, forms a whole that says something about who you are at this moment. You will be able to have good insight, especially if you have managed to get in touch with your shadow, into the things that make you emotional, the things that you reject, and the things you prefer.

The situation in which you now find yourself, with an activated unaspected planet or yod, will give the feeling that you have to choose from among evils, and it would seem as if there were only sticky options. However, this is not what it is primarily about. What it is about is that you realize the kinds of compromises you are capable of making without harming yourself and where, for you, the absolute limit lies. An unaspected planet or yod just happens to have a moral conflict with customary values sooner, and has different feelings about particular situations than most people have. This is what you have to be aware of, and it is important to remain true to this sincere, real feeling inside. As soon as you start compromising it, it will seem as if things are getting even more obscure or problematic. Of course you may doubt whether what you think or do is good. Doubt and insecurity are, after all, integral components of yods and unaspected planets! Also dare to doubt, but be careful not to end up in a mental merry-go-round of thoughts. Stand by what you feel is good at this moment. You can only get to that real feeling inside if you have also kept in touch with your feelings and your emotions. This is one more reason to take to heart what I pointed out in Number 1.

Standing by yourself and being true to yourself may result in temporarily feeling misunderstood and isolated. Just let it happen. Think of the fairy tales where the hero or heroine stays in the forest all alone, deprived of warmth and contact, having to resort to his or her own devices. Then just look at all the miraculous rescues that take place in these fairy tales and how important it was that the hero or heroine was alone.

3. Watch out that you don't start attaching exaggerated (religious) value to something outside yourself.

Stand with both feet firmly on the ground. Whenever you get into a jam or stalemate because of a yod or unaspected planet, you will be liable to escape into another reality. This is frequently an unconscious escape in the sense that you aren't really aware of it. However, you are diligently searching for a particular type of handle and believe you can find it in an ideal, a religion, or an ism, just to name a couple of examples. All the more because particular yods containing trans-Saturnian planets may also offer perceptions and experiences of a different reality. You may have powerful dreams or visions, suddenly notice that you have magnetic or healing abilities, and this kind of thing. With activated yods and unaspected planets, it's as if the dividing line between the everyday world and that of invisible reality were actually to become permeable. This causes you either to rack up impressive experiences and undergo profound emotions, or else to become detached from reality and "escape" into a world of pretense. There, "on the other side of reality," you feel better, more calm, and you can get away from all the problems for a little while.

You can easily be infatuated with this other reality, as well as with a particular image of God, or a particular religion, which may be either a world religion or a sect. Some people even establish one! Like Jim Jones, the cult leader who dragged the members of his "People's Temple" movement into a collective suicide during which he also opted for death. He had a duet between Mercury and Neptune in his horoscope, and he set up the "People's Temple" when transiting Pluto became stationary in conjunction with his Neptune duet! (See Chart 7, page 138.)

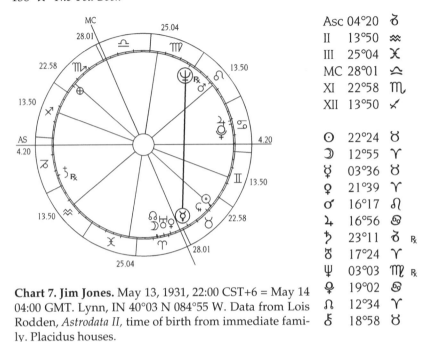

Chart 7. Jim Jones. May 13, 1931, 22:00 CST+6 = May 14 04:00 GMT. Lynn, IN 40°03 N 084°55 W. Data from Lois Rodden, *Astrodata II*, time of birth from immediate family. Placidus houses.

4. Try not to do anything radical and try to pick up the thread of your life as much as possible.

Whenever you get caught up by a religious thought, or utopia, or take a step toward "another reality," you run the risk of making decisions that will make deep inroads in your life, and these decisions are frequently irrevocable—maybe much too rigorous. I saw many times that people were suddenly gripped by an ideal or idea and completely changed the course of their lives; in some cases abandoning home and hearth, children and all, and diving headfirst into a process that, in the eyes of those around them, was an illusion or full of uncertainties. Of course, I have seen people finally end up well after taking a drastic step like this. For the great majority, though, it turned out to be too forceful and too rigorous, and in retrospect to have destroyed more than they might have wanted and more than was necessary. Some of the people who had to come to grips with this tried to avoid feeling guilty by escaping into a mental attitude of "it must have been good for something on a spiritual level," or "the others should have learned something from it," and the like. This, too, is a kind of radical act away from reality and not particularly an attitude by which you can limit or repair the damage done.

My warning not to do anything radical has sometimes been directed at deaf ears, without the person who activated the yod or unaspected planet intending to be contrary. The oncoming energy is sometimes so powerful and strong that you are driven in a particular direction and something else simply doesn't count anymore, isn't important anymore. This can take on such forms that the person involved gets the feeling of not being able to get out of it and usually doesn't want to, either. The chance at messing things up is very real then, but there is also always the chance that this "leap in the dark" will finally lead to the light. It's impossible to say ahead of time. In any case, I have seen in by far the most cases that needless damage was done and that it took considerable energy to recover after "the outburst."

5. Don't be afraid to run into a jam.

With unaspected planets, but particularly with yods, running into a jam turns out to be precisely the way to get out of the situation again, as paradoxical as it sounds. Imagine that when everything seems hopeless, senseless, or without prospect, something deep inside you is germinating. It will soon be of great value. In the outside world as well the first seeds of change, movement, and resolution will slowly become distinguishable, or come to light, only after the yod is completely past, or when the unaspected planet is completely out of orb. The solution presents itself very often automatically, and in a good number of cases without your having had to do anything for it; but you do have to discover the seeds. The solution often starts announcing itself in small signals, small incidents, and combinations of circumstances and if you see them, you will be able to bend with them. You'll have to have patience, though, because a yod period can sometimes last years!

In our society there is an overriding tendency when there is a problem, or when one threatens, "to do something about it." We are supposed to think in a solution-oriented fashion and grab problems by their roots. The problem with yods and unaspected planets is precisely that this doesn't work and will only make the problems worse. Yods and unaspected planets need a period during which the whole business has come to a halt! Trying to remedy or prevent this only spins everything deeper into the mud. However, if we listen to the message of the yod or the unaspected planets and *let* things temporarily take their course (without throwing in the towel), we will have to deal with an attitude of reproach from the outside world. We will, for example, be reproached for "not doing enough," or that we "don't want to do anything," "aren't cooperating," "are lazy," or that we are dumping it on others. These are all remarks we're best ignoring, because they won't improve the mood. And as far as that "dumping" is concerned: oftentimes others will tend to interfere in our problems and come up with all kinds of solutions, and in some cases they will take things in hand to solve the business. Aside from the question of whether they are really capable of offering solutions, the tendency to take others' affairs onto our own shoulders is a form of projection and frequently a mirror of our own piece of shadow. There are a lot of people who therefore cannot tolerate seeing us in trouble, in a stalemate, and who have the impression that we're not doing anything about it.

These people who keep wanting to interfere in our business may therefore be an extra burden during a yod period or during a period when unaspected planets are having effect! We automatically arrive at the next point.

6. Dare to wait and dare to let things take their course as they will.

This has been inspired not only by reason of the fact that working against things or taking an active approach to them often leads to more problems, there is yet one more reason. Oftentimes during the period of an activated yod or unaspected planet, talents, possibilities, or new needs awaken inside and once they have clearly come to light, involve a very different way of living and working. During the period (which may last years) that yods and unaspected planets are activated, everything is sticky and ambiguous on the outside; there may be opposition, things don't want go right, and we are faced with impossible choices, as we already saw. We can't speed this up—it will come in its own time. If, just to have some security, we should tie ourselves down to something for longer, this will mean that we won't be able to or will have a harder time heeding what is new and dormant. It will then take a lot more effort to return to ourselves than if we had simply waited.

Does this mean that we can't do anything at all? No, that's not it. Remain open to what presents itself and make sure that there are no expectations whatsoever of how things should (have to) go—because things will usually just happen to go differently. Initially it's hard to expect absolutely *nothing*, because hope and longing are always haunting our minds. Still, we had better let go of these, because hopes will be dashed more than once, expectations don't come to fruition, and longings aren't satisfied.

Activated yods and unaspected planets will force you to stand simply in the here and now. You really can still do fun things! Once again it is important to stay close to your feeling, *very* close to your feeling, and to ask yourself: What do I think would be fun to do *at this moment*? Nothing more. So don't hope on the sly that something grand will grow in the future; have no expectations whatsoever. Simply step into the activity that appeals to you at this moment, if it is at all possible. Surrender to this with all the joy that is in you and savor it. Don't force yourself "to finish it," "to become good at it," or whatever. In other words, avoid any form of pressure. Be involved with what you're doing and simply *do* it. Maybe another idea or another activity will cross your path. Do you think it might be fun? See if you can't do something with it. Maybe you'll have to give the previous things up. Just step over to the next activity and again become totally involved with it and enjoy it as well. In this way, all kinds of things can cross your path, where the only criterion for stepping into it is the question whether it is what you think would be fun to do in the here and now. Any other motive won't work. Finally, often only after many years, it will turn out that you may reach back to the experiences you accumulated during this period. In fact, you will gain a lot from them, except in a totally different way than you could have foreseen at the time!

An example from my own life: when a sturdy yod including a sextile between Pluto and Neptune was active for me, I received a request to design a CD-ROM about the tarot from a large company. The emphasis was to lie on symbolism, one of my favorite topics. I knew that everything that crossed my path could be influenced by the yod and so could happen a lot differently from the way I might hope or plan. I discussed the proposal with my husband and noticed that I found it was a lot of fun to be working with tarot symbolism and to work it out further. Since it appealed to me so much at that moment, I accepted the proposal, knowing that all kinds of things might go wrong. So I did not try to imagine anything about the form and also didn't wonder whether it would be a success. If it were to be called off, I would simply have had lots of fun being involved with the symbolism. In retrospect this turned out to be the appropriate attitude. For, it turned out that at this big company, the coordinator of the plan was a man who was out for power. He kept trying to polarize people and belittle them so as to aggrandize himself. This also led to avoiding responsibility for payment. The yod was formed between Neptune, the planet of symbolism, and Pluto, the planet that has to do with power. I never saw a penny and also tried to submit as little material as possible, forewarned as I had been by the diminishing possibilities. I did, however, enjoy down to my very toes sifting through and working out the symbolism! And without intent or plan, this naturally led to my writing my first book about the tarot and a book about its profound psychological symbolism will certainly follow.

In that situation it made no sense at all to make threats, start up a lawsuit, or whatever. It would have cost a lot of energy and money and what would I have gotten out of it? On top of this, it turned out that this man treated a lot of other people in the same way and always covered himself legally.

If you look at this from the customary social opinion, this man was on the one hand doing wrong, and it is "stupid" on the other "not to do anything" about it. Couldn't you approach or tackle it at a higher level? None of this is very certain during the period of a yod. The chance of strange bouts of adversity or being confronted by the situation where people inside the company would protect one another is great, not to mention the risk of getting caught up in other, more difficult situations involving power struggles. I simply wasn't in the mood for any of this and was having a great time working. I consider the request that was made of me at the time as the beginning of a new activity that had been dormant for so long already, and that evidently wanted to be born.

If we are aware of this facet of activated yods and unaspected planets, we will once again see the important, deeper meaning they hold for us. Considering that the only thing that works comes down to absolutely not planning or longing, and only being involved in the here and now, the immediate environment, and in this short passage of time, we are forced to sail a course that is totally counter to that of society. Out there we have to plan, after all. Both for our careers, as well as for our retirement, we have to make long-term decisions, invest time, money, and energy in longer-term affairs, and most of all, work hard (meaning keep chasing along). Activated yods and unaspected planets *force* us to step off this merry-go-round and suddenly feel again the silence of our own inner self, to be able to enjoy little things in the here and now, and to start paying attention to the subtle beauty of the moment's "everydayness." This may almost seem Buddhist.

Somebody who knows how to deal well with this dynamic may experience the paradox of turbulence and insecurity on the one hand, and on the other get closer to a kind of inner peace.

In this peaceful attitude we can nevertheless feel joy and sadness, but it no longer sweeps us away. We stay close to our essence. We can wait, because life isn't worthless or hopeless, just *different* from usual. If we stay open about what is happening, and stay close to ourselves, if we expect nothing and simply ARE, the new road that fits with us will reveal itself.

7. Drop egotistical displays and try not to force anything.

If you are accustomed to function using a particular, phony attitude because you are trying to derive security from it, better stop now, because activated yods and unaspected planets will usually remove a mask. It simply won't function anymore. The exposure may be the result of events in the outside world, but could also just as easily be the effect of inner restlessness and change. The same thing applies here: you need to dare to be open to what you really feel. Wait a time and try not to play a compulsive role, or try to force all kinds of issues with the idea of rescuing what's left to be rescued. After all, what are you supposed to be rescuing? You are in the process of concluding a period of time, even though you still don't exactly understand what's going on while the progressions and transits are in play.

This really doesn't have to mean that you are going to divorce, move, change jobs, or undergo other drastic changes in your living situation. Of course all of these things *do* belong to the realm of possibilities. Many times, though, you will see activated yods and unaspected planets more often associated with inner developments and changes (caused by external events or not). You will start looking at life and at yourself in a very different way—and through this way of looking, you will also be dealing with life in a very different way. This may even greatly benefit a marriage or your work! No matter what kind of turbulence you may feel or experience, stay close to your own inner truth and dare to wait.

Every pompous display will have an adverse effect, although exaggerated modesty isn't being demanded of you, either. It is only that you should not try to get into situations in which you would enjoy honor and respect, nor should you try to get your name on the front page of the newspaper. So don't work at celebrity status or fame! Not that you couldn't become famous during a period when a yod or unaspected planet is at work. People may spontaneously cross your path from the outside who will bring you out in the limelight or run a campaign for you. You can go along with this as long as you, *yourself,* don't try to capitalize on it, gain an extra advantage by it, or milk the opportunity, and as long as you just realize that things are just not going to go the way they were planned. Stay yourself, waiting calmly with regard to things to come, and simply do what has to be done. That is the best attitude. Here, once again—be involved and live in the here and now. Try to enjoy the way in which you have been helped or possibly received honors, then change over as quickly as possible in all happiness to the order of the day, modest and unadorned. This doesn't mean that you're supposed to go running around with an inferiority complex! An activated yod or unaspected planet, however, will punish you pretty sorely if you start getting too big for your boots. That's what it's all about.

Realize in everything that happens to you at these times that, as a rule, a yod or unaspected planet is not in a hurry to provide a solution. Paradoxically enough, much will still come out all right of its own accord with a yod, but often differently than we thought at first. So just let things take their course, let the fixations go, and relax. Times during which yods and unaspected planets come into play may be times when you will experience not only turbulence, insecurity, and problems, but precisely also an intense profundity and be very happy.

CHAPTER TEN

Yods and Unaspected Planets in the Astrology of Relationships

People who have a yod (or one or more unaspected planets) in the natal horoscope will have a hard time settling down into an acceptable, smooth-sailing pattern just because they will always be searching. This also applies to their relationships, and this means that they will have a hard time with what we are accustomed to calling a "middle-class" life, or a "homey" relationship. There will always be something gnawing at the back of their minds, "So is this it?" or "Life must have more to offer than this!" and the like. If they don't understand where this is coming from, they run the risk of abandoning a good relationship, or what is in itself a decent marriage, in search of something else. For what? They don't know, but "something" is beckoning them and they "know" or "feel" that there simply has to be more. There is a sizable danger here that they will run into the arms of a person who, for them, conjures up something very special which, in fact, has no content to offer, with grievous and painful experiences as a result. And then they ask the classic question those with yods and unaspected planets ask. "Why does this have to happen to me of all people?" It's that feeling of hunger that drives people like that, but does this also mean that these people can't have a good relationship?

Not at all! I have seen the most beautiful relationships between people when one or both had a yod, one or more unaspected planets, or a duet. However, they were relationships where both partners had gone through some kind of crisis (either during the relationship or not) and who both were capable of dealing flexibly with the fact that neither of them can make any definite plans. The couple can lead a "normal" life, one or both may have a normal job and kids, but they will both notice from time to time that as soon as they have made specific plans, something will intervene. Some of these changes may be unpleasant, but some are also a lot of fun. The point is that there seems to be something that directs life, something neither of them can grasp, but which they can learn to live with just fine by yielding, approaching things flexibly, and particularly by not blaming each other for changes that keep popping up that demand adjustment.

These are also relationships where the partners have learned that the restlessness and insecurity they feel is not the other's fault, but is an integral part of themselves. This means that no energy is needlessly wasted in "did-so-did-not" quarrels, but that both can look for solutions together. This forges a firm bond, particularly when both stimulate each other and are allowed to adjust. Accepting the other's help regarding issues that need solving can give an enormous depth to a relationship.

Thus in general we can say that people with a yod (or an unaspected planet) are equally as capable of having deep and meaningful relationships as people without them. Only the form they find inwardly and outwardly for it will be different. There are a number of issues that should be kept in mind in analyzing the relationship, some of which will apply to both yods and unaspected planets, and a number of which are specifically oriented to one or the other of these horoscope factors.

Personal Insecurity

Those born with a yod, a duet, or an unaspected planet will, on the level of these horoscope factors, exhibit the hallmarks that we already saw in detail in the previous chapters. These hallmarks include insecurity, restlessness, or uneasiness. We have already seen that a relationship is not the source of these things, but that they are part of the person in question who has to come to terms with them and managed to find a creative form for them. A partner can be very helpful with all this. Since a yod or unaspected planet can be so perceptibly dominant in the personality, it will tend to play up in the context of a relationship, even if neither Venus nor the ruler of the 7th house have anything to do with it.

Somebody, for instance, who has Pluto in a yod will somehow or other have to take on a challenge from time to time, even if he or she gets tired of it and actually does not intend or want things this way! This quite simply has consequences for a relationship. A partner will have to be very aware that this is not directed specifically at him or her, but that it is a dynamic that will play up for everyone. Nevertheless this dynamic can surely cause inevitable fireworks from time to time if it actively erupts, or it will cause tensions when the Pluto yod of this example can't budge or yield an inch, even if it is apparent that this person is definitely on the wrong track. It's as if something gets blocked and all the turbulence of the yod starts to act up. The person needs time to collect himself or herself, in order to be able to revitalize at a later point in time. If the partner then says something along the lines of, "You could have said that earlier," the same dynamic of inflexibility will come up again. Although the edges get worn off over the years, it will remain a sticky point of discussion that may well cause the relationship to suffer. This is not a question of unwillingness on either side, it is the dynamic that the people who have the yod often don't understand, never mind their partner!

An unaspected Pluto, or Pluto in a duet causes the same problem, as it happens. There is basically a deeply-rooted fear of losing a grip on life and the course of things, which may even drive some people with a horoscope like this to shake off important contacts and relationships when these get too close. This, however, comes into play particularly in those cases where the person involved does not want (or is unable) to be aware of his or her inner conflict and wants to maintain a grip on the environment at all costs. The person who does become aware of this will, in a particular period of inner conflict, come face to face with fear, and has to come to terms with it. This is very possible, but it does require considerable effort and a confrontation with very deep layers and with the past. Not everybody is prepared to enter into this confrontation. If it does happen, you will see besides the "eternal inner restlessness" of that same Pluto in a yod (or as an unaspected planet), a kind of mildness and deep insight start to grow. This will cause the person to start experiencing this inner restlessness as a kind of "divine intervention," and he or she will start to realize that precisely by *surrendering* to the confrontation, it can be overcome. Getting a grip on the situation solves the problem because the original basis of the fear and insecurity will have disappeared.

Every planet located in a yod, or that is unaspected, will be able in some way to spoil a relationship by being overly present, without realizing this (as is the case with unaspected planets), or by unintentionally undermining it through insecurity (as is often the case with yods). Imagine, for example, a field of tension in a relationship that is heading for a climax and finds expression in a fight. While tossing blame back and forth, the one with the unaspected planet will not be able to place a number of things at all, and so will get very angry about "all those lies." If this person were acquainted with psychology, he or she would say that the other person is "purely projecting," without seeing that the other

is saying something from which he or she could gain some benefit. The other person may get furious about the suspected "unwillingness of the other person to look at himself or herself and
shifting the blame *because of this.*" It should be clear that these arguments will remain interminable, and will finally drive two people away from each other.

It is only in a relationship where both partners dare to step
back from the argument, realizing that their love for each other is
larger than the occasional urge to hurt each other in fits of emotion, that a conversation about how one experiences the other's
behavior, how it comes across and feels, can start. Then both can
begin to understand in a deeper way that there is a dynamic at
play that has nothing to do with the relationship itself, but does
entail consequences for it. Here, too, partners can help each other
recognize and learn to deal with these expressions and the consequences of this dynamic.

A yod or an unaspected planet, whichever one, always entails
consequences for a relationship, but does not have to destroy it.
Mutual respect is a prime requisite to bring out the positive energy and allow both partners to work on the sore points.

Dependence, Particularly with Unaspected Planets

The restlessness and insecurity may make someone with a yod (or
an unaspected planet) approach another person in a dependent
way, as it were, to gain security by means of the other. This is absolutely the case when the horoscope of that other person dovetails harmoniously or in a relaxed way with your own horoscope.
Then the other will be experienced as a more relaxed person, and
sensed to be a little piece of stability in the sea of inner restlessness. However, this is precisely why problems come peeking
around the corner.

Imagine the following situation. Person A offers relaxation to
Partner B (who has a yod or unaspected planet). Person A will experience that he or she is very important for Partner B, on the one
hand, and that Partner B may even look up to Person A as a guru
or other model. Of course this is flattering. However, at the same
time Person A will experience that Partner B will unconsciously,
but loudly and clearly bring in his or her unaspected planet. Partner B will not notice this. Partner B will unthinkingly display a
dominance that gives Person A a feeling of being walked all over,
or the feeling that whatever he or she does, Partner B, with the unaspected planet, always will respond with, "Yes, but. . . ." This
seems stubborn, but really is not meant that way.

Then you'll get a situation where Partner B, with the unaspected planet, feels restless and insecure, which compels Partner B to say to Person A that Person A is so important for her or him, and that Partner B always needs the other's help, can't live without Person A, and so on. At the same time, though, Partner B is exhibiting behavior that really negates Person A, whose advice doesn't get followed up on, or whatever. Whatever it is you feel with an unaspected planet detracts from what you show in your actions, as we already concluded earlier. This is already tricky as far as you're concerned, but for your partner it can be very confusing.

If the issue is a yod instead of an unaspected planet, you'll have trouble picking up on a lot of the things your partner tries to do for you. You'd like to very much, and would also very much like to experience the calmness that would be the result of doing so. However, you're a master at finding exactly those things that manage to undermine, chip away at, or bring into doubt the other's remarks, help, or authority. You don't do this on purpose, it just seems to happen like that. You can learn to become aware of this, but it will take time to lend it a somewhat more creative form. In the meantime your partner will have the feeling of living with someone who is building a dependency, but who, at the same time, appears to be fighting the partner.

There is more though. How do you feel when your partner lets you know about a particular piece of herself or himself that is very unsure, whereas your partner often appears dominant to you? This is a problem that comes up particularly with unaspected planets. To give you an example: an unaspected Mercury may have the problem of not responding adequately to conversation. However, on a regular basis that same Mercury may be unstoppable. A cascade of words may flow out—the content sometimes being a string of inconsequential stories—although this certainly isn't a chief feature. It may also be a beautiful discourse, or an analysis of a particular situation or problem that evinces a talent. If you don't realize that your partner doesn't feel that way inside, simply because you have no knowledge of how an unaspected planet feels and works, you will not be able to understand, in the first place, why your partner keeps his or her mouth shut or stammers when you ask for a repetition of that brilliant analysis. And if your partner then says that he or she is insecure, you will think about how supple and self-assured the partner can be at times. Thus another enormous contradiction and reason for aggravation. The partner with the unaspected planet feels met with a total lack of understanding, whereas his or her partner (without the unaspected planet) gets the idea that some game is being played, on the one hand, and on the other, has no idea what to do with this confession of insecurity. After all, that person sees very different expressions. Result—instead of a helpful, understanding reaction, the other person exhibits a testy one, causing the partner to draw back even farther into his or her shell.

Can you imagine what it means when people say they are so insecure all the time, and still show ability and power in a given area? And that no matter how often you say everything *is* all right, the other evidently doesn't seem to (want to) hear this? This can exhaust you and you may start finding fault with the person about all kinds of things—saying that they are manipulative, unwilling to listen, play the masochist, and so forth. It will be obvious that this doesn't help the partner with the unaspected planet and misunderstanding after misunderstanding can pile up, without there being a primary party to blame. This involves nothing more than ignorance of this particular aspect dynamic.

Without realizing it, you will often be the point person in the life of your partner if your partner's unaspected planets make aspects with your planets. The easiest are conjunctions, sextiles, and trines, but in fact, each aspect can offer a way out. Those whose unaspected planets are picked up by their partner's horoscope will experience something very double-edged. On the one hand, that other will be "everything," on the other, the urge to become oneself and discover one's own individuality will be churning in the unconscious. The other will therefore be a "danger" at the same time, because if you put too much on the other person, you will never get close to yourself. There is now a risk that you will start projecting your inner problems onto the other person and start undertaking all kinds of actions *against* the other person in order to be sure to show that you are *not* bound to that person; or you will accuse that person of interfering in your concerns, etc. Thus, that person won't understand anything at all about any of this. The person has done nothing, and still gets dumped on. Your behavior is filled with paradoxes, because you can't let the other person go, either. Then you'd lose the caretaker of your planets! For those who remain unaware of the real dynamic, this will involve a kind of compulsive bond, from which you frantically attempt to break free, although you are never able to cut the knot all the way. Having affairs can become a strategy to let the other see how unattached you are, but this will never be experienced as a true solution or as something truly relaxed or pleasant, because it will be coupled to the energy of resistance.

Another problem with unaspected planets is that if they are picked up by the horoscope of another person in a pleasant way, you may feel so nice and relaxed with that person that you *think* you're in love. If you start up a relationship, of course all the other things that concern a relationship start coming into play, and then things can turn out a lot differently than you thought. That easy relaxed feeling you get in the presence of the other makes you imperceptibly dependent on that person. However, if you know what kind of process is now coming into play, you can use your contact with that other person precisely in order to get closer to yourself. Then there will be a temporary dependence on the other person, but it has been consciously chosen and is not going to lead to all kinds of erratic actions. After all, you are choosing to use the other as an instrument to learn to get to know yourself better. In a good relationship it is certainly possible to share with the other person the process in which you find yourself. In this way, certain people can temporarily play a very important role in your life, and although you feel very good in the company of such a person, this is not the same as being in love.

Another Kind of Dependence with Yods

Another kind of dependence can come into play with those who have yods as well. It will be of a different nature, because if the horoscope of the partner makes a harmonious aspect with one of the yod planets, he or she will immediately activate the yod. If that harmonious aspect is a sextile, then it will form an extra yod with the other person in synastry! Imagine that you have a yod involving Cancer and Virgo (the sextile) inconjunct a planet in Aquarius. Now, if somebody else had a planet in Sagittarius that creates a sextile with your planet in Aquarius, the same planet immediately forms an inconjunct with your planet in Cancer, and squares your planet in Virgo. A new yod is formed: your planet in Aquarius moves inconjunct to your planet in Cancer, and the planet of the partner in Sagittarius moves in sextile to your planet in Aquarius and inconjuncts your planet in Cancer. (See figure 6, page 131.)

In other words, that friendly "caretaker" turns out to activate your yod and form a new yod in synastry. The partner stirs up your inner turbulence even more, and this can cause that typical inner restlessness. And in addition, that partner can, because of this, be instrumental in helping you take another step. Instead of spinning in circles, you may, by means of confrontations with the partner that are crazy, not to be understood, and not by any means easy, somehow reach a point where you succeed in breaking through your own fear and defensiveness and start functioning in a different way. This doesn't mean that there won't be any more inexplicable misunderstandings. Yods are still yods. These things will turn out to be unsolvable, without having to hurt the relationship.

So as soon as you have a yod in your horoscope, there is a reasonable chance that other people will make additional yods with it. This is the big difference between a yod and an unaspected planet. The content of the latter's horoscope doesn't have to find a point of contact with everybody, by any means. After all, it only revolves around one point, where the three points of a yod have a greater chance of being aspected. Let's look again at the example of the Cancer-Virgo-Aquarius yod. Somebody simply has to have a planet at the corresponding degrees of Sagittarius, and there is a new yod (as we already saw: Sagittarius-Aquarius-Cancer). However, the corresponding degrees in Aries can also form a new yod: Aries-Aquarius-Virgo. Somebody can also have an inconjunct that connects with the yod of another person, such as an inconjunct between Aries and Scorpio, for instance. This might connect with the Virgo portion of the yod the partner has, and make another yod between the two partners. So a yod has more chance regarding points of contact and a bigger risk with movement. This is tricky, but there is also something exceptional going on, and I will again go into synastry for a moment (placing the horoscope of one person into that of the other person to see which aspects are made with each other, which planets fall into each others' houses, and so on).

I have noticed that when people make a lot of yods between them, they have a very special bond, and they can play a very important role in each others' lives as far as fulfilling a small piece of destiny. Of course there are requirements for this, such as being open and having respect for each other. It's just as if these people are drawn toward each other by a magnet, and somehow *have* to be involved with each other. As it happens, this doesn't have to be a romantic relationship, per se. These kinds of processes can come into play in a friendship, or in the relationship between boss and employee. I have seen extremes in these yod synastries. Things either ended in a drama, complete with a pile-up of misunderstandings, where fate also lent a helping hand to help things get out of control, or something special came about.

Regarding the first possibility, this is an example of how things can also get out of hand without it being anyone's fault. This example concerns two people who feel attracted to each other for some reason, but who don't know what to do about it. She is Belgian and he is Dutch. They meet abroad and they agree that he will come to visit her in Belgium. On the appointed day, he leaves at the crack of dawn just to be sure to be there on time and get ahead of any traffic jams. He arrives, much too early, in her village. There is no sign of the street she had mentioned, never mind the house. He combs the whole village and the vicinity, and decides, deeply disappointed, to go home. He is convinced that she wanted to play a trick on him, and decides not to communicate anymore.

She sat and waited for some time, though, but he just wasn't showing up. Deeply disappointed, she thinks that he is evidently the type of man who wants something for a moment, but won't make any effort for the rest. She decides to shut him out of her thoughts and not to get in touch.

Years later, the man finds out that there happen to be *two* places in Belgium with the same name. He had gone to the wrong one. When he goes to the right place anyway, she has meanwhile found someone else.

Or else there is the situation where two people meet each other and immediately fall in love. They exchange addresses, but for inexplicable reasons, they both lose the slip of paper.

Sometimes with lots of yods in synastry, life seems to be out-and-out against you. I have encountered many cases where people who had a number of yods between them had the feeling that they were supposed to have "something with each other." This may be the case on the level of love as well as work, friendship, research, or whatever. There is something that binds, something that can't be named, and neither of the parties can point out precisely what it's about. So don't bother pursuing it. It is there though. If they give each other space, a process becomes discernible where each means a lot to the other, but in an entirely different way. As a rule there will also be moments to be pointed out in this relationship where one party played a decisive role in the other's life, or helped the other's life significantly change course, something the other could not foresee, but which had major (and often positive) consequences for that person's future. A deep bond can arise from this that one can never label, but it feels very good. A longstanding, deep relationship will then be possible, precisely because of the yod.

My husband's horoscope forms many yods with mine, and since we have gotten to know each other, we have had a not-easily-described feeling of closeness. Initially it seemed as if it were a kind of brother-sister relationship. We stirred up a lot in each other and interacted in trust and camaraderie, surprised that on the one hand we were so much the same, and on the other, so totally different. Until important progressions of Venus entered the picture and a spark leapt across. Then we understood that we had actually loved each other all the while. And those around us let out a sigh of relief, "Well, well, so you two finally caught on?" So, one of those crazy situations: being in love without being aware of it, being a unit for a long time without being such consciously, which of course could easily have led instead to misunderstandings. Confusion and the impossibility of grasping a yod are always playing somewhere in the background. With the yods between us, our life together couldn't be called particularly peaceful, although this applies mostly to outside worries. Within there is a bond that neither of us can express in words. It's simply there and it is deep.

I have seen others who experienced similar developments as well. When partners create a lot of yods between them in synastry, there will be lots of things to work out, things they would need to address together. It may involve problems with each other, but more often than not, it boils down to finding a way together for each to shape their own life, apart from problems either family may have wrestled with for generations. Supporting each other in looking for that new form, only to discover that if you can allow things to happen and give in to what crosses your path, the answers will come of their own accord.

This is another kind of dependence—one that can easily misfire if the parties don't treat each other like adults. In the successful cases, though, the yods create a situation where both people can be themselves and at the same time realize that, despite the ups and downs, they don't want to make do without the other, and often *can't*.

Some people who create yods between them also encounter sticky situations they run into together or they end up as a couple. Precisely in these impossible situations it would seem as if the relationship were being put to the test, on the one hand, and on the other that it is finding starting points precisely for deeper involvement. In my experience it is not unusual to see "yod partners" go through a series of difficult experiences where they keep finding each other at a deeper level. Needless to say, such a bond gets to a point where it can no longer break. However, I have also seen "yod partners" end up in a mutual drama where they dragged each other down.

An example of this is Linda Tripp, Monica Lewinsky's friend, who recorded all her conversations with her on tape, and who, as it turns out in retrospect, asked Monica pretty suggestive questions, practically placing the answers in her mouth—all due to her hatred for Clinton. It led to a situation that ran massively out of control, about which, looking back, Monica Lewinsky was dreadfully unhappy. Tripp has a number of planets that form yods with Lewinsky's Saturn-Venus duet (see chapter 12). The yod friendship between Linda Tripp and Monica Lewinsky became a nightmare, first for Lewinsky, but later also for Tripp, who was accused by special prosecutor Kenneth Starr of intentional manipulation and distortion of the truth. This unbalanced yod friendship dragged both of them down and was the inevitable cause of tumult!

No matter how it turns out, the normal dynamic of the yod remains, both in cases where things go wrong (abundantly obvious here), and in cases where the involvement becomes deeper and matters are positively addressed. In this last case, the yod is finally dealt with differently because a learning process has come into play within the relationship. Nevertheless, one thing is certain: snoozing through a sluggish relationship won't be possible; it will remain varied and dynamic to its last breath.

Compulsion and Pressure

Yods and unaspected planets cannot deal very well with situations where pressure is exerted or things have to be done under compulsion. This is tricky because people with yods and unaspected planets often enter situations where something has to be done at the very last minute, so where the pressure is mounting. They may perform excellently, as it happens; that isn't the issue. However, they *cannot* tolerate "being besieged" by a partner, or being placed under pressure. As soon as the partner starts with, "You'll have to do thus and so," this elicits an inexplicable restlessness or uneasiness in the person with yods or unaspected planets. The same thing applies to the partner's clearly defined patterns of expectation. When people with a yod or unaspected planets notice that certain behavior is expected of them, this will quickly be experienced as compulsion and may set into operation an entire mechanism of changeableness, insecurity, uneasiness, and the like.

Yods and unaspected planets work best in relaxed situations, of which there aren't very many, and then they themselves have a knack for creating tension. Our society also scores low regarding relaxation, which creates extra pressure for those with this aspect. However, if they can lead a life that really fits them, they can withstand an unbelievable amount of pressure! They won't perceive it to be pressure, then; they see it as a stream of creativity finding an outlet and stimulating them immensely.

In a relationship, the person with unaspected planets or a yod will need to have space to perform an activity or hobby that forms a channel for her or his ability or talent. An enormous amount of energy will be released, thus providing inner relaxation, which will in turn benefit the relationship. So, your own activity or hobby outside the relationship may actually bring you back to your relationship.

Unaspected Planets in a Composite

The composite chart is created when you make a single horoscope out of two people's charts by creating new planetary positions by taking the midpoints of both MC's, both Suns, both Moons, etc., to create the composite chart. There are two schools: one creates the MC from the midpoint of the two MC's and obtains the Ascendant from the place where the relationship is located. So you look up the ASC for New York City, for example, and create the house cusps from the table of houses. In the second school, you create the new MC from the midpoint of the two MC's, but the ASC and all the other house cusps are created by also taking the midpoint from the natal charts involved. Most people use the first system (of location).[1] No matter which system you prefer, yods and unaspected planets can also occur in composite charts.

A composite concerns not one, but two people in relation to each other, and together in relation to the outside world. So you need to interpret it differently. A planet in a composite says nothing about any personal psychic dynamic, but about a dynamic between two people.

---

[1] For further reading on the subject, see Rob Hand's great book, *Planets in Composite* (Atglen, PA: Whitford Press, 1975).

Therefore, Mercury in a composite can tell us something about the way the couple communicates with each other and how they behave outwardly, as a unit, regarding communication and the exchange of information. An unaspected Mercury may indicate a risk of confused speech, often in ways you couldn't imagine. Take, for instance, a couple with an unaspected composite Mercury. The two experience that they talk about a particular subject, only to find out later that each meant something totally different than the other thought. So the conversation has to take place again. One couple decided to buy a house in a newly planned neighborhood. They had the choice of a number of duplexes; the husband was unable to go see the developer because of his job, so his wife goes, receives the blueprints, and by circling in red and with a written explanation indicates which of the two houses it's going to be, and then writes some more comments. She sends this to her husband who, to her amazement, turns out to understand that the house circled in red is the one precisely *not* chosen, and also doesn't get the idea from her descriptions that this is a mistaken idea. The wife said with a sigh that their entire married life had been this way (and they've been married for decades!) and that from time to time she has to check to see whether her husband understands everything or not.

An unaspected Sun in a composite may cause both partners to be unable to form an image of the identity of their relationship. They may not have a very good idea of what they're supposed to be doing with it, in spite of the fact that they love each other.

Each planet that is unintegrated in the composite forms a problem to start out with for those involved. It's as if the energy were to demand extra effort and extra attention in order to be able to function. Things really don't have to stay like this, but, when both parties become aware of what's happening, it still usually takes a few years at least.

As a rule, lots of things are happening in any relationship when the unaspected planet in the composite is temporarily affected by a transit, certainly if it's a slow transit. If the problems surrounding this content still remain unconscious ones in the relationship, the craziest complications can occur, and it would seem as if fate were playing a little joke on the two lovers. Where this entails a partial awareness of the problem though, a slow transit may offer precisely the necessary turbulence that will finally lead to a clarification of where the rub is.

A composite is only one component of an astrological relationship, so problems there can still be fielded through synastry, for one.

An unaspected planet in the composite is also an indication of a kind of "assignment" both partners will have to address together in order to help each other move ahead. An unaspected Sun, for instance, may indicate the urgency of stopping to think about the themes of self-confidence, identity, space, and the support that you give each other. The unaspected planet may finally grow out into an important, positive distinguishing feature of the relationship, as it were, in the same way an unaspected planet can do that in the natal chart, where it may represent an ability waiting to be awakened.

Yods in a Composite

As I already mentioned regarding yods in synastry, a yod in a composite often means that both partners were brought together somehow by fate, and have something to work out or have to do something together. Here it is also true that this can contribute to an exceptional relationship with great power and focus if both partners know how to deal with it maturely. It can also become an out-and-out drama where everything goes wrong, the partners project all kinds of things onto each other, and do the most radical things. Yods in a composite may make a relationship get way out of hand, but can also make for a very special relationship. It seems there aren't too many flavors in between regarding yods in a composite. For example, Prince Charles and Lady Diana had a yod in their composite.

It is difficult with a composite yod, just as with a yod in synastry, to point out what is actually causing friction in the relationship. There is "something," but it's indescribable. It can also be easily misunderstood as a "call from on high" to go do something grand together. People who come to the table with this run the risk that they may try to outshout, as it were, the real dynamic that belongs to the yod, by lending it a kind of divine dimension. You may end up with your feet only slightly touching the ground. So be careful not to start seeing that special, unutterable thing as a mission in the outer world. The goal lies inside you!

You can approach the interpretation of a composite yod in the same way as you would one in the natal chart. You take the planets involved, also in their function as house ruler, and interpret this within the specific yod dynamic. The only thing you should always keep in mind is, as I just indicated, that the issue is now two people vis-à-vis each other and both together vis-à-vis the outside world. I will clarify this in the chapters containing examples.

Transits may also cause temporary yods in a composite. They often mark a time when the relationship is going through a special kind of turbulence, or is facing almost insolvable problems, or confronted by something in the face of which both partners are powerless. It is important not to get thrown off track as a couple, and it is good to recall for a moment the rules for dealing with yods. The solution will happen of its own accord, even though you can't see it yet, or see how it's going to happen.

Many examples come to mind: somebody tries to break up a relationship through manipulation, gossip, and intrigue, but so subtly that everything becomes chaotic and incomprehensible; or one partner goes into a depression, placing pressure on the relationship; or both partners have to fight a fate both consider unfair, and so on. However, it is equally possible to have the feeling that your relationship is totally renewing itself and that, after a low point, you can move ahead, together.

CHAPTER ELEVEN

Yods, a Duet, and Unaspected Planets: Diana, Charles, and Camilla

Much has been written in astrological litera-
ture regarding what should have been the fairy tale of the century,
but became a drama: the relationship between British Crown
Prince Charles and Lady Di. In this chapter, I will not analyze the
whole relationship; that would be a book in itself. The emphasis
will be on Diana's yod, Charles's duet, and the yod in their composite horoscope. As Camilla played a role that was both of direct
as well as indirect consequence, her horoscope is also of interest.
She has an unaspected planet.

Diana's yod has the following participating planets:
Jupiter in Aquarius, inconjunct Mercury in Cancer and Pluto
in Virgo.
As rulers of houses, they are:
Ruler 12 and Ruler 1 (Jupiter) inconjunct Ruler 7 and
Ruler 9 (Mercury) and Ruler 11.

As Ruler 1 and Ruler 7 are in the yod, the relationship theme is an
important factor.

Charles has:
A duet between Uranus in Pisces and Jupiter in Sagittarius.
As rulers of houses, they are:
Ruler 7 (Uranus) in duet with Co-Ruler 5 (Jupiter).

With Ruler 7 in this duet, the relationship theme is an important
factor for him as well.

Camilla has:
An unaspected Uranus.

Uranus rules both her 7th as well as her 8th house (as it does with
Charles).

All three thus have the ruler of the 7th house involved in a yod, or a duet, or it is unaspected, and this gives them the chance of finding their way in their own, individual manner in the area of relationships, and to break through old family patterns. If they don't succeed in this, the yod, duet, or unaspected planet may create a big problem in the area of relationships. The dynamic is usually complex and may offer a pretty chaotic image, as we saw in all the commotion over Charles, Diana, and Camilla.

Diana

In Andrew Morton's book, *Diana: Her True Story,* the book that Diana helped to write, we read a number of remarks made by Diana that point directly at her yod: she always felt different. She didn't know why, but had the feeling she was carrying something and that she was therefore different. She was unable even to talk about it, but in her head it was there. (See Chart 8, page below.)

Elsewhere in the book she lets us know that her intuition told her that her life would be a winding road. She always felt herself to be very separate from others. She knew that she would go some-

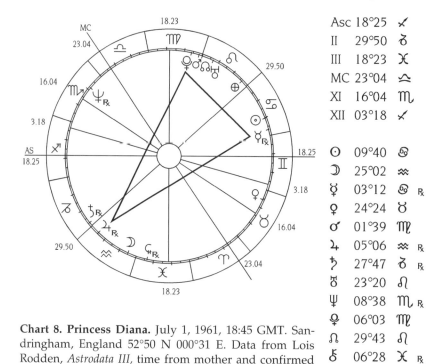

Asc	18°25	♐
II	29°50	♉
III	18°23	♓
MC	23°04	♎
XI	16°04	♏
XII	03°18	♐

☉	09°40	♋	
☽	25°02	♒	
☿	03°12	♋	R
♀	24°24	♉	
♂	01°39	♍	
♃	05°06	♒	R
♄	27°47	♑	R
♅	23°20	♌	
♆	08°38	♏	R
♇	06°03	♍	
☊	29°43	♌	
⚷	06°28	♓	R

Chart 8. Princess Diana. July 1, 1961, 18:45 GMT. Sandringham, England 52°50 N 000°31 E. Data from Lois Rodden, *Astrodata III,* time from mother and confirmed by Diana. Placidus houses.

where else and that she wasn't in the right place. A yod can hardly be better described! She had the feeling of carrying something, but wasn't able to name it. The yod indicates a theme in her family, lasting over several generations, and the participants in the yod can help unravel this theme. The past comes peeking around the corner in a yod, and in Diana's family many a relationship dynamic came, and still comes into play. There was also something else going on, though. It is common knowledge that Diana's grandmother secretly cherished the wish to become Princess of Wales someday. Diana's mother also had this wish. Both never saw this wish fulfilled. Diana, with her Ruler 7 in a yod with Jupiter and Pluto, *did* become Princess of Wales, and thereby fulfilled both her mother's and grandmother's deepest wish, without herself being the happier for it. (In the old literature, a connection between the 7th house and Jupiter is interpreted as "marrying above your station," and the combination of Pluto with this shows what a power and confrontation can accompany it.)

She knew from the beginning, though, that she would never become queen. She articulated this premonition more than once in intimate circles, but she also "knew" that she would have to go through this episode of being queen-on-deck. She simply sensed this.

Diana also has Ruler 12 in a yod with Pluto and Mercury. As the ruler of somebody's 12th house comes into play, we have to direct our attention to the person's earliest experiences. The newborn is very sensitive to the mood at home and notably to the unconscious of the parents: the repression, the pain, the unspoken, *as well as* their dormant or unaddressed talents and abilities. If Pluto is taking part, you will often see that part of the mythical phase of the child—roughly the first seven to eight years—will be marked by crisis, life and death, intensity or power struggles, or marked by some parental problem that isn't addressed.

In Diana's case the theme of "death" literally came into play. A year-and-a-half before her birth, a little brother had been born, but he lived only ten hours. He was the third child, but the first son. He should have borne the family name, but he died. The family exerted a great deal of pressure on the mother, and even had her examined to see "what was wrong" with her, because she only produced daughters.

When Diana was born, there was such a great fixation on a son, which is what everyone was counting on, that they didn't even have a name for a daughter. The atmosphere surrounding her dead brother entered her very powerfully, and so gave her feelings of guilt early on. As a young child, however, it was impossible for her to understand those feelings, and she created an image of herself that she was troublesome. She saw herself as a failure because she had disappointed her parents. Only much later would she learn to understand and accept this. However, in her childhood she played the role of the ugly duckling for a long time.

Ruler 1 in a yod doesn't make it easy to open up, primarily because feelings of insecurity continually crop up. A connection between Pluto and Ruler 1 will, however, not at any price let the outside world see this, and also Saturn in the 1st house needs to maintain a poker face. But Ruler 1 in a yod gives a feeling of insecurity regarding your role and how you function in the outside world, and you therefore have little need of showing your face much. She will undoubtedly have received a lot of support from the flair of her Sagittarius Ascendant in order to make something of it anyway, but she wouldn't have had an easy time of it.

Ruler 7 in the yod may be an indication that a pattern of several generations had to be worked out and brought to resolution in her marriage, although countless other possible effects are imaginable as well. You might fall in love with somebody with a very different kind of character, or with somebody whom others would least expect, or with somebody who involves you in a very troublesome situation because you are made to face impossible choices. Or with somebody with whom you go through a lot at a particular point. One can say this definitely involves a great love or a good marriage—it really doesn't have to be as extreme as the crisis between Charles and Diana. Whatever may be the case, the issue is that the relationship is "different" than the average one or is experienced as being "different."

The relationship Diana had with Dodi was, moreover, also one that bore the hallmarks of a yod. Everything indicated that Diana was really very in love with him, as was revealed in phone conversations she had with a few of her girlfriends and other intimates. However, the possibility of her marrying Dodi would have brought enormous turmoil. Diana was the beloved princess who was worshipped by the British public. The fact that after all the vicissitudes of crisis she managed to bear calmly, she had been so abandoned by the outwardly unmoved British royal house only gained her more sympathy. Besides rebellion against the stiff upper lip, she also symbolized what was human, she symbolized self-sacrificing care for people the British royal family had until then kept at a distance: the poor, the sick, people with AIDS, and so forth. Because of this she seemed to be a mixture of saint and martyr, with royal polish. Here we see again the exceptional ability of her yod: Ruler 12 means being involved with people in need and people on the edge, those living marginally or on the fringe of society. Pluto as the planet in connection with this indicates, on the level of inclination, a psychological capacity and insight to deal well with these things. At a very young age, she had already shown evidence of exceptional feelings for those in need, and an exceptional capacity to deal with them naturally and comfortably. The indomitableness of the efforts she undertook on behalf of the victims of landmines, in direct opposition to all kinds of political forces, can be linked to Pluto and Ruler 12 in her yod.

A relationship and a possible marriage of the princess who represented this image in a predominantly Anglican-Christian nation, with a man of Islamic background who had, in addition, built a reputation for being a spoiled, rich playboy, would have had major and undoubtedly harmful consequences for the collective projection onto Diana. Then there is also the fact that Diana's oldest son, Prince William, who is also much loved by the British public, was not a proponent of a marriage between his mother and Dodi. The British public showed it was *more* than interested in seeing a possible candidate for marriage in Diana, for after her divorce, every man with whom she was friendly had to "pay" for this, as it were, because he would be the center of attention in the media and be discussed at length in the papers.

When Charles wanted to have a modest but public party for Camilla's 50th birthday, Diana decided to go on vacation. She accepted an invitation to vacation in Saint Tropez with Mohammed al-Fayed, owner of the fashionable London department store, Harrods, and she visibly enjoyed a carefree time. The British media, however, let it be known in sharp criticism that they thought the princess's host was a dubious and improper choice. Diana was under vicious attack even before Dodi entered the picture. She became acquainted with Dodi, her host's son, on that vacation.

Andrew Morton wrote of Dodi that in the world at large he was *the* prototype of the frivolous playboy, who skimmed over the surface of life, bought fame and friendship, and purchased five Ferraris on a supposed allowance of 100,000 dollars per month that he received from his father.

On the other hand, Diana was able to look through this mask and see what was behind it. The similarities between Dodi and Charles on a deeper level were striking: both adored polo, both men lived in the shadow of a strong and dominant father, both expressed themselves by proving themselves in dangerous sports, both characterized themselves in moodiness and deep sadness

behind their masks. Charles suffered from the death of his beloved grandfather, Lord Mountbatten, Dodi from the death of his
mother, who died very prematurely.

It was common knowledge that Diana immediately felt warmly if she sensed someone was suffering, and if somebody like that
also treated her warmly, this could easily produce deeper feelings.
She has Ruler 12 and Ruler 7 in a yod, which always offers the risk
that one confuses love and pity.

The big difference between Charles and Dodi was Dodi's surprising warmth, the attention he gave her, and the fact that he
frankly, plainly let her see that he adored her. This stood in sharp
relief to the cool and distant attitude on the part of Charles, who
had really pledged his heart to Camilla. Diana yearned and hun-
gered for love and warmth. Dodi gave her those things.

Had Diana not died in the accident, the yod in her natal chart
would have put her in a very nasty place. For Dodi and her love,
she would very probably have paid the price of a great change in
the British people regarding her (just look at the attacks in the papers on her choice of vacation!). However, choosing Dodi would
have brought her into conflict with what for her was the most important thing on Earth—her children. Thus an out-and-out stalemate for Diana, and a practically impossible choice for her. So it's
not surprising that when she fell in love with Dodi, this yod was
activated by two surprising outer planets in transit: Uranus approached her radix Jupiter, so the top of her yod was activated. In
the sky, Pluto had arrived at 2°55" Sagittarius, creating an inconjunct to Mercury in her radix yod, and so forming a new yod. (See
figure 7, page 167.) Pluto and Uranus were in sextile by transit:
here again we see that a sextile in the sky can form a temporary
yod in the natal chart. Pluto, in addition, had been stationary at 2°
Sagittarius, so that it lent extra emphasis to the temporary yod.

If Pluto by progression or transit starts interfering with content, whatever is buried deep down often rises to the top. Pluto by
transit has a significant transforming effect on the planet with
which it comes into contact, regarding the planet itself and as a
house ruler. Repression, erroneous conceptualization, immature
behavior, and problems that have not been worked out in the area
of that planet or that house will then be laid on our plate—demanding a solution. Now, Pluto is not a planet that does this with
velvet gloves. As a rule we get caught in a situation that confronts
us with all the significant facets within a theme. Along with this,
entanglements concerning power and shadow may also come into

play. Pluto will straighten out any notions that are too naïve or romantic. Its content forces you to grow up quickly and become mature regarding the points it aspects. And Diana still had plenty of
things to work out concerning her 7th house.

Diana yearned for love and warmth and for a father figure.
This last also certainly had to do with the cold upbringing she
had. For, even though she may have been the apple of her father's
eye, her parents had their hands too full with each other to have
much time for the children, and they separated before she was 7,
which Diana experienced as something exceptionally traumatic.
She hardly ever saw her father. Eating meals together never happened—that took place in the company of an endless series of
nannies. She yearned for a family life, something that is very important for a Cancer, but she received only presents.

Diana has the ruler of the 4th house, Mars, located in her 8th
house, where Pluto is. This is a double indication for great sensitivity and vulnerability in the area of feelings and emotions. Children
with such a connection often have an enormous need for warmth,
attention, and emotional security, which they have a hard time

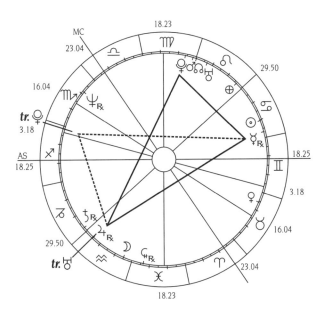

Figure 7.
Transiting Uranus activates the yod;
transiting Pluto forms a new one.

expressing, but that often comes to light in unconscious but insistent or claiming behavior. If parents understand that this entails a great deal of insecurity that will decrease over the course of years if they are able to give the child sufficient security—often at the most impossible moments!—the child may grow up to be an emotionally stable adult.

Many times these expressions and fears are not understood though, and we see the child shut himself or herself off at an early age. They do this to avoid experiencing the fear and pain of possible rejection. Children will often put on a tough front, or a semi-cheerful or busy mask. This last is something Diana did, as she was always very busy. Under the surface, though, the fear of rejection remains and even just the slightest rejection will be felt very keenly.

If the problem is not recognized and tackled, then in adult life something unconsciously demanding or even claiming (the longing for security) will start to come into play under the surface. Without being aware of this themselves, people with this combination can radiate something that gives their partner the uneasy feeling of "having to do something," without knowing exactly what is expected. On top of this, to the question of what's wrong, the partner will get to hear that they aren't asking anything at all. They are usually not aware of this deeply hidden piece of themselves.

Diana possessed great vulnerability which, as mentioned, made her highly sensitive to rejection and to situations in which she didn't feel secure. This may also have been a factor in her bulimia, an eating disorder, and because of it she may also have impressed Charles as more demanding than she was aware of herself.

Pluto in transit was now aspecting her Ruler 7, and it was time to face this problem and work it out, all the more because her Pluto had earlier been aspecting in stationary transit her Ruler 12—early childhood. The lack of warmth and security in her childhood and how that had affected a relationship was thus a theme that became prominent now the yod had become activated.

Although Diana, as mentioned, was the apple of her father's eye, she almost never saw him. Anyway, he and her mother had so many problems that there wasn't any time for the children, or a family atmosphere, either. Her parents' divorce was a big blow to Diana and was primarily the cause for her initially not wanting to divorce Charles, in spite of all their difficulties, because she didn't want her children to have divorced parents.

The yearning for a fatherly man, for warmth, security, and tenderness (an extension of the longing of her early years) was very great during the years following her divorce. She had felt trapped in the cold marriage with Charles, and now overcompensated by giving her love and warmth to her children, whom she took under her protection, and to her friends, to whom she gave the most expensive presents, and through her work for charities. A friend once remarked that she, who did so much for others, should for once start doing something for herself. "She wants to be praised and admired as a martyr because she's so tremendously unsure of herself," he said. If these factors are coming into play, you can just see Pluto coming along.

Pluto isn't very gentle, just like Hades who brought Persephone to the underworld. Persephone hadn't asked for it, but in one fell swoop stood face to face with a world that had eluded her perception until then. So also with temporary Pluto aspects: you can maneuver yourself into totally unexpected situations where all manner of confrontations can come into play. It brings up matters from the past, as described above, but also themes that conflict with power and manipulation, with fear *and* force.

At the activation of this yod, Diana was powerfully confronted by the emotional dynamic that went together with her inclination and her past. However, with the yod, she may also have become a pivotal player in an unintentional power struggle, of which she may not even have been aware while being in love, but which, had she not died in the accident, could have created enormous complications in the future.

The power struggle went together with Dodi's father. As owner of prestigious Harrods, and as a multimillionaire, he couldn't swallow the fact that he hadn't been granted full British nationality. He always felt, as he put it, like a "grade B citizen." It is said of him that he does everything to play an important role in the highest circles. He had known the Spencers for years and had been friends with Diana's father (meanwhile deceased), and had taken Diana's stepmother into his employ at Harrods. It was a public secret that he bribed members of the British parliament.

The *New York Times* publicized a number of unusual revelations on August 28, 1997, only a few days before Diana's death. The *New York Times* reported that Al-Fayed had purposely taken revenge on the Tories, the British conservative party, by bribing officials, taking care to make this known. Indeed, Al-Fayed had succeeded in influencing the elections with his opposition to the royal family. It is generally accepted that it was partially because of Al-Fayed that the conservatives lost the elections. Al-Fayed wanted to avenge his "second-rate citizenship" and also wanted to take revenge on the royal family. Taking Diana into his "camp" was, of course, a big trump card for him: Diana, the mother of a future king! It is also understandable that Al-Fayed stimulated the friendship between Diana and his son, Dodi, and that he was enjoying the prospect of a joining of his family with the highest ranks of British society.

Certainly if Pluto comes into play in a yod, you can imperceptibly become part of a power struggle that can make your position very sticky. It can give you the feeling that there is something larger being battled out over your head. As we saw in the general indications, the best way to deal with a yod, holding still and waiting, is the only way to get through a time like this. But just try to do that when you're in love up to your eyebrows and are finally getting what you've been yearning for since early childhood!

Charles

In Charles's horoscope (See Chart 9, page 171) there is a duet between Uranus and Jupiter, and Uranus is the ruler of his 7th house, Jupiter is co-ruler of his 5th house. If that doesn't point to tension between marriage (7th house) and romances, affairs, or lovers (5th house)! Of course many other interpretations are possible, but this is a classic one, and Charles's life has clearly shown this.

In a psychological sense, a duet involving the 7th and 5th house brings up questions along the lines of: "What do I want out of my marriage? What role do I play (5) and which does my partner play (7)? How much freedom do I have to express myself the way I want to (5) and how far do I have to conform to my partner or take my partner into account (7)?"

Charles, too, was stuck with a psychological inheritance from the past, an inheritance in which Camilla Parker-Bowles plays an important role. Her great-grandmother, Alice Keppel, had once been Charles's great-great-grandfather, Edward VII's mistress. Camilla (her maiden name is Shand), who married Major Parker-Bowles, seems to be pretty proud that she was the first one to seduce Charles (in 1971). Charles didn't realize then that he might someday fall very much in love with her and want to marry her. He realized that only when Camilla was already married. Camilla seems to have waited for him for a long time, but Charles was very unsure and still very young, and didn't dare to commit himself; he wanted to keep the door open. At this, Camilla married someone else. After Lord Mountbatten's death, she got in touch with Charles again and helped him in many ways. She also appears to have frequently taken on the role of hostess for him (it seems her husband was having an affair with another woman at the time).

The stubborn rumor continues, moreover, that Camilla once told Charles at a party, "Your great-great-grandfather and my great-grandmother had an affair. When are you going to start one with me?" The relationship between Charles and Camilla was un-interrupted after that, and as it turned out, even the marriage to Diana couldn't put an end to it. So, an out-and-out stalemate: marrying the woman you know you will never be able to love as much as the woman with whom you (according to Camilla) had your first sexual experience, but who is already married. And then to be the successor to the throne, by virtue of which it wouldn't do for you to divorce and keep on with Camilla. On top of this, the British public adored Diana and saw Camilla as an evil witch who was disturbing the fairy tale. If that isn't a stalemate! When Charles and Diana married, a duet Ruler 7 married a yod Ruler 7, and playing in the background was Camilla's unaspected Ruler 7!

I have seen the ruler of the 7th house, unaspected or in duet, work out in the sense that the person involved often didn't know what "really loving" meant, and is often in search of the answer to the question of what marriage actually means. You may have been married for years and still sometimes be overcome by doubt. That doubt is often ungrounded; it's just that you can't get

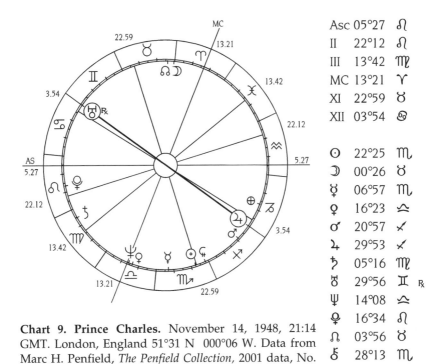

Asc 05°27	♌
II 22°12	♌
III 13°42	♍
MC 13°21	♈
XI 22°59	♉
XII 03°54	♋
☉ 22°25	♏
☽ 00°26	♉
☿ 06°57	♏
♀ 16°23	♎
♂ 20°57	♐
♃ 29°53	♐
♄ 05°16	♍
♅ 29°56	♊ ℞
♆ 14°08	♎
♇ 16°34	♌
☊ 03°56	♉
⚷ 28°13	♏

Chart 9. Prince Charles. November 14, 1948, 21:14 GMT. London, England 51°31 N 000°06 W. Data from Marc H. Penfield, *The Penfield Collection*, 2001 data, No. 358, birth certificate. Placidus houses.

to your feelings of love at all for a time. Or else you can't imagine that somebody loves you (we can meet up with these same expressions with an unaspected Venus). Also there is a fear of commitment and then finding out afterward that because of it you passed up a great love: I have seen that more than once! This also seems to be confirmed by Charles's life, as is having a difficult relationship with "the wrong person," where what is necessary does break free inside you so you are able to keep going in a better way. All kinds of inner and outer complications crop up, though, before it all starts running smoothly.

Unaspected planets, or planets in a duet, absolutely cannot tolerate pressure from the outside. "Having" to do something, or being forced into something, can temporarily totally block this planet. Regarded in that light, it was for Charles no party that he was considered the world's most eligible bachelor, for the older he got, the more his parents exerted pressure on him to fulfill his royal duty to insure a successor to the throne. His father, Philip, finally ran out of patience, and Charles later said that he asked Diana to marry him under pressure from his father.

In public, Charles let it clearly be seen that he saw marriage as something very different from falling in love. And he once said, "If I should decide with whom I would want to spend fifty years, well, that would be the very last decision in which I would let myself be guided by my feelings instead of by my common sense." When he asked her to marry him, Diana said yes, and immediately added, "I love you so much, I love you so much." To which Charles promptly responded, "Whatever love means," before calling his mother to tell her the news of his pending marriage. That one little phrase, "Whatever love means," is very telling for the way a Ruler 7 works out in a duet.

Still, Charles did to some extent care for Diana and love her, in spite of the fact that his bond with Camilla held firm. In the first year of their marriage, Charles and Diana did argue a lot about Camilla, and yet they wrote each other touching love letters and also experienced fine moments together. However, Charles never came to Diana's aid in the big transition from common society to the royal family, where any show of feeling or emotion was considered improper. We shouldn't ascribe this to the duet with Ruler 7, this is simply the result of the upbringing and "training" that Charles received. Once a fixed sign (Scorpio with Moon in Taurus and Ascendant in Leo!) gets into a rhythm or a pattern, you won't get it out again very quickly as a rule.

In the duet, Uranus is not only the ruler of the 7th house, but also of the 8th. This means that Charles's 8th house may also start exhibiting an all-or-nothing response, a response that is so typical of unaspected planets.

In practice, an unaspected ruler of the 8th house means that when it comes down to coping with things, you *feel* for a long time—sometimes for years—that there "is" something, or that something is coming into play that you just can't reach. Even though you may try from time to time, it's "as if you get bounced back by an invisible rubber wall," as someone with an unaspected Ruler 8 succinctly put it. Then if you think that nothing more is going to happen, you're suddenly surrounded by problems. You can walk into a situation with open eyes and suddenly realize everything has been dumped on your plate.

If you have an unaspected Ruler 8, it so happens you will be able to cope with things pretty well, except this will happen in fits and starts, and with big ups and downs, and a crisis may all of a sudden significantly worsen. This can by tricky, but it can also lead to your coping with your problems more rapidly if you dare to be open to this, *once* the pit suddenly does open up.

The themes that encompass several generations and that find expression in Charles's horoscope are, with regard to houses: relationship dynamic (7th house), the role of repression, masks, and power (8th house), and questions of self-expression and self-confidence (5th house). And what also comes out with planets like Jupiter and Uranus is, of course, that there is a great tension between the straitjacket of everyday life, on the one hand, and the need for individual expression and space for the duet planets on the other. Moreover, Charles has a (co-) ruler of the 5th house in a duet. His mother, Queen Elizabeth, has an unaspected Sun. The theme of "self-expression" and the question, "Who am I and what do I want?" have already been in play for a time in the family, with the risk of an all-or-nothing expression.

Camilla

The theme of the 7th house finds expression for Charles in two relationships: the one with Diana and the one with Camilla, both with a ruler of the 7th house connected to generational problems and patterns. It is also known that relationship problems and vicissitudes have been prominent in Camilla's family. Thus Charles once again has a relationship with somebody who is part of a greater family dynamic. In this way, however, both are getting the chance to find their own form of relationship, and to build their own lives, although the beginning for all this is typically distorted by stalemates.

Diana had gone to St. Tropez so as not to be in England when Charles had a party in the honor of Camilla's 50th birthday. Because Diana had spoken in a slightly more friendly way about Camilla in the press, and her relationship with Charles had significantly improved, the British public hesitantly, although reluctantly, began to accept Camilla more. Meanwhile, Camilla had divorced and was living a stone's throw away from Charles, but in reality the two are living together. Charles maneuvered things very cautiously to make sure not to push Camilla to the forefront too quickly, but now the time seemed ripe for the next step. (See Chart 10, below.)

How differently everything went! The party was celebrated, but right after, Diana died, and for many British citizens, this brought back the memory of Camilla as the one who disturbed "the fairy tale."

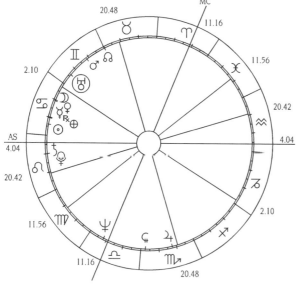

Asc	04°04	♌
II	20°42	♌
III	11°56	♍
MC	11°16	♈
XI	20°48	♉
XII	02°10	♋
☉	23°47	♋
☽	09°59	♋
☿	19°55	♋ ℞
♀	10°34	♋
♂	11°17	♊
♃	17°42	♏
♄	09°57	♌
♅	23°50	♊
♆	08°14	♎
♇	12°23	♌
☊	29°42	♉
⚷	02°31	♏

Chart 10. Camilla. July 17, 1947, 05:05 GMT. London, England 51°30 N 000°05 W. Data from Caroline Graham in *Camilla: The King's Mistress* as shortly past 7:00 A.M. I used 7:05. Also in England in 1947 there was double daylight savings time, so two hours difference with GMT! Placidus houses.

At Diana's death, Uranus was located by transit at 5° Aquarius, exactly at Charles's Descendant! Uranus is part of his natal duet and so can have a very unpredictable effect. It can be this way also on the basis of the fact that it is Uranus, but this tendency is reinforced by its not being aspected. This planet now plays an acute and sudden role, right at the moment that everything seems to be somewhat easier for Charles. Typical of Uranus, but equally typical for a planet in a duet that demands one pay attention to patterns from the past.

Since the division of Camilla's houses is pretty much identical to those of Charles, the transit of Uranus also comes into play over her Descendant. For both Charles as well as Camilla, Uranus is the ruler of the 7th house, and this means that Ruler 7 is entering the 7th house, which for both can generate a powerful focus on building a relationship. Uranus by primary progression was in the process of passing over Camilla's Ascendant. This planet, unaspected in her natal horoscope, activated the Ascendant-Descendant axis at the time of Diana's death. The unaspected planet stepped out, in both its Uranian quality as well as that of Ruler 7. The paradox of the unaspected planet is powerful: just when the British public was starting to be more accepting of her, its attitude changed due to Diana's death, so she had to start all over. And although Diana's death was a liberation for her, on the one hand, it was, on the other, an enormous limiting factor because of the negative projection with which she temporarily had to cope.

Uranus as an unaspected planet was thus active for Charles and Camilla and this could have offered the following expressions, in short:

As *Uranus*: a sudden event, scare, or nervousness; also self-liberation and outwardly being more yourself;

As *Ruler 7*: an opportunity for a relationship or marriage;

As *Ruler 8*: chance of a confrontation with the theme of life and death, along with the urgency of having to cope with problems, as well as confrontations with the consequences of past behavior;

As *Unaspected Planet*: an expression that may become more significant, paradoxical, and unpredictable.

We can see that at the time of Diana's death, Charles, Diana, and Camilla's planets in a duet, or yod, or unaspected, were activated, or were themselves coming into play: and the planets all indicated fate(ful) connections through patterns from the past.

Charles and Diana's Composite

If we create the composite for Charles and Diana, we see the Moon in the 12th house in Pisces as the top of a yod whose base is formed by the sextile between Neptune in Libra and Pluto in Leo. (See Chart 11, page 177.) The Moon is also inconjunct Mars in Libra, and Mars is sextile Pluto, so this entails a double yod in the composite:

Moon–Neptune–Pluto
Moon–Mars–Pluto

In addition there are two unaspected planets: Venus and Mercury! In other words: six of the ten planets are involved in the dynamic of yods and unaspected planets.

If Venus is unaspected in a composite, it is hard to understand in the beginning what you are looking for, and it is also harder to find a form for a relationship. Expressing feelings and love may produce difficulties, or there may be circumstances that cannot be influenced that throw a wrench into the works, and that demand both parties be more resourceful in finding their own form. This might be a situation where you would like to hug each other, but have to keep a straight face because you have to conform to protocol. Or you're in the middle of relationship troubles and have to take part in an official function together, which the public expects you to do while treating each other amicably, or whatever the case might be.

Mercury without aspects in a composite may provide plenty of problems with conversation and communication at the beginning of a relationship.

A yod with the Moon in Pisces in the 12th house is an indication of the risk of emotional instability, with intense projections, emotions, and deep longings coming into play.

Mars in a yod may charge a theme like sports or sexuality (think of Charles's interminable polo playing, which annoyed Diana so much, and of both their little trysts, typically revealed in the press).

These are the troublesome sides, although we have seen that yods and unaspected planets are also associated with abilities and talents. Now, in a composite the issue isn't just one person, but two people, so we have to interpret this a little differently. What is now at issue is what they can do together, and that's a lot!

With a yod where the Moon is in Pisces in the 12th house, in-conjunct Neptune, both could have gotten along by placing general humanitarian values and the environment in the foreground. Environmental problems are close to Charles's heart and he is actively involved in tackling them. Diana's heart went out to caring for the poor, the sick, and the disadvantaged, including those in the third world. If they had combined forces and focused on this dynamic, then they would have formed a golden link that could have done a lot of good.

Venus and Mercury, unaspected, meant that they could have stimulated the arts, sciences, and education, or could have brought problems there to the public's attention. In short, a lot of good things could have been possible as well, although a composite like this does indicate initial difficulties and demands a mature approach on the part of both partners, and an open, honest attitude toward themselves and each other.

At the time of the accident, the yod had been activated: Neptune had reached 27° Capricorn and was creating a sextile with the Moon at the apex, and Neptune had just been inconjunct Pluto. A "stretched-out" yod by transit, but still totally active.

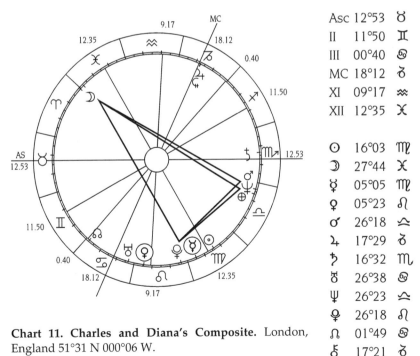

Chart 11. Charles and Diana's Composite. London, England 51°31 N 000°06 W.

Asc	12°53	♉
II	11°50	♊
III	00°40	♋
MC	18°12	♒
XI	09°17	♒
XII	12°35	♓
☉	16°03	♍
☽	27°44	♓
☿	05°05	♍
♀	05°23	♌
♂	26°18	♎
♃	17°29	♒
♄	16°32	♏
♅	26°38	♋
♆	26°23	♎
♇	26°18	♌
☊	01°49	♋
⚷	17°21	♒

By transit, Uranus created an opposition to Venus, at 5° Leo in the composite. Venus as planet of the (former) love, and ruler of the 1st house. With regard to Ruler 1, Uranus by transit says: the relationship may gain some other outward expression as a result of a sudden or unexpected event. That same Uranus by transit created an inconjunct with likewise unaspected Mercury in the composite: the sudden, shocking, and almost incomprehensible report. The news of Diana's premature death is a suitable effect.

It is striking that the relationship between Charles and Diana was so strongly colored by yods, a duet, and unaspected planets. The composite actually emphasizes all the more the dynamic that was already present in both horoscopes demanding to be worked out. Thus, this is a relationship that inherently bore the potential for extremes. The fact that things escalated to such an extent is one possible expression; it could also have taken a very positive turn.

Prince William

If an important theme is at play in a family for several generations, not all the children that are born into this family, as it happens, will reflect it in their horoscopes in the form of a yod, a duet, or an unaspected planet. Oftentimes you will see that one child in a family "gets to carry the burden," sometimes more children, and only very rarely, all the children. With Prince Harry, the second child of Diana and Charles's marriage, you find no indications, but with Prince William all the more! (See Chart 12, page 180.)

William has a yod in his horoscope. It includes Venus in Taurus, Pluto in Libra, and Neptune in Sagittarius. He also has an unaspected Saturn.

The yod that includes Venus seems to have everything to do with the relationship dynamic within the royal family in general, and those of his parents in particular. William will feel inside that he will have to make his own way, but he hasn't had a very good role model. Feeling around and searching, he will have to find out what essentially fits with *him*. It may be that a pattern will repeat itself, one that also came up in the past, but this isn't carved in stone, and he certainly doesn't have to have such a dramatic marriage as his parents did. One of the (very) many possibilities with this yod may be: to decide for love of a woman to renounce the throne. In any case, for William, too, the relationship theme will be prominent. Along with this, he will want and need intensity and authenticity in a relationship (Venus-Pluto) and will have to watch out not to confuse love with pity, or to romanticize (Venus-Neptune) it. Venus in Taurus can, however, help him keep his feet on the ground.

Venus is Ruler 4 and Pluto Ruler 10. The 4-10 axis is the axis that reflects the parents, also the axis that has to do with growing toward a balanced comportment in society (10th house) through safety and security (4th house). William, however, was born at a time when his home was everything but stable, and when the extended (royal) family was depriving his mother of the emotional support she so craved. His father changed William's diapers with love, but was often away the rest of the time, and his parents' marriage quickly ended on the rocks.

The 4-10 axis in the yod forces William to resort to his own resources: he will have to figure out, cautiously feeling around, what he expects and wants later on regarding family life, and how he wants to present himself to the outside world as future king. One thing is sure with a yod: somehow or other you *can't* follow the beaten track. It simply *has to* be your own form, if things are to go well. And this is why William is preeminently a leader for a period of transition for the British royal family. Another issue with a yod is that the second half of your life as a rule looks different from the first half. This is oftentimes on the outside, although it may also have to do with a completely different inner viewpoint as compared to earlier in life. It is within the realm of possibilities that William, should circumstances lead that way, could decline to be a king. However, there is just as big a chance that he will give unique and personal meaning to being king, apart from existing protocols and structures.

Venus is also Ruler 9, an indication of the role of higher education or foreign countries. A yod including Ruler 9 may indicate that because of some involvement with foreign countries, your life takes an important turn. For William, this could also have to do with the death of his mother in a foreign country (Pluto and Ruler 9 in the yod).

The House of Windsor, at Diana's arrival, is undergoing a crisis of form. It hasn't come out clearly yet, but the old-fashioned and standoffish ways of the royal house no longer suit modern times. In her speech at the occasion of her 50th wedding anniversary, the British queen let it be known that the response of the British people to Diana's death had set her thinking. Henceforth, a couple of formalities were done away with.

Distance and formality belong to Saturn, a planet Queen Elizabeth has at her MC. And it was precisely to this image that Diana managed to introduce change all by herself. She was seen by the public as "one of us" and viewed as a symbol. She was the one who managed to endure the pressure of the formality and the structure, and to succeed in getting closer to the public.

William's unaspected Saturn may very well have to do with this dynamic. He witnessed his mother's flexibility, how she just took her kids to an amusement park or to a movie, exposing them to common life and the suffering there. She took them to institutions where people were not well off, and let them see that it was all right for a member of the royal family to throw an arm around the shoulders of "the common man." On the other hand, William is all too familiar with the strict rules and the etiquette of the court, and with the great distance between Elizabeth II and her people.

William will have to find his own form and structure. He has two extremes as models, and will have to steer his attitude in between what is permitted, what needs to be broken through, and what he himself feels that he should do.

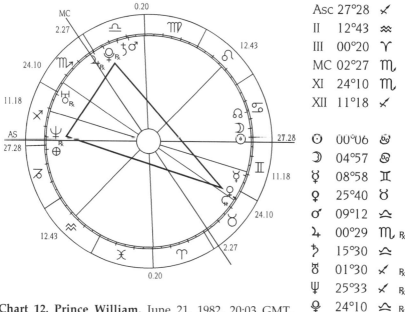

Chart 12. Prince William. June 21, 1982, 20:03 GMT. Paddington, England 51°31 N 000°11 W. Data from an offical press release on the day of his birth. Placidus houses.

Saturn is the co-ruler of his 1st house, which indicates that his unaspected Saturn may also have a very keen effect on the way in which William will come out in his environment as a person. Both the yod and the unaspected planet make him vulnerable, insecure, and sensitive, something that he shares with his mother, whom he resembles to a significant degree by way of character. Other horoscope factors also reinforce this sensitivity, such as Neptune on the Ascendant, Ruler 12 on the MC, and Ruler 12 aspecting both Sun and Moon.

If we take a bird's eye view of the thread that runs through the story, we will see the following components:

Basic situation

- In the British royal family there has been a relationship dynamic going on for generations—since Henry VIII, according to some!
- In the family into which Diana was born, there has likewise been a relationship dynamic going on for generations; and in Diana's female line there has been the wish for generations to become the Princess of Wales.
- The British royal family is stuck in a form that the people experience as too standoffish and too far away, no longer fitting with modern times.

Developments

- Evidently life or fate has in store that the aforementioned patterns need to be broken through, and the factors to do this start to distinguish themselves in the horoscopes. Elizabeth is born with an unaspected Sun. When she was born it was far from probable that she would become queen; it happened all of a sudden because of a variety of circumstantial changes. She also has an inconjunct between the Moon (her Ruler 7) and Venus. When transiting Neptune forms a yod with these two emotional contents, including the ruler of her 7th house, Prince Charles is born. In synastry, his Neptune forms a yod with his mother's Moon and Venus. He may undermine her carefully built relationship image, and at best may also bring her closer to her feelings.
- The son Elizabeth bears has a duet between Uranus and Jupiter (freedom and space, so counter to the straitjacket!) and they are Ruler 7 and Co-Ruler 5.
- This son marries Diana with Ruler 7 in a yod.

- A lot of turbulence is the result, and on account of this marriage, the crisis in form and the relationship dynamic of the British royal family as a whole is suddenly public knowledge; they break through, and this demands change. In other words: Diana turns up on the scene with her yod at a turning point for the British royal family, and in spite of herself is part of the process of change. Precisely because she is who she is, the matter is set in motion.
- Diana and Charles's composite contains a yod and unaspected planets which only reinforce the *turning-point* concept inherent in Charles and Diana's marriage.
- Charles and Diana's oldest son has a yod that includes Venus, and the rulers of the 4th and 10th houses, and an unaspected Saturn. William will have to find a way to resolve the whole of the theme that burst forth through the marriage of his parents, but which had been dormant for generations. He may become the transformer and bring about the realization of the turning-point.

And as if it had to be so, the turbulence in the marriage between Diana and Charles was also caused by Camilla's presence, likewise "saddled" by fate with an unaspected Ruler 7.

So Diana was the factor that appeared on the scene when a turnaround and change were necessary. She was the pivot in that process, notably in breaking open and making the problems public. She appeared, with her yod, at a place and time that involved a turning-point situation.

People with a yod don't always witness its positive results, but again it isn't out of the question. Diana passed away too soon for her to see the turning-point her entrance into the British royal family brought about.

CHAPTER TWELVE

Yods and Unaspected Planets in Action: Lewinsky, Tripp, Starr, and Clinton

As the Dutch edition of this book was going to press, President Clinton was facing impeachment proceedings or censure. The astrological magazines elaborately went into the astrological backgrounds and contexts. However, the theme of yods and unaspected planets was actually barely addressed there. We will now study the entire affair through this lens.

During the course of 1998 Monica Lewinsky, Linda Tripp, and Kenneth Starr's birth certificates surfaced, so we have good horoscopes at our disposal. There is some discussion about Clinton's horoscope, and more about that later. We will take the players in the game one by one and look at them closely, and will then see how their horoscopes relate to one another—so, some synastry.

Monica Lewinsky

Prologue

Spring 1995: Monica Lewinsky receives a B.A. in psychology from the Lewis and Clark College in Portland, Oregon, and shortly thereafter, in June 1995, gets an unpaid internship at the White House. One of the officials responsible for screening interns, who interviewed her, even said right after the interview, "There goes trouble, or there goes something special." He was not totally confident, but because the FBI found no objectionable data in Lewinsky's past, she was accepted. She kept eliciting conflicting opinions, which is sometimes described as "the problem of the two Monicas." Some called her hard-working, nice, polite, and intelligent. Others described her as arrogant, spoiled, and immature. She enjoyed making off-color jokes and was also known for spending hours on the phone.

Two years later she will tell a friend, Linda Tripp, that in November 1995 her relationship with Clinton started, that this relationship lasted eighteen months, and that it involved oral sex. In December 1995, her job in the White House changed from unpaid intern to a paid position in the Office of Legislative Affairs. This is, according to her, one month after the relationship began. In April 1996, Lewinsky was transferred to the Pentagon by White House officials, who more than once let it be known that they felt uncomfortable regarding Lewinsky's comportment toward Clinton; she seemed to be obsessed by him. It is a fact that *after* her transfer she was also regularly at the White House, as the tidy visitors' book shows. In the Pentagon, moreover, she flirted with various officials as well, all a good deal older than herself. She also had a romantic relationship with a highly placed person there, about which she talked indiscreetly. This man did not want to go into it with journalists, but did remind a reporter that he was not married, in other words that he would not have overstepped any bounds by having a relationship.

In the Pentagon she became friends with Linda Tripp, who had also been transferred there from the White House because she had become too critical of Clinton's administration. The friendship between Lewinsky and Tripp became a fateful one for Clinton, because Tripp played the lead in publicizing the affair.

A journalist at the *Washington Post* who tried to form an image of Monica Lewinsky based on conversations with people who had known her in various stages of her life—from old neighbors to teachers, students, and coworkers—also sees "the problem of the two Monicas." He summarizes the image as a strange collision of power and glamour, on the one hand, and willingness and hard work on the other, coupled with steady ambition and naivete. (See Chart 13, page 187.)

And then her horoscope. Venus and Saturn are both important in Monica's horoscope: they form a duet, an "unaspected aspect." Within their signs, Venus and Saturn each aspect only each other and no other planets. They therefore gain the hallmarks of unaspected planets, and that is, first of all, an "all-or-nothing" attitude and second, the connections with generations of preexisting, covered-up family problems.

For Monica this has to do with the area of Venus: relationships, affection, beauty, and such, and that of Saturn: stability and structure, feelings of responsibility, and endurance. The Venus-Saturn contact gives her a great need for safety and stability in a relationship, which, in an unbalanced upbringing, may also express itself in the preference for a father figure. The fact is that

Monica established relationships with men who were a good deal older than she and who also held high positions.

It is difficult to review what her family dynamic is concerning these themes. A theme may notably be something that has been repressed so that its content doesn't come to life for generations, although this can only be discovered when you know enough about the family. The theme may also, however, come out only in a very exaggerated version, which is just as unbalanced, in principle, as the repressed theme. There are, however, some points from which to begin.

Her parents divorced in 1987. The documents about her parents' lifestyles describe an extravagant life of luxury with pricey vacations and pricey cars, a house in Beverly Hills, etc. The excess of it may fit into the image of Monica's Venus duet. When more facts about Monica's life surfaced, it turned out that at a very early age Monica had been forced into a kind of "Venus role" by her mother. Monica was dressed like a fashion manikin, wore makeup at a very young age, and one gets the impression that she had to play a role in everything as if she were "the height" of femininity. When a mother requires that her child do this in an excessive manner, it is an expression of an unbalanced form of the mother's own Venus. It seems as if Monica always had to be the sweet little girl for her mother.

Another unbalanced Venus expression on the part of her mother seems to be confirmed by the following facts: Monica's mother, Marcia Lewis, is a writer, and in 1996 published the work *The Private Lives of the Three Tenors: Behind the Scenes with Placido Domingo, Luciano Pavarotti, and José Carreras*. During the publicity campaign, Marcia Lewis more than once made veiled allusions to having had a relationship with Placido Domingo. "How else would I have gotten all that inside information. . . ?" was her consistent reply to journalists' questions.

A mother who makes veiled allusions to an affair with a world-famous singer, during the time when her daughter is making veiled allusions to an affair with an even more famous man, the president of the United States—what's at play around the relationship theme in Monica's family? Why do mother and daughter exhibit identical behavior? Is there perhaps some facet coming into play of rebelling against her mother? Or doing her one better? This is possible, the more so since there is an involvement not only with an unaspected Venus, but Venus is also ruler of the 8th house, the house of complexes and repression. And the unaspected Saturn is ruler of the 4th house: home and hearth, family and past, emotional security.

Thus two water, or emotional, houses are involved. An un-aspected (or duet) ruler of the 8th house produces specific problems where coping with experiences is at issue. However, if you start playing hide-and-seek with Ruler 8, then you will tend to maneuver yourself into the most impossible situations, where you will encounter in the outside world a mirror of what you are en-countering inwardly. Your need for attention and power becomes substantial, so does your manipulative capacity, and the chance that you will start playing a double role increases: an attitude you are aware of that is riddled with unconscious behavior.

If the ruler of the 4th is unaspected, you will often have a great need for security, care and nurturing, togetherness, and emotional attention. You are looking for a homey form of security and togetherness. Monica, for instance, loved organizing birthday parties for anybody who wanted one! In a positive sense, you are capable of helping a lot of people by offering them warmth and care (although you run the risk of overdoing it). In a negative sense, you are constantly looking for somebody who will be a father or a mother to you, somebody who gives you special emotional attention. With an unaspected Saturn, this may possibly also indicate a replacement of a father figure.

Over the years that were leading up to all the commotion, the duet between Venus and Saturn had been steadily pushed into prominence by temporary yods by transit. It is, however, also a sextile, and although the planets within the sextile are working to a more extreme degree, they are also working on each other. The same thing applies to the house connections they indicate. She has Ruler 8 (Venus) in aspect with Saturn. This is a connection that may provide a great fear of intimacy, and at the same time a great longing for intimacy in a stable relationship. I have seen extremes of this in people who withdrew from sexuality (including a monk and somebody who joined a small New Age movement that had sworn off sexuality). And extremes in people who behaved very promiscuously in fact. In both expressions, there was a fear of intimacy deeper in the psyche. By swearing off sexuality, we don't have to get into a confrontation with it. And by exaggerating it, we are really only proving to ourselves that we're not scared of it, although there is never any substantial involvement. Of course, we can, at some level, arrive at a deep and intimate bond with this aspect, but it will take time and we have to overcome an obstacle.

Saturn is Ruler 4, as we already determined, and Venus, Ruler 8. Each connection between the 4th and 8th house will give somebody a great emotional vulnerability and a deep need for attention, for a hug, for security. There is an almost compulsive need, and at the same time, a fear of expressing it. If we then happen to have a Libra Ascendant with Uranus at that point and Mars in Aries in opposition to it, we look unconventional and sharp, although at the same time, we need to be liked. So, an excellent horoscope combination to hide any possible emotional hunger or insecurity.

In all the studies and descriptions I reviewed and requested, I discovered nothing about forms of aggression, intensity, causticity, or resistance, nor about any independent attitudes. Lewinsky was good at school and worked hard, and she also studied hard at college. Uranus at the Ascendant in opposition to Mars in Aries, and Mars opposing the Ascendant, with both squaring the MC should have given Monica other traits as well. A number of her supervisors were charmed by her "intensity" and "youthfulness," but that's just about the only qualifications I came across.

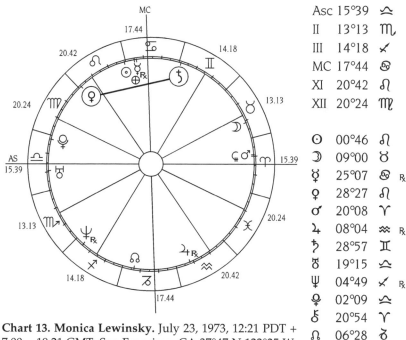

Chart 13. **Monica Lewinsky.** July 23, 1973, 12:21 PDT + 7.00 = 19:21 GMT. San Francisco, CA 37°47 N 122°25 W. Data from birth certificate. Placidus houses.

It is very possible that a dominant Mars doesn't come out, even while aspecting two Angles, the MC and the Ascendant. I have encountered this a few times. In therapy it turns out that this involves deeply hidden anger. The energy is blocked and the planets start leading their own lives. They are still at work—except we don't see them. Instead of leading our own life, with renewal, inspiration, and activities (positive opportunities for expression of Mars and Uranus), we unconsciously maneuver into situations where we become the pivotal point in a process of aggression, change, and possible destruction (negative expressions of unlived planets). We, ourselves, get dragged into this as well.

She has the Sun in the 10th house, astrologically an indication that she will certainly be ambitious. The Sun in Leo reinforces that again. Her ambition is, in fact, mentioned by many who know her. Uranus as Ruler 5 in the 1st reinforces that ambition, and the need for centrality also in the personal realm.

The Sun creates important aspects, notably an opposition with Jupiter, a trine to Neptune and a sextile to Pluto. Someone with a Sun-Neptune-Pluto connection always has something "extra." It's as if we were somehow more noticeable, we can't do anything about it. These are powerful energies, with which we can do a lot, but they can also take us for a ride. A child with a Pluto-Sun connection will have an attitude, something like: "I'll raise myself, thank you." There is a kind of challenge to authorities, by nature: on the one hand, not caring about the highest authorities, and on the other, wanting to be seen as one. With Neptune added in, we may be exceptionally empathetic and inspired, but also have a more difficult time staking out personal identity. This also means we need to avoid getting swept away by illusions and (false) hopes from outside, or by dreams and fantasies from inside. When these two outside planets are linked with the Sun, we tend to be quite dynamic. And if they are also all connected with Jupiter, this is again reinforced, because Jupiter, as the principle of expansion, tends to plump up, enlarge, and flesh out the direction in which the development is taking place. So if Jupiter is involved in a scandal, it will be a *big* scandal!

That Jupiter is now located opposite the Sun, sextile Neptune, and trine Pluto, but also squaring the Moon (Ruler 10). With this Jupiter, she may become an enthusiastic, stimulating personality who will lead a creative and dynamic life. However, if it becomes a life riddled with repression and problems, Jupiter will manage to enlarge these as well.

Back to Monica's duet. With this background, we can also better understand how the very diverse reactions to Monica fit in.

The one extreme side of Venus is being nice, correct, and sociable, and taking care that we are liked. The good side of an unaspected Saturn is a feeling of responsibility and wanting to work hard. We ran into both descriptions of Monica. The opposite is spoiled, off-color jokes (another face for Venus), and immaturity (a negative, escapist Saturn).

Let's look at June and the fall of 1995. The Pluto by transit is at 28° Scorpio, square Venus, and inconjunct Saturn. Uranus is also in the process of making a yod with Venus and Saturn. So, two heavyweights by transit aspect Monica's duet during the same period of time.

Uranus is the ruler of the 5th house, the house to which classically all possible forms of romantic relationships have been ascribed. It's not for nothing that it is called the house of romance. If the *ruler of romance* creates a yod, you aren't going to seek out the safest relationship! There is a good chance that it will be one that isn't average, and one that can lead to trouble. Moreover, if you take a look at the journalistic climate in the U.S.A. since Watergate, you can be sure that sooner or later an affair involving a president in office would come out and be discussed at length in the often shameless press. In pursuit of juicy detail, it will publish any rumor—and then typically has to make retractions.

In June we also see Pluto by transit creating an aspect with Venus, a connection that is occasionally associated with impetuousness or with significant sexual experiences. The aspect may also express itself less dynamically, although even then emotions or sexual dreams may come into play. Pluto aspecting an unaspected Venus can have significant effect, and considering that Venus is Ruler 8, repression and disguises may also surface and let you do things that will start to produce inner confrontation or commotion. The inconjunct with Saturn may indicate that Monica had a problem with setting boundaries and she didn't know where she should have drawn the line. She didn't. This would also be difficult when your actions are being dictated by the invisible motivation that goes together with complexes.

In June, Neptune, by transit, was moving into an opposition with Mercury. Whenever you have a temporary connection between those two, there is a chance that you won't see things very clearly. You forget certain things, don't hear things, or don't hear correctly—this isn't the same thing as intentionally lying, although that may also happen—and you run the risk of creating illusions and imagining that situations are nicer than they are. It is a fine aspect for getting involved with music or the arts, with poetry, dreams, and fairy tales, or studying homeopathy or mythology. For an administrative job at the White House, though, it isn't an ideal aspect. What was she dreaming of when she was accepted?

Some sense of reality is restored by Saturn, which was then creating a trine to Mercury, but Saturn is a duet planet in her horoscope and because of this can produce extreme effects, even by transit. This means that she was able to show diverse faces, with both planets by transit making aspects with Mercury: the dreamy, fanciful side and the serious, hard-working side.

By secondary progression, Mercury arrived to trine Neptune, exactly on October 8, 1995. This accentuates the transit of Neptune in opposition to Mercury even more.

By primary and secondary progression there are a couple of other aspects that are worth mentioning. She starts her job at the White House with her primary MC squaring the Moon. The Moon is Ruler 10. In itself, a connection with Ruler 10 is appropriate, and the conflict may indicate that extra activity is needed to move ahead. Beginning as an intern and shortly thereafter getting a paid position can happen with an aspect like this, or entering a partnership. Occasionally, the MC squaring the Moon can involve being confronted by the inner question of how emotionally secretive we really are, or the desire to start a family and motherhood; or we may feel an urge to come to terms with the past. Considering we have no information about Monica's psychological background at that time, the depth of the effect of this aspect cannot be indicated.

Monica arrives at the White House with her yod formed by Uranus with both Venus and Saturn. Uranus again moves toward this yod, in November: the month Monica claims her relationship with the president began. Transiting Pluto is then at 0° Sagittarius, trine to her Sun, which might indicate a hidden power factor.

Venus by secondary progression is sextile to Mercury, which made some people chuckle: Mercury is Ruler 12 and Venus aspecting Ruler 12 has the possible outcome of a secret (12th house) love affair (Venus). Although I have seldom seen the connection work out this way, it does belong to the realm of possibilities. This aspect became exact on September 21 and was still exercising full effect in November.

The Years 1996 and 1997

In November 1996, Venus enters her 12th house by primary progression. It would have been such a good thing if Lewinsky had started to develop herself in a somewhat more artistic direction! In August, however, Venus also enters into an inconjunct with Mars, a field of tension regarding the male/female theme or relationships: Venus is Ruler 1 and Mars is Ruler 7.

Neptune by transit has now taken over the role of Uranus and is in the process of creating a yod with Venus and Saturn (April). No longer Uranus, Ruler 5, it is now Neptune (dream, illusion) and Ruler 6 with an unfeasible situation as far as her functioning at work.

April is also the month during which she was transferred to the Pentagon. Jupiter is then located by transit at her IC and in opposition to her MC: it is a well-paying job. In that same month the primary aspect between Neptune and Mercury becomes exact: an inconjunct. This aspect will continue in effect for at least a year.

We saw that in 1995 Mercury and Neptune were also connected, both by transit as well as by secondary progression. Now a primary aspect joins in, which also had a running start in 1995. The risk that a lot of fantasies, illusions, and dreams played a role is considerable and this doesn't make it any easier trying to figure out what actually happened. And transiting Neptune returns again: in the fall of 1996, Neptune is once again in opposition to Mercury. Lewinsky herself once said during one of the secretly recorded phone conversations with her friend Tripp, "I've lied my whole life."

After this, there is again a yod created by Neptune with Venus and Saturn, which repeats in February, July, and August, as well as in November and December 1997. As far as that goes, the entire autumn of 1997 is characterized by this yod! Now, Venus is a planet in her 11th house that can offer information about friendships. There is a remarkable relationship between Tripp and Lewinsky. They are good friends and Lewinsky calls Tripp a lot. They were both removed from the White House: Tripp because she criticized Clinton too much and didn't like him at all, and Lewinsky precisely because she was so in love with Clinton, so the exact opposite! This didn't ring a little bell in Lewinsky's head though. Venus may refer to Tripp, but Neptune as well: Neptune is Ruler 6. Considering Tripp is a coworker at the same establishment, the Pentagon, without this entailing any direct working together (that would be the 7th house), Tripp falls into Monica's 6th house in another sense. So there are two planets that can indicate Linda Tripp's role, and both are involved in a continually returning yod in 1997! The situation that unfolded is indeed as complicated, sticky, obscure, and "fateful" as a yod can be!

Thus, we have a "complex" relationship between Tripp and Lewinsky, whereby the woman who was in love with Clinton was lured into the trap laid by a woman who hated Clinton, in order to pillory him. It was Tripp's hatred that drove her to *Newsweek* magazine. In the summer of 1997, an article appears there where

Tripp is quoted. She makes mention of how she suspects the president of having had sex with a volunteer at the White House, Kathleen Willey. That was in 1993. She describes how she saw Willey leave the Oval Office with her makeup all smudged and her clothes a mess. Tripp claims that Willey herself told her she had just had sex with the president. This revelation was a big risk for Tripp. She was suddenly in the spotlight and she ran the risk of being fired. Her credibility was thrown into doubt by lawyers. Tripp became furious, and vulnerable.

Tripp then tells Lucianne Goldberg, a literary agent in New York who detested Clinton with a passion, that she has another instance: with Monica Lewinsky. To be able to convince Michael Isikoff, reporter for *Newsweek*, about this second case, there must be proof. So, says Goldberg, "You have to prove it. You have to record the phone calls." Tripp does this, without the knowledge of Lewinsky, who recounts one detail after another about her relationship with Clinton in her long phone conversations. In this way, Tripp collects some twenty hours of phone conversations. Tripp receives an offer of two million dollars from a tabloid to be allowed to publish the audiotapes, but this doesn't happen.

Lewinsky now becomes a pawn in a larger game because of Tripp, where Tripp's contempt for Clinton, Goldberg's hatred for Clinton, and the need the Republicans have to work against Clinton all come together. And Neptune creates with the Venus-Saturn duet a continually returning yod for Monica Lewinsky! Things are starting to run out of hand! They are going to get even more complicated though.

Lewinsky, herself, approaches Vernon Jordan, a very good friend and close colleague of Clinton's, and tells him that she wants another job, out of the Pentagon. Jordan is very influential and recommends her to various companies, including Revlon, where he is on the board of directors. She does, in fact, get a job offer from Revlon in January 1998, but when the affair comes out, Revlon withdraws the job offer, on January 21.

In January, Neptune is once again located in the yod with Venus and Saturn, and Saturn enters into opposition with her Ascendant. This has happened before, but is now repeating. In addition, there is a stationary transit of Pluto that will inconjunct her Moon in March, but it is already having a strong effect in January. No pleasant aspects for being all over the news with a sexual affair! Pluto can blow the thing all out of proportion and make things emotional, and the yod speaks for itself with its opacity and the risk of everything getting out of hand. In fact she was betrayed, not only by somebody with whom she had become friends, but also by her own talkativeness, naivete, and fantasy.

This combination of aspects is reflected in a still more complex plot. The investigation of Clinton for improper financial practices, which became known as Whitewater, is still underway. The legal investigator, Kenneth Starr, has started hitting a dead end. Although it is written that he is neutral-minded, it turns out more than once that he actually belongs to the anti-Clinton camp. The matter threatens to slip away from him, and that could cost him his good name. He therefore made several new attempts to drag something more out of it. His newest argument is that he also needs to investigate all of the president's sexual affairs, since "Whitewater facts may have been pillow talk"! He receives permission to do so.

The Paula Jones sexual harassment suit against Clinton is also still pending. It has been in the works since 1992, and should come to court in May 1998. Tripp has to testify for the Paula Jones case about the Willey affair, which got her into *Newsweek*. What she does, though, is deliver the twenty hours' worth of tapes to her attorney. Those tapes also contain Lewinsky's claim that Clinton and Jordan advised her to deny the sexual relationship with the president. Lewinsky signs a statement in the Paula Jones case that she never had sex with the president. Tripp's legal team advises her to bring the tapes to Clinton's attorneys. Tripp doesn't do this, instead bringing them straight to Starr, Clinton's prosecutor.

Starr in turn arranges a meeting between Tripp and Lewinsky in the Ritz-Carlton Hotel where Tripp records their conversation by means of a hidden microphone. The tapes become a powerful weapon in Starr's hands. He received them on January 12, 1998 and the meeting at the hotel was the day after.

On January 16, Lewinsky is questioned by the FBI and public prosecutors for ten hours. After that, the matter was not to be stopped and the press jumped on it. In February, however, Neptune is located in opposition to Lewinsky's Sun and that won't be the last time. This is not a good position for being labeled reliable in public.

By transit, Uranus went back and forth across Jupiter, and Pluto was moving back and forth in sextile to this. Neptune, too, will pass over. Jupiter is Ruler 3 in her horoscope—the press! Suddenly she's in the news (Uranus over Ruler 3) about secret matters and sexuality (Pluto in stationary sextile with Ruler 3): all according to the book!

Uranus and Pluto by transit also involve conflicts with Monica's Moon. Uranus in a square, Pluto in an inconjunct. The Moon, as her Ruler 10, has to do with her outward image, her social position. This makes for a big chance of damage due to the affair, regardless of whether she is speaking the truth or not. And inwardly, it may cause her a lot of tension and doubt about exactly who she is now. A Pluto connection with Ruler 10 may, in addition, also be the first step to freeing yourself from old projections and patterns of expectation in your childhood, such as the direction in which her mother drove her.

And then, she's stuck with an affair she started under the influence of a yod, kidnapping both her duet planets. She was betrayed through secretly recorded tapes by a friend under the influence of the same yod, with Neptune aspecting her duet, and her self-image receives a blow at the transits just described. However, with the media-aspects in her horoscope and the activated yod configuration, still more can come into play. At the moment of preparing this book for press time, Monica Lewinsky was trying to get in touch with Andrew Morton, Princess Diana's biographer. She will tell him *her* side of the story. . . .

Linda Tripp

In 1990 Linda Tripp comes to the White House to work under President Bush, which she considers a true honor. When Clinton becomes president, she continues to work there, but feels a growing annoyance toward Clinton. Tripp begins to rebel against the new president. Not openly at work, but outside it was no secret that she didn't think much of him and his administration. She thought it was all just trivial business. She began to have contempt for Clinton, and her resistance to Clinton was reinforced after Vincent Foster, a man she liked who worked for Clinton, but who became involved in serious problems because of the investigation into the Whitewater affair, committed suicide. On the day that Foster was found dead in a park, it was Linda Tripp who had brought him lunch at his office, and was the last one to see him alive. That was in July 1993.

Linda began to get more and more involved with conservative movements that Clinton wanted to combat. At school she had been somebody with old-fashioned norms and values, and therefore now had increasing difficulty "with Clinton's roaming eye spying for young women on staff," as she said later.

When her supervisor's replacement brought staff, Tripp was no longer given any work to do. During this period she agreed to a meeting with Lucianne Goldberg, a literary agent in New York who was looking for sources to be able to publish a book on Foster. Goldberg was known to be harshly critical of Clinton and not averse to using any means possible to attack Clinton. She would like to see nothing better than a book about his affairs. Ms. Goldberg began to come into play in the background.

In August 1994, Tripp was transferred to the Pentagon, to a job she really didn't want, but she did everything for work, being a divorced mother caring for two children. She took this appointment as a step backward because she had always been proud that she was allowed to work at the White House (to which she had come already under Bush).

In the fall of 1996, she entered into a friendship with Monica Lewinsky who, as we saw, had also been removed from the White House. Coworkers at the Pentagon indicated that both women were soon exchanging lots of stories. That fall, Neptune by transit was located stationary opposition to Mercury in Lewinsky's horoscope—talk about gossiping!

Linda Tripp's Horoscope

The way Linda Tripp went to work was not really inspired by noble motivation. Her annoyance with Clinton kept growing and she was only too ready to play a role in bringing down or pillorying the man whom she disdained. If such mechanisms are at play, we always need to look at the natal 8th house. This house is connected with things we repress, our problems, the accompanying emotions, and our projections. Everything we repress concerning whatever facet of the horoscope will finally end up in the 8th house and will have its effect from there. Moreover, our hidden abilities and talents are also in the 8th, but as long as they haven't been discovered or developed, they, too, can come out in more extreme projections.

The repression and the hidden abilities and talents that are in the 8th usually come out in the open strongly whenever Pluto, by transit or progression, creates important aspects, or whenever the ruler of the 8th house does that, or whenever contact is made by transit or progression with either Pluto or Ruler 8 in the horoscope. There is a big chance then that we will end up in sticky, complicated, and often also emotional situations that are connected with the unconscious content inside that is yet to be revealed and discovered. I have often seen that during periods of time when transits or progressions like this are coming into play, we can make a "fatal decision" or follow up on "fatal advice." By "fatal," I mean that at that moment we have no idea that this decision or advice is irreversibly going to get us into a jam, regardless of how well the decision was thought out! It's as if Pluto, or the 8th house, were to make sure that we couldn't foresee the true consequences of our actions at that moment. We may also, unintentionally, become part of a much bigger dynamic, like a pawn in a power struggle. And the end of the story may be that everything turns against us. Tripp is a textbook case of how these psychic dynamics work. (See Chart 14, page 199.)

If we look at her 8th house, we see Pluto, and Pluto is Ruler 11 and Ruler 12. The ruler of the 8th house is the Moon that is located in conjunction with Jupiter (Ruler 1). But watch out: the conjunction of the Moon with Jupiter is a duet. This means that these two tend to work through an all-or-nothing basis, and to manifest themselves forcefully, although not particularly comprehensibly for Tripp. An unaspected ruler of the 8th house—wasn't that exactly the same as for Lewinsky, who also has Ruler 8 in a duet?

If an unaspected or duet Ruler 8 enters a negative projection, it can quickly take on more extreme forms, with the chance of everything getting rather out of hand. It is a smoldering but powerful energy that can give a strong orientation, so that life begins to revolve completely around the theme of this projection. As with Lewinsky's aspected (duet) Ruler 8, we feel the problem and the projection are somewhere, but have the feeling we can't get at them, only to notice all of a sudden that we're right in the middle and forced to tackle them. With an unaspected Ruler 8, coping with problems is more irregular and unpredictable. We can maneuver into the most impossible situations, may start manipulating things more, or play a double role. This came into play—at the same time—for Linda Tripp as much as it did for Monica Lewinsky. The fact that Tripp has Pluto in her 8th house can heighten the effect. Pluto in the 8th may be briefly earmarked by, "Why should we do things the easy way if there's a harder way?" The why of this remark I will clarify later, and to do this, we first need to sidetrack to some of the distinguishing features of the 8th house. For backgrounds and theory, I refer you to my book *Astrologische huizen* (not yet available in English).

Planets in the 8th house and in aspect with Ruler 8 are planets that both fascinate us as well as instill fear in us.

We have a kind of love-hate relationship with them. The fascination causes us to keep returning to the domains that have to do with them, the fear can cause us to play hide-and-seek with them anyway, or not dare or want to see them all. These same planets play a double role in another way. We can use the planets in the 8th and in aspect with Ruler 8 as instruments to get through to our inner selves and to learn who we are and what we want, and as instruments to cope with problems. On the other hand, those same planets are also instruments that help repress our problems!

In this way, Jupiter in the 8th, or in aspect with Ruler 8, may, in a positive sense, mean that we are looking for the sense behind events, and in this way, we learn to see the connection between inner and outer, so that we gain more perspective on ourselves. However, that same Jupiter may escape into constructing an artificial theory about meaning, so that the person involved remains out of range. Or else Jupiter, being an enthusiastic and optimistic planet, takes things much too lightly, so that it thinks it's already there whereas the coping still has to start. In the first case, we can build up true wisdom about life and become deeply philosophical in a gentle way. In the second case, we can cause a lot of destruction due to thoughtless optimism, or harm people with pompous and opinionated words.

Pluto in the 8th, or in aspect with Ruler 8, has a profound capacity for growth, using anything dredged up from the depths working with the hidden aspects of something, including things that can't take "the light of day."

It doesn't matter whether these are forensic sciences, whereby evidence from minute indications can still be collected for a crime, or that the issue is psychology, parapsychology, or whatever. In all these cases, by involving ourselves with deeper backgrounds, whether they be all facets of the human, or of matter, or life (think of physics and such), we can gain a deeper feeling of connection and an awareness of how things fit together. If we look at ourselves with those eyes, we can gain insight for our own depths, fears, shadow, and unknown possibilities. However, that same Pluto may use the knowledge of these areas as a means of power, without looking at itself, and even as a means to "bring others down a notch" in overcompensation for an inner fear. Then we see that people like this succeed in somehow using all their knowledge, including gossip, "strategically," in order to stay out of range themselves (until it goes on too long and we've dug our own grave). Or else we radically change our attitude regarding certain other persons, who then get a negative projection pinned onto them, all just not to have to see how we ourselves are on the wrong track.

Pluto in the 8th, or in aspect with Ruler 8, has, if we look at the positive side, incredible endurance when fighting for a cause.

However, we will only benefit if we are absolutely honest with ourselves and are willing to face all the facets. Then we can overcome even the most difficult situations. That same Pluto, if it is working negatively and we are dishonest with ourselves and others, or are playing hide-and-seek, will likewise give us a long suit, but we'll see that we are gradually digging our own grave and maneuvering into a nearly hopeless inner (and often also external) situation. Remember that we can be dishonest regarding ourselves and at the same time be convinced that our motives are pristine! Dishonesty, as I mean it here, has less to do with lying (although that's perfectly possible), than with not wanting or daring to face what we are really doing, in fact, and what our unconscious and hidden motives are.

For Linda Tripp, considering her growing and intensifying hatred of Clinton, this means that she could have asked herself which part of herself she so hated. The greater the emotion toward someone, the stronger the unconscious complex that has to do with this projection—and so, with this emotion. Instead, she utilized Pluto's manipulative capacities to make the object of her projection, Clinton, black.

If we suppress the shadow side regarding a planet in the 8th, or in aspect with Ruler 8, we may develop a keen fascination for the shadow, which can start ruling our lives.

This is an important consequence of the 8th house and of projecting repression. We are sucked toward it, as it were, or keep getting caught up in situations surrounding that theme. And this, too, can start ruling us a good deal. In this way, Pluto in the 8th house—already a position that creates sensitivity to unspoken power problems—without thinking, may keep being involved in these kinds of problems. Our own behavior also contributes to this, but not always in an obvious way. Somebody may have a way about them, though, and may send out subtle signals that others pick up. I have encountered a number of cases where someone with Pluto in the 8th was seen by others as being arrogant, with the result that the person got involved in particular forms of resistance or with shadow projections. A man once told me he had a feeling that his coworkers didn't take him seriously or understand him. He couldn't figure out why they found him arrogant and standoffish, because he didn't see himself that way and he wasn't like that in his own opinion. However, I noticed that he did radiate something of that nature, of which he obviously was not aware. In this way he also elicited responses, and the only thing he could do about it was not to start fighting the outside world, but to go in search of the source of his own subtle messages. What is the background of the *wall* of standoffishness? What is the background of the slightly arrogant attitude? What fear is the cause of that shield? As long as this man hasn't managed to answer these questions for himself, he will be confronted from time to time by situations where he will feel himself misjudged, situations where he has the feeling of being rejected. He may also be confronted by situations where he has the idea that people are talking about him, or situations where he feels something or someone is challenging him to a fight, wants to bring him down, and more of these kinds of sentiments. The crux, however, lies in a fundamental feeling of insecurity and fear somewhere in the man himself. Pluto in the 8th, or in aspect with Ruler 8, may even feel that it is being persecuted by others. A persecution complex often combines with strong feelings of inferiority in the consciousness, that are unconsciously overcompensated for by the idea that everything in the world revolves only around us.

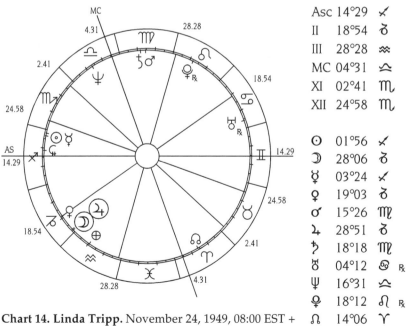

Asc	14°29	♐
II	18°54	♑
III	28°28	♒
MC	04°31	♎
XI	02°41	♏
XII	24°58	♏

☉	01°56	♐	
☽	28°06	♑	
☿	03°24	♐	
♀	19°03	♑	
♂	15°26	♍	
♃	28°51	♑	
♄	18°18	♍	
♅	04°12	♋	℞
♆	16°31	♎	
♇	18°12	♌	℞
☊	14°06	♈	
⚷	11°18	♐	

Chart 14. Linda Tripp. November 24, 1949, 08:00 EST + 5.00 = 13:00 GMT. Union City, NJ 40°47 N 074°01 W. Data from birth certificate. Placidus houses.

One last point that I want to bring out here is that the 8th house gives nothing for free; we have to fight for everything. In fact, we have to want to fight for issues that relate to the subject matter of the 8th house, because otherwise they have no value. This doesn't come from the feeling that we don't *deserve* these things. However, the 8th house wants to feel (emotionally) involved in issues in a positive sense, and the more we are engaged in something, and the more we put into it, the greater the involvement and the emotional value. In a positive sense, we then have at our disposal a great capacity to take on the situation with a lot of energy, input, and involvement, and will also enjoy—down to our very toes—the success we experience.

This involvement may also exist in a negative sense. Then the person onto whom we are projecting will receive an enormous negative charge and we may even unconsciosly feel that the projection itself is not enough. It's as if something smoldering inside is looking for another way to intensify or worsen the situation by, for instance, undertaking activities that will reinforce the problem for the other person. What we don't see is that the situation also gets more significant for us. So we may really sink our teeth into a matter, and not let go.

No matter how we look at it, planets in the 8th, or in aspect with Ruler 8, want to feel the depths, whether our consciousness likes it or not. So, if we don't undertake an action to experience depth or to be involved in a "deep" domain, the unconscious will make sure we run into it in the external sense. Instead of sticking energy into gaining depth and learning to yield, we then have to stick our energy into external problems. In both cases, we will be very involved with planets connected to the 8th house, even though we might not see it that way. This is the background of the remark, "Why do things the easy way, if we can do them the hard way?" The easy way is simply too superficial for the 8th house!

Back to Linda Tripp's horoscope. It is evident that she used her manipulative capacities to the utmost in Monica-gate, and somehow sank her teeth into the matter. A couple of moments were, for her, of great importance in this:

1. A little foretaste was her transfer to the Pentagon, which she felt to be a step backward, and which only fanned her anger and negative projection onto Clinton. Her MC had to cope with a square with Pluto by primary progression.

2.   After this, the friendship with a "companion in misfortune," Monica Lewinsky, who had also been "promoted out." It is common knowledge that if you are troubled by a particular complex and you meet someone who is wrestling with the same theme, this can offer a remarkable kind of recognition, and even lead to temporarily "close" friendships. In the year that Lewinsky arrived at the Pentagon and got to know Tripp, we see Neptune by transit at the end of Capricorn moving back and forth over Tripp's Ruler 8 (while also inconjuncting Monica's Ruler 8!). In April 1996, Neptune stood still within a 1° orb to Linda's Ruler 8 (which intensifies and extends its effect), and so activated her 8th house. During the years that follow, Neptune will keep moving back and forth, making contact with that point again. So in that year she gets to know Monica, and at the next transit of Neptune she assisted with the following.

3.   The article in *Newsweek* in which she accused Clinton of having sexual relationships. Earlier, I indicated that if Pluto or Ruler 8 become activated by an important transit or progression, you can make a "fatal decision" or follow up on "fatal advice." Tripp did both: the fatal decision was assisting *Newsweek*, so that she was all over the news and was, of course, dealt with harshly by the presidents' attorneys, who attacked her in all possible ways. She was furious about this (which only intensified her projection onto Clinton), but she could have known beforehand that things would go this way, because they have been happening like this all along in the U.S.A., where many issues are battled out in the media. If she wanted to be left alone, she should have kept her mouth shut. However, Neptune is her Co-Ruler 3, and when Neptune came to be located at her Ruler 1 (Jupiter) and her Ruler 8 (Moon), she used the information she had (3rd house) to inform the press (likewise 3rd house). In doing so, she definitely entered the arena, but certainly didn't anticipate things being like this.

4.   The fatal advice that she followed up on during the same period of time was Goldberg's advice (see above) to record her conversations with Monica. In the state where Tripp lives, this is a punishable offense, and it has been reported that she will be prosecuted for this and will herself appear in the defendant's box. The spot in which she wanted to put Clinton is the spot she prepared for herself, unintentionally, unwittingly, and unforeseen. And it all revolved around

secretly recording (Neptune) and the theme of phone calls and tapes (Co-Ruler 3). So we see that Tripp, with the transit of Neptune, alias Co-Ruler 3, at her duet Ruler 8, received all the choice ingredients to make things difficult for herself and others.

5. Pluto, too, takes a dive into things in the summer of 1997, and may have assisted in these "fatal decisions." Pluto becomes stationary by transit at 2°50" Capricorn and is conjunct both the Sun and Mercury. A Pluto transit will dredge things up from the bottom, and will mean a confrontation with the shadow and other repressed material. If the Sun is involved, and you already have a dislike for a man holding high office or a position of authority, there is a very good chance that this projection will intensify in a troublesome way. In retrospect, this was also clearly the case. And Mercury is also taking part: again the press and the audiotapes. However, the Sun is the ruler of the 9th house and Mercury is co-ruler, a house that has to do with the legal profession, with jurisprudence, and such! In October 1997, Uranus becomes stationary inconjunct with itself (at 4° Aquarius) and sextile Mercury, which is already located in an inconjunct to Uranus in her natal horoscope. We now have a yod in transit! It contains Uranus (Ruler 3) by her radix, and Uranus (Ruler 3) by transit, and Mercury. Not an easy transit for throwing your lot in with the press. And Mercury as Co-Ruler 9 has to do with judicial power. A yod with a doubling of your Ruler 3 in combination with the judiciary is asking for trouble if you submit fishy information and tapes to the judiciary. The apparent victory might well turn into a Pyrrhic victory! In the coming years, Neptune will be creating the same yod: sextile Mercury and inconjunct Uranus. Then she herself will have to appear before the judge for unlawfully and secretly acquiring information.

Pluto will by then have moved past the Sun and Mercury, but will be progressing toward the Ascendant. Moreover, it is increasingly evident from the voluntarily submitted tapes that Tripp was extremely manipulative and put a good number of words in Lewinsky's mouth. This was during the time when Pluto by transit was still wobbling back and forth over her Sun and Mercury and inconjunct her Uranus (Ruler 3). She found another form for her manipulative capacities this way.

It is impressive to see how Tripp's horoscope fits with Lewinsky's. If we lay the two horoscopes on top of each other in synastry, we see that Lewinsky's Venus (Ruler 8)-Saturn duet forms a yod with Tripp's Moon (Ruler 8)-Jupiter duet! A yod containing two unaspected rulers of the 8th house and two women driven by their unconscious. That's a display of fireworks!

The transits of Neptune over Tripp's Moon-Jupiter duet meant a yod in transit with Lewinsky's Venus-Saturn duet. And in this transit, both women became "fatefully" intertwined.

Kenneth Starr

Kenneth Starr had always been known as the epitome of integrity, and he was strongly influenced by his strict and religious upbringing. He always promptly did what was required, even as a schoolboy, and was a kind of model pupil and model child. His professional life began for him by selling Bibles. Up until now, nobody has been able to discover even the tiniest indecency in this devout man or his past, something of which his mother is very proud. She told the press that she raised him that way and knows that he will finish any job, no matter how unfortunate.

It was precisely because of Starr's reputation for integrity and honesty that he was chosen to be the special prosecutor in the suit against Clinton, and this turned out to be a big mistake on Clinton's part. Namely, if somebody identifies so strongly with a particular attitude and has turned it into a powerful starting point for his actions, very likely the opposite attitude—dishonesty and manipulation—has been repressed. Now, somebody may on the inside have a particular manner of conduct and consciously held attitudes that are basically sincere and honest, and at the same time be aware that nobody, including himself, can be perfectly honest. Being aware of the fact that dishonesty may become a shadow trait and over the course of time may simply break through, is of great importance in order to remain truly honest.

Whenever we invest a lot of energy into maintaining a particular image of ourselves, it is exceptionally likely that we *don't* want to see that in fact we, too, can make a mistake. Memories of such moments are quickly hidden away deep down and often forgotten, or "explained away" with rationalizations and motives that aren't correct, but are supposed to justify the behavior. By believing these rationalizations and justifications, we are able to keep holding on to the ideal image we have of ourselves. Our consciousness is forced to pay for this with some amount of effort, and this process entails major consequences. The *unconscious* will not agree to this way of doing things, and becomes mutinous in various ways, of which the most common are:

- *Restless or uneasy feelings:* Inside we have a latent feeling of not being comfortable in our skin. This is often misunderstood by consciousness, and the cause of this is sought in the outside world. Something or someone has to be at fault, and this will become the object of the projection.

- *Projection:* Any subject matter that has been repressed—and that the consciousness therefore doesn't see—it will spot in the outside world. So we get pretty annoyed with people who exhibit the hallmarks of the repressed subject matter. Somebody like this has to offer only a little finger for us to bite the whole hand. Typical for projection is notably that the greater the repression the bigger the complex, and the stronger will be the emotion that is elicited by "seeing" this in the outside world, and the more fiercely we go for it.

- *Fascination:* A mysterious kind of fascination arises for precisely those subjects that are repressed. Of course the fascination has to have a justification, so it's "ideal" if we can involve ourselves with it on a professional level. And we will, of course, deny this fascination in every possible way.

Although there is more to the projection mechanism, these hallmarks are enough to describe Starr's behavior. The way in which he sank his teeth into the matter, all under the pretext of "proper legal proceedings," etc., surprised many people. It is very clear that Clinton is the embodiment, as it were, of Starr's shadow. Whenever we identify with a powerful marital morality from a religious standpoint, then the playful, the sensual, the sexual, and an open morality will, of course, be repressed and taboo. A president who sleeps around becomes the personification of evil, which has to be combated.

Also people who enjoy things, who maintain a somewhat looser and more flexible lifestyle, won't cut the mustard from the point of view of strict morality, and so may also elicit plenty of irritation. Only virtuousness, working hard, and sobriety are the values that should be admired. Clinton, however, has a flexible style, and despite his working hard, has something flamboyant that Starr utterly lacks. So again a little piece of Starr's shadow, now given meaning by Clinton.

If someone else is a personification of what we have repressed, seeing this person will each time cause inner unrest. After all, the repression and accompanying complex buttons are being pushed! Restless feelings arise and we may even be thrown off balance by them. The logical conclusion is, thus, that we want to combat the outer source of these disquieting feelings. In Starr's case, this has gotten to the point where he also wants to prosecute Clinton as soon as the latter is no longer president, and wants to drag him before the court on account of perjury. The fact that Starr doesn't know when to stop lets us see how big his complex has gotten.

Kenneth Starr has loudly and clearly revealed to the world his fascination with what he represses. When we can't find anything, not a thing, regarding the issues for which we were hired, and instead we end up presenting such a long report (thousands of pages) containing very detailed sexual information, it does make a person wonder. The Dutch paper, *NRC/Handelsblad* wrote this about Starr's investigation: "Starr's argument that the affair is not about sex is a tough sell, since he himself reported on the affair in September in language that made pornographers envious. Besides, Starr cannot get around the fact that the whole business stems from a desire to keep a relationship secret." Whenever a repression is strong, we will not be able to muster any understanding for the emotional stalemate in which somebody finds themselves when an affair comes out in the open. That this person will initially beat around the bush is only human. Starr, however, can look at it only as an obstruction of justice, and will hang the entire impeachment proceeding on that—including in it the Paula Jones case as well as that of Monica Lewinsky.

Typical of projections is that the picture of the other is clouded, that the resultant actions are not in proportion to the incident, *and* that people will try to justify their actions as much as possible, pointing out an objective motivation for them.

Another hallmark of repression is that occasionally, sometimes only a little, sometimes a little more, we *ourselves* exhibit the very behavior that we condemn or with which our consciousness absolutely does not wish to identify. Kenneth Starr turns out to have intentionally kept quiet about the fact that he was an advisor for the attorneys in the Paula Jones case against Clinton when he asked U.S. Attorney-General Janet Reno for permission to expand his investigation to include the Lewinsky matter. Monica Lewinsky complained she had been unfairly treated, and that Starr had tried to prevent her contacting a lawyer, and in addition placed her under severe pressure. And then,

Starr held up information that was advantageous to Clinton for months, until after the election.

In other words: the "honest and unimpeachable" Mr. Starr, himself, withheld information about his role in a previous sex case, attempted to deprive Lewinsky of her legal rights by placing her under pressure not to find an attorney, and also withheld positive information that might spoil his case. In what way is he honest? He will no doubt have a "clean story" and not want to see what is really at play.

If we now look at Kenneth Starr's horoscope from this psychological analysis, we see that he has Venus and Mars in Virgo in his 8th house. Indeed a very good position for analyzing people's sexual lives in detail! The subject matters of planets in the 8th, and in aspect with Ruler 8, as we already discussed are those with which we have a love-hate relationship. We are scared of them and at the same time fascinated by them. The themes of relationship and enjoyment (Venus) and assertiveness and wanting to show yourself (Mars), possibly also the macho thing (Mars), then, are themes to which Starr will have an overreaction. (See Chart 15, page 208.)

He will have the need to experience a relationship deeply (Venus in the 8th) and will need assertiveness, militancy, and to stand up for himself (Mars), but be afraid to express these things at the same time. The fear may make him seek out a "safe relationship," which will find form according to customary norms and values (all the more so because Saturn is also in conjunction with Ruler 8). However, Venus' deeper desire for real depth and passion keeps on smoldering, even though it is so repressed. In that case, passion in the outside world will have to be dealt with very firmly so he won't remember his own deep needs. In addition, the fact that Venus creates no major aspects, so is unintegrated, makes Venus's expressions and needs subject to greater extremes.

With Mars in the 8th, his fearful side may lead to outflanking initiatives—not standing up for himself right away, but seeking out strategic moments. This can produce exceptional militancy for a supposedly objective case, which is by nature, however, always emotionally colored. Mars is also the planet that has to do with the sexual act: penetration. This will fascinate Starr and he will be made uncomfortable by it as well.

Ruler 8 is located in conjunction with Saturn. A planet in the 8th, and in aspect with Ruler 8, can be used in two ways: as a mechanism to tackle his problems, and also—paradoxically enough—as a mechanism to push his repression further down. If Saturn is involved, life according to the rules, and according to traditional values, is a perfect way to play hide-and-seek with himself. By adhering to values of sobriety and simplicity, of restraint and duty, he is at any rate "justifiably" enabled to crush the eruption of the deep longings of Venus and Mars, and also use "duty" as an excuse to intervene in every detail with someone else's expressions of Venus and Mars!

Matters like beauty and art (Venus), sports and assertiveness, sexuality as well (Mars), and granting himself the time (Saturn) might at the same time, however, be able to help Starr cope with problems and arrive at a balance. However, Starr exaggerated his Ruler 8 conjunct Saturn. No wonder: it's a duet! The thing that is striking in the entire Lewinsky affair is that we are involved with:

- Starr: a duet that includes Ruler 8;
- Tripp: a duet that includes Ruler 8;
- Lewinsky: a duet that includes Ruler 8.

Tripp's duet created a yod with Lewinsky's duet and an opposition with Starr's duet, all pretty exactly. A "fateful" intertwining of three overcompensating rulers of the 8th house!

Starr, however, has the sign of Virgo intercepted in his 8th house, and therefore we have a second Ruler 8: Mercury. In addition, the position and aspects of Co-Ruler 8 play an important role. Mercury is conjunct Pluto, sextile Jupiter and Uranus. Therefore these planets are mechanisms that both cope as well as repress. And they will fascinate and elicit fear at the same time.

We have already discussed Pluto in Linda Tripp's 8th house at some length earlier. Pluto in aspect with Ruler 8, or co-Ruler 8, will receive a similar interpretation. And an 8th-house Pluto connection can make a person grab hold of a situation like a terrier, with no intention of giving up. Tripp has Pluto in the 8th, Starr has Pluto in aspect with co-Ruler 8, and Clinton has Pluto in aspect with Ruler 8. Three terriers that are fighting. Monica Lewinsky plays a very different role. She has no connection between Pluto and her 8th house.

Jupiter in connection with the 8th house, in the positive sense, may give us a person who can handle problems well because of an optimistic attitude to life. There is the risk that because of that very optimism we think that there aren't any problems, when, in fact, they are lying in wait. Being involved in areas that belong to Jupiter's domain present an opportunity to come close to ourselves, as well as opportunity to repress things. Jupiter has everything to do with jurisprudence. Being involved with judicial matters may confront us with the human dynamics that give pause for reflection and that also confront us with our inner substance. We may grow psychologically by being involved with judicial matters. However, we may also use those same judicial matters precisely to cover up problems, by waging war against the evil that we project into others. From all the reports in the media, it seems Starr chose primarily for this last expression of Jupiter in aspect with Co-Ruler 8.

Uranus is another story. Of course it has to do with the urge for individuality and originality. In connection with the 8th house, this is also something that strongly appeals to us and which we would ever so much like to realize, and at the same time it again involves some fear. Always that polarity regarding the 8th house! The fear can produce a projection onto everything that is original, alternative, and different, and everything that doesn't toe the line. This is something that has to be combated!

However, Uranus has other distinguishing features that are important in order to understand the planet, and that have been set forth fantastically by Liz Greene in her book *Uranus: the Art of Stealing Fire*. She shows that Uranus has emotional problems and

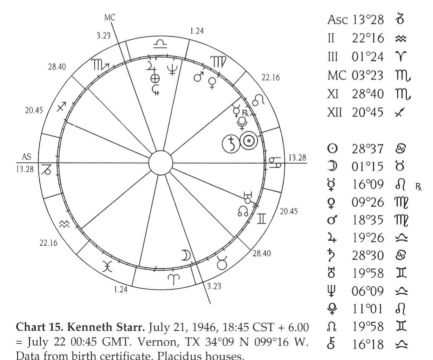

Chart 15. Kenneth Starr. July 21, 1946, 18:45 CST + 6.00 = July 22 00:45 GMT. Vernon, TX 34°09 N 099°16 W. Data from birth certificate. Placidus houses.

is a planet significantly involved in what is utopian. Any perfect model of a state, or society, or any other kind of elaborate mental construction has to do with Uranus. Adhering to any kind of teaching that is significantly permeated by utopian and idealistic characteristics, and that is a mental and reasoned construction, is a hallmark of Uranus. The paradox is that adhering to that teaching makes us collective and demands we sacrifice a portion of our individuality, in the name of freedom, in fact! Movements such as, for example, the Red Army *Fraktion* in Germany were not just revolutionary movements; there was a whole ideology behind them with specific opinions about how a state should function and what the rights of citizens should be.

Religious teachings can also have something to do with Uranus. With Uranus, what counts is not so much the content as the total construction of the teaching. If a religious school has constructed an ideal image of how people should be and how the world should ideally be put together, this is a Uranian phenomenon. The *content* of the teaching belongs to Neptune.

If Uranus finds expression in an idealized and perfected form, it is stripped of every human element (like the Greek god Uranus, who wouldn't accept his children because they weren't perfect!). Then the system becomes the most important thing. There may be a connection here with the fact that Uranus is the second ruler (also called the nocturnal ruler or dispositor) of Capricorn. A normal, practical structure belongs to Saturn, the utopian-mental structure to Uranus.

Uranus in connection with the 8th house may, by way of escape, provide an almost cool identification with utopian thought, regardless of whether it is religious or social. It is known that Kenneth Starr is well-versed in the Bible and has very strict opinions. Such an attitude is also associated with the opinion that we better learn to control ourselves. There won't be any understanding for the array of human expressions, fears, and missteps then.

With Uranus connecting with the 8th house, psychological growth and coping would be very possible, particularly through the Uranian domains—from astrology and the alternative healing arts, to technical matters and computers. Starr shows little sign of doing these things, which is why I will discuss at greater length the expressions that he does exhibit.

Starr has enough unaspected planets in his horoscope: a duet consisting of the Sun and Saturn, and then an unaspected Moon, an unaspected Neptune, and an unaspected Venus. Five of the ten planets! These force themselves very insistently into the forefront and are important motivators for Starr. Themes of the Sun are, for instance, identity, honor, respect, and authority. Saturn is structure, law, and order. The Moon is the feminine, the nurturing, and the caring. Neptune, that which empathizes and is sensitive, the musical, and the religious. Venus, the relativizing, the tender and erotic, the artistic, as well as the enjoyable. All of these themes have to do with dynamics over several generations in the family which brought him forth, and that want to find an individual solution in him. With an unaspected Sun, this may mean looking for your own identity and your own authority, which you unconsciously accentuate, but don't consciously understand that way at first. Of course, Starr may learn to deal with this well in his life, but then he will need to become aware of the fact that it is important for him to build up a sense of self-worth, and to be able to show this to the outside world. As long as he isn't aware of this, he may even have an "allergic" reaction to people who display self-assured authority. This is an attitude that Clinton has, which may make Clinton even more of an object of projection for Starr.

Starr's significant religious need may be related to his unaspected Neptune. In a positive sense, an unaspected Neptune may lead to a feeling of oneness with all that lives, a great bond with nature, and a sense of the mystical and dreamy side of life, as well as a deep, personal spirituality. In a negative sense it may lead to religious fanaticism and dogmatism, and to living in a world of illusion. In short: Kenneth Starr is an extremely gifted person, should he develop the abilities of his unaspected planets, but a pretty problematic person if he plays hide-and-seek with them.

Starr had to testify at a hearing of the U.S. House Judiciary Committee. He was under fire for twelve hours and was firmly dealt with notably by the Democrats. The American public, however, didn't have much of an appetite for it anymore. The live television broadcast attracted so few viewers that one station after another stopped the broadcast. This didn't make Starr any the more popular. The fact is that actually lots of Americans have a dislike for him. This doesn't bode well for Starr in his coming progressions and transits.

A transit he should really watch out for is that of transiting Pluto squaring Venus. The theme around which it all revolves in large part! It may produce plenty of inner tension, but it may also very well be that stories come out where Starr doesn't come off so properly, or stories where he doesn't deal with women particularly courteously. Now that Lewinsky has gone to Andrew Morton (Lady Diana's biographer), to tell him her story, Starr may have something to worry about, because Monica is furious with him. Venus is the ruler of his 9th house, the house that has to do with litigation. Pluto will create the square for the first time in January 1999, and then repeat it a couple of times. Uranus by transit will then just have been exactly inconjunct to that same Venus, before heading into Aquarius. There it will hang around in stationary transit at 16°, in exact opposition to the second ruler of Starr's 8th house—Mercury. This may involve sudden confrontations and tensions for him and will happen in May 1999, also a month when Pluto will be located at 9° Sagittarius, again creating an exact square with Venus. For Kenneth Starr, the story hasn't ended.[1]

Transiting Saturn was square Starr's Sun-Saturn duet in November 1998, and it didn't inspire the general public to be more sympathetic to him.. Neptune became stationary in October 1998 at 29°31' Capricorn, still within the 1° orb, in opposition to his Sun, thus his Ruler 8. This effect lasts many months, and the hearings where Starr himself was questioned began under a transit of Saturn square Saturn opposing Neptune, his duet Ruler 8. Kenneth will probably not be as calm and assured on the inside as he outwardly lets on.

Earlier I pointed out the danger of making a "fatal" decision or following up on "fatal" advice if your 8th house becomes activated by transit or progression. We saw that Linda Tripp, with transiting Neptune conjunct her duet Ruler 8, took Goldberg's advice to record her phone conversations with Monica and later handed the tapes over to Starr. It seems that Neptune came into play for Kenneth, as well. It was common knowledge that he had come to a complete standstill regarding all the investigations of Clinton and that he wanted to stop. However, he was placed under pressure by the Republicans to continue and decided to do so. Shortly thereafter Tripp came along with the audiotapes.

The decision to continue had huge consequences, consequences that Starr was unable to see at the moment of his decision and they may well have further repercussions.

Starr might also make another decision under this stationary transit, or follow up on particular advice that may again entail significant consequences for him. Transiting Saturn will still pass over his Moon and be in opposition to his MC. Neither aspect will gain him any popularity. And Neptune will soon follow with a square to his Moon and a square to his MC, as Neptune continues on its

---

[1] Readers should note that this copy was written prior to 1999, so Karen is actually predicting events here. Publisher's note.

march through Aquarius. In transit, contact will thus be made with a number of important horoscope factors for Starr, of which the majority have the potential for getting him into a nasty fix.

A salient detail: Pluto in the horoscope of the U.S.A. is located at 27°34′ Capricorn, thus over Linda Tripp's Sun-Jupiter conjunction, Kenneth Starr's Sun-Saturn opposition, and is creating a yod with Monica Lewinsky's Saturn and Venus.

✩ ✩ ✩

In brief, what do we see coming together? Lewinsky, Tripp, and Starr all have a duet in which Ruler 8 participates, and for all three this duet is activated during the years in question by transiting Neptune. These three people become intertwined in a process that revolves around everything that has to do with a negative Neptune: from dishonesty and secret recordings (also by order of the impeccable Mr. Starr), betrayal, undermining, and so forth. The activating of the ruler of the 8th house for all three gave their own repression and complexes lead roles in the drama.

There is more going on though. Ever since Watergate, which caused Richard Nixon to resign, the press has looked at presidents in a different way. They are seen as normal people as far as their passions and character traits go, and the press tends to publicize as many scandals as possible. Due to the Monica Lewinsky affair, for the first time we are hearing powerful noises from the public that it would like to be spared this kind of gossip. People are fed up with this way of "waging war." I have seen on many occasions that when somebody's duet or yod leads to controversies in the news, that the yod ushers in a new attitude on the social level. It may be that the Lewinsky affair is finally the beginning of a somewhat more nuanced approach to news about people in high positions. It will probably still be a while before this becomes noticeable as well, but the first signals are evident. Activated yods often occur at crossroads or turning-points in somebody's life. If that life has a public function, the activated yod may also accompany a changing undertone in society, or that yod may activate the makings of a change. Particularly people with yods and unaspected planets will come to the forefront or have a pivotal function during times that entail a turning-point, or in important transitional situations. American society is at a stage of change in which religious fundamentalism plays an important role. Kenneth Starr is now functioning at such a crossroads as an officer of the court, and the overcompensating nature of his 8th house and his unaspected planets are making news all over the world. In many countries one can say there is an absolute amazement at the manner in which people are carrying on in the U.S.A., and many government leaders, on being asked, have declared they find it strange or, in fact, like Helmut Kohl, the former chancellor of Germany, a nauseating display. The whole business reveals a black spot, a piece of shadow, and a critical problem in American society, and it won't let itself be covered up or hidden away. With all the extremes and absurdities we now see in the spotlight, the seed has been sown for change in American society. Starr had a large role to play in this, as did Tripp (Moon-Jupiter duet) and Lewinsky (Venus-Saturn duet), and as we saw, all three have the ruler of the 8th house in their duet. (See figure 8, page 214.)

William Jefferson Clinton

I have until now said very little about Bill Clinton's horoscope. The reason for this is the enormous debate taking place in America about the precise time of his birth. Diverse variants have been brought to the table, but there are two that jump out and each one has its fervent followers: time of birth at 3:44 A.M. or at 8:51 A.M. In the light of yod configurations, the 8:51 A.M. horoscope jumps out. There is no yod in the radix itself, but during the period of time that was so critical for Clinton, when exposure was inevitably approaching and he was standing with his back to the wall, Pluto and Uranus by transit were together creating a yod with his MC. Very appropriate. Using the time of 8:51 A.M., we thus see the following transits:

February 1997:
Transiting Pluto inconjunct MC, and stationary at that! Transiting Uranus likewise inconjunct MC. So, together a temporary MC-Pluto-Uranus yod. Transiting Saturn is located in opposition to his Ascendant.

November 1997:
Transiting Uranus inconjunct MC and:

December 1997:
Transiting Pluto inconjunct MC, so a repetition of the yod.

August 1997:
Again a stationary transit of Pluto inconjunct his MC.

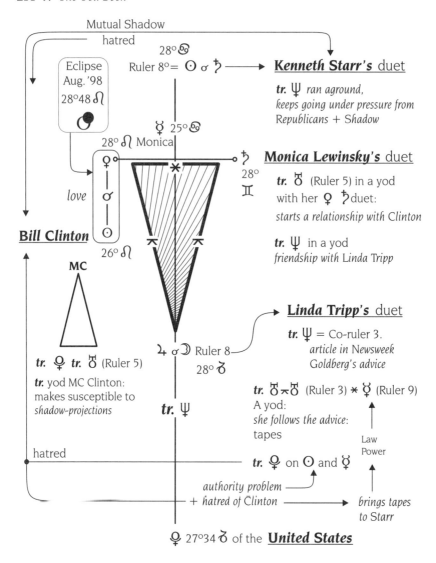

Figure 8.
The power game in the Clinton-Lewinsky affair.

If Pluto is stationary by transit, you can easily count on the effect lasting six months. If Pluto meanwhile forms a yod, as in 1997, the full effect of that yod will travel along with it during this period of time.

During the effective term of this yod, the previously mentioned article, where he was accused by Linda Tripp of sexual acts with Kathleen Willey in 1993, appeared in *Newsweek*. The country began, from that moment on, to become preoccupied with the sexual escapades of its president, who had, after all, also been entangled in the Paula Jones case.

During that same period of time, special prosecutor Kenneth Starr was in the process of running into dead ends in his investigation and announced his resignation and acceptance of another job. The next day, however, he was already withdrawing his statement, under heavy pressure from Republicans, who wanted Clinton to "hang" some way or other, according to reports. From this moment on, an all-or-nothing mood stole over the Clinton investigations. Clinton was made to stand with his back to the wall more and more. (See Chart 16.)

The planets that created this yod in Clinton's horoscope were Pluto and Uranus. Pluto concerns themes that have to do with power, and it also knows a thing or two about sex. Uranus rules Clinton's 5th house (in the 8:51 A.M. horoscope) and this is traditionally the house of "romantic affairs and amorous experiences." (See Chart 17, page 216.) If this were the case, a yod composed of these planets with his MC at the time the sexual affair hit the front

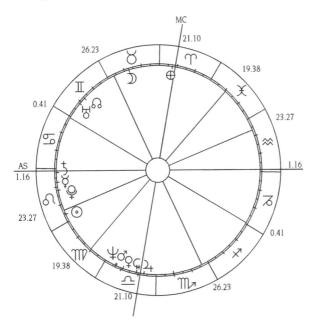

Asc	01°16	♌
II	23°27	♌
III	19°38	♍
MC	21°10	♈
XI	26°23	♉
XII	00°41	♋
☉	25°48	♌
☽	17°18	♉
☿	07°26	♌
♀	10°53	♎
♂	06°13	♎
♃	23°11	♎
♄	02°07	♌
♅	21°08	♊
♆	06°51	♎
♇	11°51	♌
☊	18°51	♎
☊	17°16	♊

Chart 16. Clinton 03:44. August 19, 1946, 03:44 CST + 6.00 = 09:44 GMT. Hope, AR 33°40 N 093°35 W. Data from an astrologer's mother who said she had seen a copy of the birth certificate in Hope, in a special book about him (as governor), which is now missing.

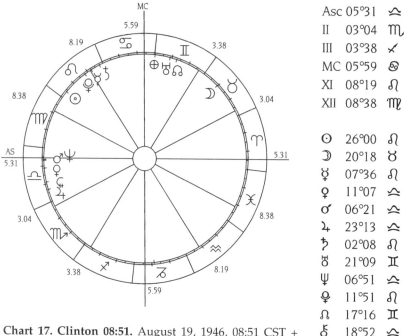

Asc 05°31 ♎

II   03°04 ♏
III   03°38 ♐
MC   05°59 ♋
XI   08°19 ♌
XII   08°38 ♍

☉   26°00 ♌
☽   20°18 ♉
☿   07°36 ♌
♀   11°07 ♎
♂   06°21 ♎
♃   23°13 ♎
♄   02°08 ♌
♅   21°09 ♊
♆   06°51 ♎
♇   11°51 ♌
☊   17°16 ♊
⚷   18°52 ♎

Chart 17. Clinton 08:51. August 19, 1946, 08:51 CST +
6.00 = 14:51 GMT. Hope, AR 33°40 N 093°35 W. Data
from Lois Rodden, who has a report from Clinton's
mother using 8:51 A.M. Placidus houses.

pages nationally and became the opening bid in a power game
that is running out of control, would be highly appropriate. The
5th house is also the house that has to do with prestige and self-
confidence. Clinton's prestige is also part of the yod!

When the yod repeats at the end of 1997, a new problem arises
for Clinton, as Tripp is making the notorious audio recordings of
her phone calls with Lewinsky which she will later hand over to
Starr. Clinton gets to stand with his back even closer to the wall.

The next stationary transit of Pluto already starts having an effect at the beginning of 1998, becomes exact in August 1998, and
continues to come into play well into the autumn. This is an extremely uncomfortable transit, one that allows the tail end of the
yod its effect. An unimaginable escalation takes place, and the
players are merciless. Pluto places Clinton in another stalemate.
Even though there isn't a total yod anymore this time, experience
teaches that if such a transit has taken part in a yod (which it did
in 1997), it may again take along in its repetition those previous
themes, problems, and stalemates. And this is what Pluto did!

Just imagine how it must feel: your extramarital sex life down to the most intimate details has just been posted on the Internet and splashed on the front pages of newspapers, worldwide. Then, as the president of a large and powerful country, you are to address a large assembly of government leaders at the United Nations! What goes through your mind?

If the 8:51 A.M. horoscope is the correct one, Clinton's temporary yod would complete the picture of the temporarily activated duet rulers of the 8th house in Lewinsky, Tripp, and Starr's horoscopes. How grotesque a situation can become, how many stalemates there are (in essence for *all* the participants), how things can get out of hand, and are not able to be stopped anymore—we were able to follow it all. However, this entire affair might, in a good number of years, very possibly turn out to have been the beginning of a turning-point in the way in which the U.S.A. deals with themes like sexuality and power, with Puritanical opinions and beliefs.

CHAPTER THIRTEEN

Life and Death

I *was eighteen weeks' pregnant with our second child. A pregnancy that was different in every way from the first one. The pregnancy announced itself completely unexpectedly for us and obviously was not planned. This wasn't a problem in itself; we really wanted another child. When I stopped breast feeding our first child after six months, my menstruation didn't resume. A month later I felt so tired and listless, it was like I was pregnant. The pregnancy test came out negative though, so I put that out of my mind. After some time, I felt my belly was starting to bulge. It worried me, so I went to my gynecologist. It turned out I was eighteen weeks pregnant! That was December 23, 1994.*

This is what Jannette wrote me, and this episode turned out to be the beginning of a very difficult time for her. Jannette is a gentle woman who doesn't step into the forefront. I have known her for years, and she has never been other than friendly and quiet, maybe even a bit afraid of demanding attention. Yet she has many capacities and lots of interests. Jannette has an unaspected Venus in her horoscope. Her Venus squares her Ascendant and is conjunct her MC, but creates no aspects to other planets, so it is unintegrated. The fact that Venus is connected with two angles in the horoscope makes Venus dominant and palpable.

An unaspected Venus really needs to be part of something, to be liked, and to make compromises. This is why you often see a great deal of tolerance in someone with an unaspected Venus, and a fear of tension and arguments, because this Venus isn't very well equipped for it. An unaspected Venus is often capable of squelching a portion of its assertiveness from fear of "not being part of things anymore." Jannette has Mars in Cancer square Neptune, and this is not the most suitable aspect for your assertiveness to come into its own! Therefore there is a greater chance that

Jannette, despite her Moon in Aries, will repress a good deal of her assertiveness and emotions, such as anger and rage.

An unaspected planet, however, has an all-or-nothing expression, and is both a problem as well as a talent. Suddenly this gentleness may be gone and what replaces it may be a feeling of not being able to communicate anymore, and of being a fifth wheel and not a part of the group. In expressing affection, love, and friendship, the image an unaspected Venus exhibits is also changeable: from being very devoted to being closed up, in alternating bouts. Things don't go as well particularly if there is any stress. In tense situations, somebody with an unaspected Venus can often have trouble showing how much she cares about somebody else, or how concerned she is about others. This can offer a significantly distorted picture, and also bring about great inner insecurity for the person with the unaspected Venus.

Venus is the ruler of two houses in Jannette's horoscope: the 1st and the 8th. If the ruler of the Ascendant is unaspected, the person involved will often be troubled by sudden feelings of insecurity when in contact with the outside world in unforced situations. It's as if these people are suddenly overcome by a feeling along the lines of "they're being very nice to me, but they don't really mean it," or, all of a sudden there is a feeling of uneasiness so that they no longer really know how to respond in a relaxed manner. This is unfortunate for Jannette, because a Libra Ascendant and her so prominent Venus give her precisely a strong need for functioning in a socially adept and friendly fashion, without complications or tension.

The ruler of her 8th house is also unaspected. Now, the 8th house isn't the simplest house and it is an area of life in our horoscope where fundamental confrontations take place. With an unaspected ruler, I often see that these confrontations can suddenly arise in an intense and intriguing or moving way, and this is often a way that causes you to wonder why this should happen to you, of all people. I have also seen that people with an unaspected ruler regularly run a greater risk of receiving the negative projection of a group. It's as if the unaspected Ruler 8 had the kind of demeanor that comes across as particularly threatening to people who aren't coping with their own problems and so who repress a lot. It's as if someone else's Ruler 8 automatically and unintentionally makes this more palpable. If this is the case, you will see that enormous projections build up regarding the person with unaspected Ruler 8.

The ability-side of an unaspected planet, however, is not misplaced! With an unaspected Venus, you will discover, sooner or later, that you have a talent for harmonizing things, or else artistic or musical talents, or design talent in general. A lot of diplomatic skill is also part of the picture.

If the ruler of the Ascendant is at issue, there is a capacity to put yourself as well as others at ease, and this may mean that once you have discovered this ability and can live with the insecurity that occasionally arises, people will quickly feel at ease in your presence.

An unaspected ruler of the 8th house has a talent for managing power, and/or a talent for working with people, considering the 8th house gives you the capacity to get through to and find hidden problems and to "grasp" (emotionally or intuitively) what's wrong with someone else or what's needed. In the case of an unaspected Ruler 8, it is a talent that manifests itself often after a crisis or real low point.

Jannette comes from a big family (nine children) and is the youngest. She always felt like the oddball. She was a child born later in life and feels she doesn't belong with her sisters. The family was strict of faith and plenty of problems regarding family issues of faith are behind her. Jannette is now still seen as the odd one out, but is accepted. As the oddball in her birth family, she always exerted every effort to fit in anyway, if she felt it was important. She writes:

> When the importance is there, all my antennas perk up to feel around to see how I can accommodate someone else. In a (larger) group, this is an impossible task because it's impossible for you to tune in to all those people. This is why I have always felt extremely vulnerable in group processes (and still do), and so my friendly, quiet, and accommodating behavior automatically kicks in. Meanwhile, I did go my own way, but I didn't broadcast the fact. I didn't share my being different, even my family doesn't know much about me in that regard.

The question of what was expected of her was a guideline for her action if she wanted to be part of things, and then she would try very hard to meet that expectation.

Jannette's unaspected Venus regularly drove her toward adaptation and friendliness, while pushing aside her assertiveness. However, whenever she was in that frame of mind, she shortchanged other parts of herself significantly, and this is a situation with which her unconscious will sooner or later confront her. It is not unusual for this to happen when there are important temporary aspects involving Pluto and/or Ruler 8. For someone with an unaspected Ruler 8, this may well be a sudden and defining experience.

The themes of an unaspected planet itself are most clearly expressed when it is activated by progression or transit, or is itself creating aspects by progression. However, there are also other moments at which an unaspected planet can make itself heard for a certain length of time. This is notably when, by progression or transit, there are temporary tendencies in the horoscope that have affinity with the theme of the unaspected planet. In this case, Pluto has great affinity with the 8th house, ruled here by Venus. This means that at the moment that Pluto, by progression or transit, is involved with the horoscope—whether creating or receiving these aspects—it will, psychologically speaking, reveal the effect with which an unaspected ruler of the 8th house can directly interfere. An example of such a situation is what Jannette experienced from the end of 1994 on.

On December 23, it was established that she was eighteen weeks' pregnant. This means she must have become pregnant when the Sun was approaching the end of Leo, so in the neighborhood of her Pluto. Pluto's previous stationary transit had been at the beginning of March 1994, with Pluto at 28° Scorpio, squaring itself and at the same time inconjunct her Sun. A stationary transit plants a long-lasting brand on your horoscope, *longer* than the 1° orb (the active part of the transit) lasts. So, for the effect of a stationary transit of Pluto you can easily reckon six months. Thus the transit already begins about three months before the exact point, and some three months afterward still has plenty of effectiveness. For Jannette it won't have been an easy time, in itself, because an inconjunct between Pluto and the Sun is often confrontational, tense, and usually accompanied by emotions.

However, what makes this inconjunct important is that it is the harbinger of an approaching yod by transit. Uranus is crawling toward 28° Capricorn, and will also create an inconjunct with Jannette's Sun. This won't happen at the same time as the stationary Pluto in the spring, however. Uranus will follow later. So here we have a "delayed" or "stretched-out" yod (and it will reappear a few more times). The beginning of this stretched-out yod in fact is coincident with the conception of her first child, and at the moment that she hears that she is already eighteen weeks' pregnant with her second child, Pluto is located at 29° Scorpio, again inconjunct her Sun. It will be the end of December 1994 and the beginning of February 1995 that Uranus begins creating its inconjunct with Jannette's Sun in Pisces. However, Uranus in Capricorn will also form an inconjunct with Jannette's Pluto in Leo and form a true yod by aspecting the sextile between the Sun and Pluto. (See Chart 18, page 225.)

In March, we see Uranus by transit in a yod with the Sun and Pluto, as well as in opposition to Mars and squaring Neptune. Transiting Saturn will be located at 16° Pisces in the middle of March, trine Jannette's unaspected Venus. If harmonious aspects are created by progression or transit with an unaspected planet, unfortunate things can still occur, according to my experience. It's as if the unaspected planet were saying, "I am incomprehensible, so I'm also unpredictable."

Therefore, the time following the discovery of her pregnancy looks problematic, particularly the period halfway through March has to be kept in mind. Jannette writes the following about it.

The months that followed were very difficult because my little boy walked very poorly and demanded a lot of attention during the day. He had ringworm and was awfully bothered by the itch.

On February 28, 1995 the obstetrician thinks an ultrasound is necessary. The circumference of my belly did not correlate with the length of the pregnancy. There isn't any panic, though, and I'm not worried, either. On Friday March 17, the ultrasound shows something isn't right. A structural ultrasound is immediately planned. The following week it turns out that there really is something terribly wrong with the baby. We know, meanwhile, that it's a girl. A serious chromosomal defect is the cause for our child hardly being viable. It is probable that she will pass away during the pregnancy.

This is a horrible shock. The next weeks are a nightmare. Countless examinations follow. It is suggested that the pregnancy be terminated, but we won't hear of it. Elise will stay inside me as long as she's alive, because in my womb things are (still) good for her. Only should she come into the world alive would a road of suffering begin for her. However, the chance that she will survive birth is small.

These were weeks of great sorrow, but also of intense contact between Elise and me. In a miraculous way, she seems to support me. Now and then when I think of her, she answers this with a series of little kicks, even if it's in the middle of the night, and once again I can't sleep. But then things in my belly quiet down more and more. The kicks get weaker, the pauses of silence in between, much longer. During the weekend of April 8, it is quiet and when we go to see the obstetrician the following

Monday, there is no heartbeat to be detected anymore. Two days later the stillbirth spontaneously starts.

It is a beautiful birth. My husband and I are together; the obstetrician is too late because the birth only took an hour and fifteen minutes. I take hold of Elise myself when she is born, and that feeling of how she is laying there in my hands will always stay with me. It is an intimate event, the three of us there together. Elise looks so beautiful, a dark child, black hair and dark eyes. She looks very peaceful and nothing indicates that she suffered. When the obstetrician arrives, we are allowed to wash her and dress her together, using baby clothes I had knit for her shortly before. Then we lay her in the crib. Her crib.

There is nothing awful or scary about her death. It is intimate, a birth at home without doctors and without the coldness of a hospital. She is in the place where she belongs, within our family. On the evening before the funeral, Richard (my husband) and I both write a farewell letter. The next day we read these letters to the grave, even though it tore our hearts out. Despite the intensely sad occasion, it gives us a good feeling, a loving and respectful saying goodbye to our daughter. I am happy to this day that we said goodbye to her like that.

Even though there is a yod at play, plus plenty of the other aspects, we can see from Jannette's example that we are still capable of responding with full devotion and of dealing very thoroughly with such a drastic situation. As it happened, the yod hadn't played itself out though, even though it was very briefly out of orb at the time of the burial. At the end of April, however, Pluto returned in Scorpio and again started up its inconjunct with the Sun. In June, Uranus, too, after entering Aquarius for a while, would return to Capricorn and repeat the yod it created previously. So, before the birth, a yod, and not long after the birth, a double yod: the sextile between Pluto in Scorpio and Uranus in Capricorn, which forms in June, creates a yod comprising transiting Uranus-transiting Pluto-radical Sun and a yod comprising transiting Uranus-radical Sun-radical Pluto. During this month and the months to follow, this yod will fully develop. This is what Jannette writes about it.

Shortly after the burial, my husband's family reproached us for shutting them out during the weeks prior to Elise's birth by not taking them up on their requests to come by and be with us.

They got the feeling they had been consciously shut out, which was not the case in the least. It was my husband's and my conscious choice to cope with this pain together as much as possible, due to the amount of time we spent in the hospital undergoing all kinds of tests that demanded a lot of us emotionally. Then if we were home, we only wanted to be together. Of course we were in touch with family and friends by phone.

This reproach was just the tip of the iceberg representing years of irritation, unspoken frictions, and disparagement on both sides, particularly between my sister-in-law and myself. We weren't able to get along from the beginning. The reason that was latched onto, notably the death of our daughter with which Richard and I coped in our own way, overstepped all bounds for me.

Here we see what we described earlier as "the feeling of injustice" entering the picture. Jannette is still totally involved in coping with the feelings about feeling a child die inside her, being able to hold on to the child for just a moment longer, and then bringing the child to its final resting place. On receiving this news fit for

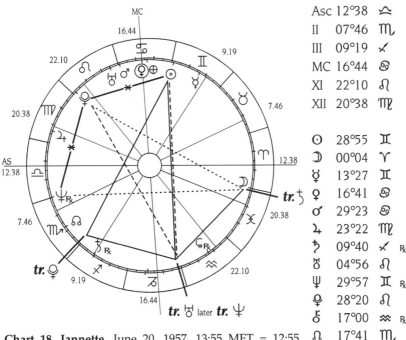

Chart 18. Jannette. June 20, 1957, 13:55 MET = 12:55 GMT. Kamperveen, Netherlands 52°31 N 005°56 E. Data from Jannette, who is also an astrologer. Placidus houses.

Job, she tried, together with her husband, to prepare as well as possible for the situation, and succeeded in giving in to it by adapting to the inevitable and still making something beautiful and moving of it. It is Jannette and Richard's experience, and only they know how hard the blow was, how hard it feels to go through a process like this. The first few weeks after the funeral they were simply involved with this on a daily basis, and a wound like that heals slowly. Besides, Jannette, like any other woman who has just given birth, is in a process of hormonal change that can make her emotionally vulnerable, on top of which she still has a very young child who needs attention. In this situation, her husband's family start blaming Richard and Jannette, but primarily Jannette, for being egotistical, and all manner of censure is flung at them. Richard and Jannette's pain is not taken into account at all, only the feeling that the family wasn't allowed to visit counted. There was no understanding of the endless hours in the hospital or the need to keep track of everything themselves. It is interpreted as an attack on the family, and when a discussion among the family takes place on July 29, 1995, Richard and Jannette are upbraided for not taking into account the family's grief.

> The discussion degenerated into an escalating argument, in which notably I was put into their bad books. They laid into me from all sides, even those with whom I thought I'd been on a good footing. They railed at Richard, too, but it was all indirectly ascribed to me, because I had supposedly caused Richard to change for the worse.
>
> . . .This is when I lost it. What are you supposed to do against so much unreasonableness and egotism while you're going through such a deep low-point in your life? This was all out of proportion, wasn't it? I was furious. And what timing. Couldn't the whole business have been put off a bit until we had gotten ourselves back on track a little? I asked myself that many times.
>
> In the years that followed, I returned more than once to this little show of lack of understanding. Still, we haven't ever really been understood, and I have to keep on living with that pain and that rage.

Her feeling of powerlessness, of injustice, of not being understood, and in particular the exceptionally callous timing on the part of the husband's family are typical of a situation in which a yod is at play. It is simply too much, and it is a situation that Jannette certainly didn't deserve. A yod, however, doesn't care about that, and on July 27, transiting Uranus and transiting Pluto were totally involved in their yods on her radical Sun and radical Pluto. Jannette now has to come to terms with the loss of a child and with the negative attitude or, rather, manipulative rejection, on the part of her in-laws. This was a situation in which she felt lonely and not understood, which was reinforced by her little boy.

> *At the same time I've got my hands full with my little boy. On an unconscious level he has picked up on everything, and is very difficult in his behavior in response to all the goings on. On a rational level I can grasp it, but can't deal with it emotionally. And because he demands all my attention, I secretly resent him for not giving me the peace and quiet to grieve. So I don't react well to him, and to lighten my load a little, he has been going to daycare one morning a week. This is becoming a big drama, so we're stopping daycare.*
>
> *Besides all the emotions, I feel very guilty toward our son. I know I'm shortchanging him a lot, but I am not strong enough to do things any other way.*

If you try to put yourself in Jannette's situation, it is more than understandable that she just had too much on her plate and simply *can't* take any more. That her little boy is experiencing the unhappy consequences is, of course, a problem, but in this combination of circumstances, she is irreproachable. She does what she can and what lies within her capacities. How differently things might have gone had she *really* received support from her husband's family! However, she keeps feeling more guilt toward her little boy, and this doesn't particularly boost her self-confidence.

Another factor, however, is also coming into play. Her little boy was born with his Pluto inconjunct his mother's Sun. It is important to realize that a child's horoscope is always a transit to the parents' horoscope. This transit "congeals" and keeps returning now and then in the person of the child. Jannette had her son during the time that Pluto was moving back and forth in an inconjunct to her Sun (which would become a yod configuration). This means that merely her son's presence, no matter how he is in any other way and whatever he may do, is already enough to make his mother wonder who she is, now, and what she wants in life. These are questions that belong to the Sun. If you have been completely discounting yourself, or are living a life that doesn't fit with you, such a child's presence will be enough to keep confronting you with your secret, repressed longings. As a mother, you may not be very aware of this; the only thing you know is that you feel more unsure and restless. You will also be overly sensitive to the child's insistence (a quality every child has) and the nonstop demanding of attention. You just happen to react more directly to this if your Sun creates a conflict with your child's Pluto. It is very understandable in this case that Jannette, who already had so much to cope with, wanted to place her little boy in daycare. His presence at home, as much as she loves him, means an extra emphasis on her inner problems, and she urgently needed to get closer to herself.

Parents who have gone through an inner process of coping can often build up a very positive and stimulating bond with the child with whom they create a Pluto aspect, and this certainly applies to the conflicting aspects as well. I have seen truly exceptional examples of this. First, a stage often has to be passed though: coping with deep-seated and deeply rooted older problems.

In fact, during this yod you see that more and more certainties, both external as well as internal, are starting to crumble away and no handle is replacing them. It is important, though, that Jannettes husband takes her side in the entire nasty situation.

In December 1995, Pluto enters Capricorn and leaves the yod. Uranus does the same in January 1996. However, this doesn't mean that there is going to be quiet on the front, because in March 1996, Neptune is making a run for a yod. Neptune will have arrived at 27° Capricorn and will create an inconjunct with Pluto. It will then come to a halt in orb; while in March 1996, Saturn will move from 25° to 29° Pisces, and from there will not only create a square to Jannette's Sun, but also an inconjunct to her Pluto. So, again a yod, this time created by the sextile between Saturn and Neptune by transit (from Pisces and Capricorn) to Jannette's Pluto in Leo.

In March 1996 there was another family talk. Jannette notices that her father-in-law is subtly ignoring her. Jannette's parents inlaw have not chosen sides until now, even though only superficial matters are talked about and the contact has no substance. Now, in March, with an activated yod, there is another family discussion which Jannette had fervently hoped would lead to improved relations, but it comes to nothing. Worse, in fact: again Jannette is the brunt of resentment in veiled terms and she gets to hear that she isn't very attentive. She senses a kind of silent agreement not to talk about any of the earlier berating, so nothing can be talked out. It also becomes obvious to her that her father-in-law is no longer neutral and has chosen the "opposing team."

In a very subtle way, as only he can do that, I am cleverly informed of how I should change my attitude. I am now getting the strong impression that I'm the big bogeyman. It makes me furious and I'd like nothing better than to break it off with the whole lot. I've still got that feeling of rage and pain, I can't turn anywhere anymore. I feel so misunderstood and I have a strong impression that this will mean a plot against me.

So she writes a letter and puts all her frustrations down on paper, but doesn't send it. That would only aggravate the situation. Again she and her husband take the initiative to talk things out, this time with Richard's brother and sister-in-law. Jannette has a significant need to be finally understood. The pain is laid out on the table and these things are discussed. However, the so fervently longed-for sympathy is absent. Jannette remains trapped in the pain of the grieving process and the rage at how things are going.

Then she becomes pregnant again. It is September 1996. In the background, there is still the fear regarding the previous pregnancy. Everything seems to go well though. Where things are not going well, however, is at Jannette's job. She is a nurse, and for a long time things have not been to her liking. This is something I also run across a lot with people who have an active yod and who are driven from inside to an entirely new life situation. They don't realize this, and so end up involved somehow in all kinds of problems at work, or their work itself becomes very difficult. This also often involves a sense of discouragement, as if both their inner as well as outer worlds were saying, "Isn't it time to look for something else?"

Jannette indeed felt discouraged. Start something new? She preferred not to think about it. In the first place was the question of what she was supposed to do, and secondly, of course, social security. Where would she end up? What would she have to do? She was in the process of finishing yoga teacher training and would like to get going with that.

Except I didn't feel I was ready for a total change. I had no idea how I would be able to teach yoga by myself and mostly preferred to work for an employer, regardless of the work. A gradual transfer from nursing to yoga, that's the way I imagined it. But I didn't get the time. I got sick and just couldn't keep going.

She tried to keep on working until her pregnancy leave, but it didn't work that way. She was burned out. So in January 1997 she reports to the company physician. Shortly after that she calls in sick. It is clear that she has to take some time off. In January 1997, however, Neptune starts creating a yod from Capricorn to her Sun and Pluto. Neptune can suck away a good deal of energy and make you draggy and absent, certainly in a conflicting aspect. As if the discouragement and the empty feeling weren't enough, Jannette starts having abdominal pain in the middle of January. It turns out to be pelvic floor strain. Walking and standing become very difficult now.

The yod will continue with pauses throughout all of 1997, and will only depart at the end of January 1998.

> *I'm getting physiotherapy, but as the pregnancy is progressing, so are the problems, so bad even that for the past months I can move around outside only in a wheelchair. At home I'm becoming very handy at doing just about everything sitting down, I roll through the apartment and into the kitchen in my office chair. Meanwhile I worry about how it's going to be when the baby's here and what if my pelvis doesn't recover (well). On top of that we live in an upstairs apartment and that doesn't make things any easier. As if that weren't enough, we have extremely loud neighbors, so the house is never quiet. We complain to the management more and more of being disturbed by the noise, particularly when our son isn't able to sleep because of all the carrying on next door.*

Jannette and her husband decide to look for another apartment, but they can't get a declaration of urgency to motivate the move. Jannette feels herself sliding away into a depression, and gets help from a therapist who works with her for the rest of the pregnancy. On May 24 her daughter is born. She is a beautiful, healthy baby and Jannette savors her joy fully during her maternity leave. Her pelvis gradually recovers. Still, she is very quickly thrown off balance, even when they suddenly do get offered a new apartment, a single-family dwelling. All the cleaning and straightening of the house looms up like an unassailable mountain. However, they get a lot of help and gradually Jannette emerges from her depression. They move September 1, 1997. After some time Jannette starts seeing what a fine house it is, even though she knows she doesn't want to live there for the rest of her life.

Then my maternity leave will be over, and what then? I know for sure that I have to call it quits at my old job, and at the same time that decision fills me with fear. How are things supposed to go from here? I have completed my yoga instructor training and want to do something with that in the future. Still, at this stage, I think it's much too early to make a definite choice. This uncertainty and my overall feeling of instability don't help. Through work I'm getting career counseling. From the tests I've taken, nothing has come up with which I can do anything.

Again, typical of Neptune in a yod with the Sun. Uncertainty, not daring to choose, and a general feeling of instability are all symptoms that are associated with this yod. Even career counseling results in nothing. Neptune has extra significance here as far as work and career are concerned because Neptune is the ruler of the 6th house in Jannette's natal chart!

Still, I see that people with a yod or an unaspected planet in their horoscope do a variety of things in their lives that all of a sudden, unexpectedly come together and shape into a new direction in life. So, too, for Jannette.

Only when I complete another, external career counseling course, a number of things become clear. All the training and courses I have done in the past fifteen years as a hobby, turn out to be so important that I have to draw my work from this. All the research results point in that direction.

However, when this conclusion is out on the table, the yod with Neptune is still active. Adversity comes knocking again: the choice is hampered because her husband is having a hard time finding work. Could they live off of Jannette's fledgling yoga studio? What about their material security and care for the family? Jannette feels guilty about this and feels she isn't a good mother. Through confrontations with her still very demanding son, she comes face-to-face with her long-repressed impatience, her rage, and her feeling of powerlessness. These confrontations have cranked up her feelings of guilt again and another downward spiral is likely.

Jannette seeks help to get a little push in the right direction. She has a very good idea of what the trouble is and what's wrong, but somehow, after all those years filled with emotions, she can't find the switch to turn. She is tired and feels little zest for life. She isn't really getting any pleasure out of things anymore. She asks for an appointment and brings her dreams along. It is January 1998. Jannette writes:

> *From dream interpretations it is becoming clear to me which direction life is "pushing" me in. The messages are clear: make more time for myself, don't hide behind responsibilities like being a mother. And as far as my family frustrations are concerned: don't expect understanding anymore, also don't be accommodating any longer, and just stay close to myself in any contact with my husband's family. Keep asking myself the question: "Why am I doing this?" so as to keep my actions and choices clear. Actually the message is: "Become independent and accept yourself." My little boy also confronts me with that part of myself that includes going your own way, regardless of whether those around you approve or not. I understand that if I pay attention to that part of myself, let it be there, that I also won't have such an extreme reaction to his behavior.*

Jannette is going to see what her unaspected Venus has been up to and how she now will need to give her anger, as well as her assertiveness and independence, a place. What gives her the most trouble in her little boy's behavior is precisely his independence, his disobedience, and his willfulness. He ignores everything, and nothing helps get him on another track. Jannette understands very clearly that her little boy is displaying behavior that is her shadow, and a portion of her intense feelings toward him are able to disappear when she manages to give her own shadow a place. Her previous attitude, when she was little, comes up in discussion. Her forever feeling around for "what's expected of me" lies in sharp contrast to her little boy's behavior. He shows her another side of herself: his Pluto is in conflict with her Sun, as we determined before.

Jannette picks up well on the message and tackles it with positive motivation. Only the sorrow over her stillborn baby still comes into play. Why did that have to happen? What role did this child play in her life? These are the questions that preoccupy Jannette.

I know from experience that it doesn't help to look for a rational answer to this question. There may be philosophies of life that provide clarification, but if they don't appeal to you, you remain empty-handed. Something that works very immediately is active imagination, a way of getting in touch with your unconscious using C. G. Jung's method. I suggest that Jannette make another appointment to try to bring her in touch with her inner images of Elise. Jannette agrees, and is also aware that this will elicit many emotions.

I ask Jannette to relax, close her eyes, and to visualize Elise in a way that Jannette finds pleasing. Jannette immediately receives images.

It's her birth. She came very quickly. She is warm and soft. She was dead, but I didn't feel that. I picked her up myself. She is dark and her eyes are open. She is very peaceful. Nothing indicated she had suffered.

Now she is lying in the cradle. It is a very pretty cradle, with embroidery.

Inside me, she was always alert, a strong little girl.

*She is coming toward me. She is big and little, the image alternates, first big, then suddenly little again. She wants to take me somewhere. I give her my hand and we walk. She takes me along. It's so good. . . . [*Jannette starts silently weeping.*]*

It's so good to walk hand in hand with her.

*She always led me. Now she's doing that again. She shows me a landscape. Flowers, mayflowers. Far and wide. I don't know, maybe she can't talk, she keeps making gestures as if she were inviting me. [*Jannette is quiet for a moment.*]*

The visualization goes further and deeply touches Jannette, but is too personal to put down on paper.

We talk about her visualization afterward. The images are Jannette's and she is the only one who can estimate their value. However, associations with those images and feelings can sometimes have a clarifying effect. Jannette herself is reminded of her unaspected Venus in Cancer.

I can imagine that she wants to teach me that: inner strength and love.

Then she continues:

The landscape had flowers that looked like violets, a gorgeous color. Elise was holding my left hand. She motioned invitingly. She invited me to take part in the landscape. . . .

I ask her for an association with mayflowers.

My childhood. When I was a little girl. There were fields full of flowers at that time of year. Until I was 8, I was on the farm, it was a really nice time.

I was often in those fields by myself, just in a little place somewhere. I have fond memories of that. I fantasized and never felt alone. I felt good toward myself. I was never bored and often played by myself. I had a big fantasy world. A very rich world.

It was particularly later on that I had more of a problem with the outside world. As the youngest girl to have to compete against the adults. To have to know you're accepted. In reality, there was a lot missing, although I had the rest in my rich inner fantasy world.

That inner world, that wealth that fed me in my childhood, I lost. It's on a very back burner. This also includes my creativity. I used to do all kinds of things: sang, danced, painted, art school, but I'm not doing anything with these things. It does eat at me. Now I have a family, I don't even have time for piano lessons, for instance. . . ."

And then suddenly it all becomes clear to Jannette. Elise took her by the hand without saying anything and brought her back to those fields filled with mayflowers. Elise showed Jannette that in order to be able to live, she needs to go back to who she was and how she felt in her earliest years, up until she was 8. Jannette writes about this later.

Elise brought me back to a world filled with inner wealth that was still there, but that I had bit by bit neglected more and more. I found it so moving that she handed this to me, it made me very happy. I also know now that I can feed myself by spending time and paying attention to this inner world. It also dovetails perfectly with being a professional in yoga, where the gaze is also turned inward.

Later I drew the field of mayflowers and the drawing has a place in my work space, or yoga studio. Mayflowers have now gained a special meaning. This spring I picked flowers and dried them.

Jannette had no need of a follow-up appointment. She was able to give Elise's life and death a place in her life. Her grief began to make way for reconciliation and a sense of meaning behind the entire event, without denying the pain. Elise's death finally brought her to a dying of her own overly adaptive and self-denying behavior, and the feeling of strength that Elise made her feel in her belly gave Jannette the strength to take into account her own choices and talents more. The process of Elise dying meant the birth pangs of the real Jannette.

This process that Jannette went through lasted as long as yods were being formed by transit. At the end of January 1998, the last contraction was over and her imagination came back to her. Everything started falling into place and answers and solutions began to present themselves. Jannette closes her letter with:

> *The time that followed was not immediately free of worry. To this day I still worry about how I'm going to be able to pay my way by myself. The financially limited situation and caring for my family I still think is hard. But something is starting to get going this way at any rate. In the meantime, I teach yoga classes and feel supported by the visualization experience to expand on that.*
>
> *I'm even going to teach yoga at my old workplace to employees and clients, something for which I "fought" for a long time, and which is now finally getting off the ground. For me, this is a victory, after months of negotiation.*
>
> *I have also started to learn obstetric yoga. The experience I went through has contributed to the connection I feel to the whole theme of pregnancy and birth, and I hope to be able to give it a form in this way. I am also granting myself the opportunity by participating in this training to be able to cope with the grief and give it a place.*
>
> *For the rest, I have a lot of other plans that who knows might take shape when the time is ripe. I am able to be future-oriented again, since to my feeling it has been merely survival for a long time.*
>
> *All in all I look back on this period of time, which has until now maybe been the blackest in my life, and even though I'm still in the process of scrambling back on my feet, I can already say that this low-point is leading me somewhere. I'm simply sure of it.*

Jannette's unaspected Ruler 8 brought her intensely close to the theme of Life and Death. The low-point lasted as long as the yods by transit were active. After going through a yod, people are never the same, and you'll see them start leading a different life in many respects. If they pick up on things well, this life will be much more appropriate for who they are than their life before that time. Jannette was able to access her old strength and left her old job. She did return, but now as an independent woman with her own vision and contribution to make, to help them, through yoga. Jannette dared to start taking on risks, making choices for herself, and is again looking forward to what the future may bring. And, as I see so many times: the problem and the low-point often lead to the cultivation of the talent or ability. Jannette is now taking obstetric yoga. I'm convinced that she has an exceptional ability to work with even the most difficult pregnancies.

CHAPTER FOURTEEN

Yods and a Duet
in C. G. Jung's Childhood

Jung was born into a family of preachers and doctors: on his mother's side there were six preachers, and in addition his father, plus two of his father's brothers, were also preachers. His grandfather, in his day, had been a very well-known and highly esteemed and progressive doctor, who was also the president of the University of Basel in Switzerland. This doctor had the local general hospital enlarged and founded a residence for those with mental disabilities.

Jung has a yod comprised of Pluto in Taurus, Mars in Capricorn, and Jupiter in Libra, plus a duet between the Sun and Neptune. Five of the ten planets in his horoscope are directly involved in themes that have been at play for generations. In his adult life, it would be religious issues (Jupiter and Neptune), his career as a doctor (Jupiter), and delving into of the dynamics of the psyche (Pluto) that would not only preoccupy him the most, but would drive him in an entirely personal direction, which made him famous in the end. Nothing was sure for him, and his life—as we may expect from a yod and a duet—was completely ruled by his seeking.

From early childhood on, Jung heard many conversations about religious topics, sermons, and theological discussions that utterly fascinated and aggravated him at the same time. He sensed the mental constructions, his father's problems, and the unreality of the way religion was experienced. With Jupiter in a yod and an unaspected Neptune, the two sides of religion are placed at the forefront: Jupiter concerns primarily vision, teachings, and studies, whereas Neptune much more concerns the unarticulated actuality and experience of the religion. With Neptune, the lines are blurred and the actual experiencing of oneness comes to the forefront.

In his book *Memories, Dreams, Reflections,* Jung presents anecdotes, feelings, and experiences that illustrate his yod and duet beautifully. I will recall a couple to clarify the dynamics of his yod and duet. (See Chart 19, page 238.)

The three outer planets—Uranus, Neptune, and Pluto—may bring us into contact with another reality, beyond the customary three-dimensional world in which we live, and which is so familiar to us. Each of these three planets does this in a different way.

Neptune is strongly connected with the transcendental and experiencing oneness in diversity, so that existing delineations can no longer be taken for granted. With Neptune we enter the world of dreams, a world filled with symbols and mysteries. The delineations of time and space are relative for Neptune as well, which is the reason why this planet is always brought into connection with clairvoyance and extrasensory perception. However, blurring these delineations may also bring to the surface general human themes, hidden away deep down in our psyches, and mix collective psychic material with personal feelings and experiences. Neptune keeps the awareness of other dimensions alive inside us, and offers a sensitivity to the mythological and religious, and for everything that has to do with inner images: from fantasy to dream, from fairy tale to vision. It is the effect of our inner nature to which Neptune lends plastic form, while it also makes us sensitive to the living reality of external nature.

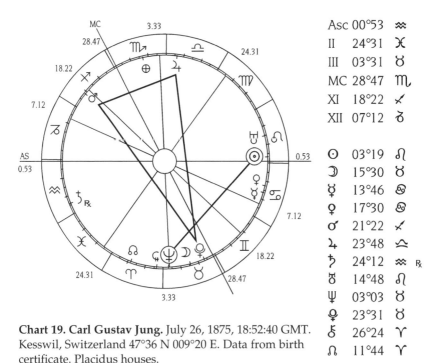

Chart 19. Carl Gustav Jung. July 26, 1875, 18:52:40 GMT. Kesswil, Switzerland 47°36 N 009°20 E. Data from birth certificate. Placidus houses.

Jung gives a number of clear examples of this from his child-hood years. From when he was 7 until he was 9 he liked to play with fire in and around a stone wall. Stretching down from this wall was a hill in which a stone was imbedded. This stone stuck up above the ground and Jung experienced this as *his* stone. When he was alone he often went there to sit, and then in his head a mental game arose according to a particular pattern which began by deter-mining that he was sitting on this stone and that he was on top, and the stone beneath him. However, according to him, the stone was also able to think "I" and to think something along the lines of, "I'm lying here, on this hill, and you are sitting on me." This inev-itably led to the question, "Am I the one who is sitting on this stone, or am I the stone on which *he* is sitting?" A question that kept confusing Jung and made him doubt and made him uncer-tain, but a remarkable magnetic force radiated from this thought game and it fascinated him. Jung was able to sit for hours on the stone "under the spell of the riddle it gave me," as he put it.

The relationship between the psyche and matter would al-ways intrigue Jung, and his experience with the stone reveals how a deeper philosophical question, that doesn't at all fit with a boy of that age according to customary standards, can pop up as a col-lective theme and turn into an actual, personal experience. The blurring of the delineations between Jung and the stone, and the confusion regarding his identity, form a nice example of the duet between the Sun and Neptune.

Another example of the blurring of the delineations between time and space is Jung's story about the "little man and the stone in the pen box." In olden days, there was a little wrapped up god, a Telesphorus Euemerion, sometimes beside Aesculapius' staff in renditions, who is reading aloud from a scroll. Telesphorus was a spirit who protected convalescents, and belongs to the domain of the god Aesculapius. Telesphorus was often depicted enveloped in a cape with a hood, the clothing of those who were newly con-valescent. Jung discovered the existence of this mythological fig-ure only when he had already been an adult for a long time, and the same thing goes for his discovering the role "magical stones" play, as he describes it in his *Alchemical Studies* (Collected Works, No. 13). In § 128, he reveals how the image of the stone is associat-ed with the image of the divine. In earliest Greek alchemy we find the stone as a symbol of the divine, and in older times we also en-counter the stone as the birth place of the gods. The idea of the "birthstone" we also find in very diverse peoples throughout time, and this is what Jung calls the *churinga*, birthstone to the Australian aborigines. These are boulders or oblong stones that are carved and decorated and used as ritual objects. These stones are believed to be "child-stones" and it is believed the souls of children live in these special stones. By rubbing the stone, the soul was supposed to pass over into the womb. The original peoples of Australia and Melanesia believe that these *churingas* came forth from their totem forebear, and that they are relics of their forebear's body and activities, and so, full of *mana*. The stones are sacred and are kept in special places.

The idea of magical stones we find everywhere else in the world, including the West, and Jung refers to digs in his day in the vicinity of Basel and also in the canton of Solothurn, where boulders were found that were wrapped in birch bark. Magical stones were used to heal, to seal an oath, and so on, and we find many traditions from which to conclude that stones were considered to be animated.

All of this was totally unknown to Jung when he was 10, but unconsciously these old themes must have continued on in him. He describes having a yellow pen box with a little lock, at that age, with a ruler in it. In the end of the ruler he cut out a small man, about two and a half inches long, wearing a coat, top hat, and shiny shoes. He colored it black with ink, cut it off his ruler, and placed it in his pen box, where he had made a little bed. With a piece of wool fabric, he made a little cape for the little man. Jung had an oblong, dark rhinestone that he painted with water color in a way that created a division between the upper half and the lower half. He placed this stone with the little man and that was *his* stone. Jung experienced all of this as a big secret and brought the little man to a forbidden place in the attic of their house (the prohibition concerned the rotten boards, so the spot was pretty dangerous to stand on). He knew for certain that nobody would discover his secret there.

The whole ritual had a healing effect on him. Until then he had felt incredibly divided and insecure, and placing this box in the attic on the beam supporting the roof gave him a feeling of safety, and his feeling of being split made way for more calm. And occasionally, when he was having a hard time, for whatever reason, he would think of his secret little man in the attic and he would be able to cope again. Now and then he would go to the attic and take up with him little pieces of paper he had covered with a kind of secret writing, and these were both letters with what Jung wanted to say to the little man, as well as the little man's "library." Jung later could not recall what he wrote the little man. The whole process gave him a new feeling of certainty, and looking back on this time, Jung writes that this was the most essential thing in the first part of his youth and of the greatest importance. In his youth he felt something like "the secret" and longed to fathom it. He sees making the little man as the first, still unconscious, childish attempt to find a form for the secret.

Jung later recognizes the little man as Telesphorus, the god who protected convalescents. Jung's health in his younger years was not fantastic, but the burden Jung shouldered during the time he made the little man was the awareness of the great big world and society, in which he felt very insecure. He experienced it as a direct threat and didn't know how to deal with it. After the ritual with the little man, things improved considerably, just as if Telesphorus had entered the scene at the moment that Jung's psyche was ready for a changing attitude. Telesphorus was also the symbolic expression of the healing process of that psychic wound. The way Telesphorus was dressed largely agreed with what in olden days had been the custom, without young Carl having even the slightest clue about this. Evidently something deep and archaic in his unconscious managed to break through, which in the old days had to do with healing, to set into operation a healing process for this 10-year-old as well!

The stone also has a big role to play in this. When he later writes *The Psychology of the Unconscious*, he encounters in the literature he is researching from different angles the idea of the "spirit-stone." He understands that this is the stone he gave his little man, a magic stone full of "power," like the aborigines' *churingas*. He then also understands the urge to hide it away in an inaccessible spot; we find the same thing all over the world regarding these magical stones. Jung writes the following about this.

Along with this recollection there came to me, for the first time, the conviction that there are archaic psychic components which have entered the individual psyche without any direct line of tradition. My father's library—which I examined only very much later—contained not a single book which might have transmitted such information. Moreover, my father demonstrably knew nothing about these things.[1]

---

[1] C. G. Jung, *Memories, Dreams, Reflections*, Aniela Jaffé, editor, Richard and Clara Winston, trans. (New York: Pantheon, 1961), p. 23.

Although Jung does not point this out himself in his book, we already see in this 10-year-old's secret and healing ritual "the finger of God" at work: this concerns Telesphorus, the god protecting the healing process—and Jung later becomes a doctor and a psychiatrist! The spirit-stone is divided into two halves: a top and a bottom. Jung's life work is about the integration of our top and bottom: the consciousness and the unconscious. In this ritual, Jung's destiny commenced and the story fits very well into the possibilities of Jupiter in a yod and Neptune in a duet.

The planet Pluto brings us into contact with the darker sides of life, with taboos and the unarticulated, with the depths and also with the intensity of experience and the renewal of the personality, once the confrontation with the darker world has commenced. Pluto in a yod is a seeker of what is hidden and this can run from antiquity and archeology (literally digging up) to psychiatry (figuratively digging up). Jung was interested in both. However, at an early age he is already involved with the troublesome sides of Pluto. He experiences dreams and images that get him into serious inner trouble, such as the dream about a giant phallus on a throne where, in the dream, he hears his mother say that it's the people eater. He is 3 years old when he has this dream, and the dream makes a deep impression on him and preoccupied him for years. He didn't dare talk about it, though. When he has been a doctor for some time, he recognizes the image as a ritual phallus, and has the impression that the phallus in his dream refers to some subterranean deity about whom no one speaks. That a child of 3 in a very devout family has a dream about a dark power and a penis is a harbinger of Jung's sensitivity to the shadow of his surroundings, and a harbinger of his search for "what lies behind the visible," which throughout his life inevitably causes him to keep stumbling on taboos that he has to bring to light, but which won't pass away without confrontations.

When he was 12, another taboo image impressed itself on Jung, just like that, on a nice summer day when he was walking to school. He was enjoying the sun that was shining on the glaze of the tile roof of the cathedral, and he was grateful for the beauty that God had provided, when he felt a very sinister image working its way up. For days he fought the "breakthrough" of this image, because he felt it would be a sacrilege, and he would not be able to reconcile it with his conscience. He fretted and racked his brains about why God was forcing this image on him of all people, and finally he sensed that God had created both good as well as evil. God created Adam and Eve and considering Adam and

Eve sinned against God, and God also created the serpent, it could only be that God had also created the possibility of committing a sin—these are the thoughts running around inside 12-year-old Carl's head. He feels he must maintain the courage to experience that which is impressing itself on him and he also thinks that if he's holding the right end of the stick, God will shed His grace and enlightenment on him. In itself this is a remarkable inner struggle for a 12-year-old who is trying to work his way through an adult theological problem with all the biblical knowledge that he has at that moment.

He then surrenders to the image he feels is working its way up and "sees" the cathedral with the blue heavens behind it, and suddenly out from under the throne of the heavens a huge heap of excrement lands on the roof of the cathedral and the church is destroyed by it.

Jung experiences a feeling of "indescribable release" now the image has come out, and he later writes that it gave him a feeling of mystical revelation. At the same time, though, he knew from that moment on, in his deepest being, that there was a power that was greater than himself and which he experienced as God. This was a power at whose mercy he was. He also writes about this later. It was at that time when he became aware that something can be expected of humans that may be contrary to religious tradition, and precisely by going along with this, one experiences a form of grace. For Jung, however, it announced a complicated time. He was implicitly aware that the divine encompasses *more* than the church taught and more than his father taught him, in particular. He had had a deeply emotional experience and missed this in all the sermons and discussions about theological issues. He had been confronted through his unconscious by a problematic image: a combination of a taboo (excrement) and something sacred (the image of the divine). This is an image that is far too comprehensive for a young child. Still he had to manage to come to terms with it. Here again we see a forerunner of his later life.

The way in which Jung is involved his entire life with religious themes is not always appreciated by the customary clerical schools. There is a great deal of criticism of his psychic treatment of *The Book of Job* and Jung loses many good contacts because of it. At the end of his life he is disappointed with the fact that he received so much resistance to themes he was working out. In fact, though, Jung's work kept touching on the synthesis of the taboo and the religious, whereby a deeper insight into psychic dynamics becomes possible. Only after his death do we see more and more recognition of these insights that Jung had.

The more religious, philosophical problems are associated with Jupiter in the yod and Pluto merely intensifies them, it being also the planet that elicits precisely the dark side and the realm of the taboo. Jung's yod reveals itself around this theme when he is 12 and this has major consequences. This is the beginning of his alienation from his father, because he feels he has experienced something that his father has not known, and he feels that his father doesn't catch on, or can't comprehend a number of things. This brings him into a kind of isolation, a feeling that is so familiar for a yod configuration. On the other hand, this experience made him serious and reflective, and he writes literally, "It casts a shadow over my life."

Jung does not mention a date, only that it is the summer of 1887 when he is walking to school. There is a big chance that it was June/July, considering summer vacation is a time of no school. If we look at the locations of the planets in these two months in 1887, we see a couple of remarkable transits. Saturn moves in June from 20° Cancer to 27° Cancer in July and during this time creates an inconjunct with Mars (part of Jung's yod), and a sextile with Pluto (another point of Jung's yod), thus forming the temporary yod Saturn (Cancer)-Mars (Sagittarius)-Pluto (Taurus). It is the learning process of pain (Saturn) that now insures a confrontation, causing him to become more serious and reflective, likewise Saturnian traits! Saturn by transit also forms a square with the third participant in Jung's radical yod, namely Jupiter. Saturn is, however, also the ruler of the 12th house, the house of inner images, visions, and symbols, and the house that brings us into contact with the deeper layers of the psyche.

Along with this, the planet Neptune is moving at this time from 28°00 Taurus to 29°40 Taurus and creates an opposition with his MC. Neptune is part of his radical duet and can thereby have extreme effects if it is temporarily active. Ruler 12 (Saturn) and the Neptune duet together bring a deep and archetypal experience that has to do with a problem that far exceeds a 12-year-old's capacity to comprehend. At the same time it is a precursor of situations with which Jung will be involved later in his life.

Jung fearfully keeps this experience a secret and doesn't feel very good about it. From the way he was raised and the way in which he tried to live, he felt this to be a shameful experience and thought he was despicable. He had the feeling he had come into contact with something evil, bad, or sinister and even though he tried to fish around carefully among other people, he received no indication that others also had this kind of thing happen to them.

As a result I had the feeling that I was either outlawed or elect, accursed or blessed, he writes, and further, my entire youth can be understood in terms of this secret. It induced in me an almost unendurable loneliness. My one great achievement during these years was that I resisted the temptation to talk about it with anyone. Thus the pattern of my relationship to the world was already prefigured: today as at that time my aptitude for relations with the world was what it still is now: now, too, I am solitary, because I know things and must hint at things that other people do not know, and usually do not even want to know.[2]

A very clear description of the yod and duet feeling!

As a result of this experience, and all his fretting and brooding, Jung starts looking at religion differently and also seriously begins to doubt what his father has said. Now, both a yod as well as a duet, by themselves, will already elicit doubts, over and over, and in addition Jupiter and Neptune embody preeminently religious doubts. Jung *searched* and wanted to go deeper; he found his father's stories boring and hollow, for the stories were told without any actual inner experience accompanying them. When he is a little older, he gets into more discussions with his father. However, he keeps running into a wall. He begins to see that his father is wrestling with his faith and with theology, and that his father doesn't understand a number of things. In order to avoid being confronted by that insecurity, Jung's father stated with increasing emphasis that one simply has to "believe," and this happens to be precisely something that a yod can't do. Jung is disappointed when he finally concludes that theology has alienated him from his father, and writes that he is shocked to see to what extent his father has become caught in the spell of the church and its theological thought, and thus incapable of experiencing the divine directly and internally. Jung can do nothing but establish himself as an independent thinker (among others, Pluto as Ruler 9 in the 3rd house in the yod with Jupiter), but does not reject faith, not even as a result of this experience. He feels himself to be a Christian all his life, but then in his own unique way.

Jung keeps on searching and digging, and in his experience of the religious, another factor also comes into play. He describes how he always experienced a split in himself and that he feels two personalities inside, which he calls Number One and Number Two. This, moreover, has nothing to do with a personality disorder; Jung

---

[2] *Memories, Dreams, Reflections*, pp. 41–42.

was aware of these two "currents" in himself and was able to give them a place in his life. He describes Number One as the son of his parents who went to school, was attentive, diligent, decent, and neat, but a bit less intelligent. Number Two was not only adult but old, even. Jung describes him as skeptical and mistrustful and far away from the normal world. Number Two represented more nature and the earth, the sun, the moon, and the seasons, living creation, and particularly also the night, dreams, and everything that "God" brought about directly inside him. (He himself places the word God in quotation marks in his description of number Two.) Number One is the schoolboy from 1890, but Number Two was involved with an area that was like a temple, where everyone who enters is changed. The way in which Jung describes Number Two can really be summarized as the awareness of a cosmic unity, an awareness of utter wonder in which you forget yourself.

He recounts that the exchange between Number One and Number Two came into play all through his life and has nothing to do with a "split personality" in the common medical meaning. Something like this takes place in every human, he asserts, and he points out that since time immemorial it has been the religions that have spoken to the Number Two of a person, thus the inner person. In Jung's life, Number Two played the most important role.

> *All my writings may be considered tasks imposed from within; their source was a fateful compulsion. . . . I permitted the spirit that moved me to speak out.*[3]

That this Number Two played such a prominent role in Jung's life is easily imaginable. With the ruler of the 10th house in the yod and the Sun in a duet, a constant doubt in one's own manifestation and identity will play in the background. In addition, the way in which Jung describes Number Two fits well with Jupiter in the yod and Neptune in the duet. It is the being situated in the yod and the duet that make this side so palpable and inevitable. In fact, with a yod and a duet it is impossible to push these feelings into the background because they will keep insisting with intensity, and not always at moments that suit the consciousness. However, it is also precisely this tension that Jung made so extraordinarily creative on the level of depth psychology, religion, and symbolism. It was, however, always accompanied by doubt and having to feel around, and Jung was even afraid for a short time that he would go insane.

---

[3] *Memories, Dreams, Reflections*, p. 222.

Jung's yod and duet can also be considered in the light of house rulers. We already saw that Ruler 10 and Ruler 9 are in his yod (Pluto), but also Co-Ruler 2 (Mars) and Ruler 11 (Jupiter). Neptune is Ruler 2 and the Sun, Ruler 7. So houses 2, 7, 9, 10, and 11 are also directly involved with yod experiences or duet experiences. I would like to go into a couple of these.

The 2nd house has to do with the literal experience of solid matter and the first thing we experience on Earth after birth as "solid matter" is our own body. I have seen from time to time that the way we experience and see our body and how we deal with it have to do with the 2nd house. Problems concerning the 2nd house are often accompanied by physical themes in childhood, particularly during the mythical phase. Jung has both the ruler as well as the co-ruler of the 2nd house in a duet and in a yod, respectively, and he did indeed have difficult physical experiences, such as general eczema, which in his book he sees in the light of the marital problems of his parents, to which it was a possible reaction. His Co-Ruler 2 in a yod with Pluto may present either a physical experience (I have often seen eczema with Pluto connections), but Pluto also enables a reaction to psychic problems. Jung also had attacks of pseudo-croup with bouts of strangling. The theme of imminent suffocation I have seen more than once with Neptune. It is remarkable at those moments Jung also saw a bright circular vision above himself that calmed him during these attacks—likewise Neptune.

With Ruler 9 in a yod, you will always be studying different things from what your instructors expect you to and the things you have to do, you'll forget about, or they will play a secondary role at best. Children with Ruler 9 in a yod are often also very obstinate and willful, and at the same time, they can be enormously inquisitive regarding nontraditional domains. With Jung, this was also the case. As a child, he studied issues that didn't fit with his age, and once he wrote an essay about a subject that was close to his heart and profound in nature. He had done his best on it and was consequently accused by his teacher of having copied it from somewhere. Since he usually didn't try as hard as he could with normal topics, they thought he was stupid and superficial. Misconceptions and misplaced accusations, and these were never put right.

Jung always felt different from others and during his school years experienced the world as a threat. Being different meant isolation and he wanted to stand out as little as possible, so as to be seen as "different" as little as possible, which caused him to try to be mediocre at school and not to excel (and he succeeded). As far as friends were concerned, his sympathy went particularly to boys of modest backgrounds and often also toward the retarded, although with this group of friends he couldn't satisfy any of his intellectual needs. This brings us to his 11th house, considering Ruler 11 is in his yod. Jung wrote of these childhood friendships that they gave him the advantage of appearing innocent, and these friends didn't notice anything strange about him, a boy who continued to wrestle internally with defining experiences, such as the dream and the little man in the pen box, etc. He had slowly gotten the idea that what he called his "peculiarity" meant that he must possess revolting traits, but just wasn't aware of them, causing him to repel friends and teachers—a yod with Ruler 11 (friends) and Ruler 9 (teachers)! Later in his life, this view balances out, and in the end Jung has a loyal circle of friends and many like-minded people around him.

Whenever Jung describes his childhood years, you keep encountering how much he is seeking an identity, on the one hand, and how bad he sees himself as being, on the other. He wrestled with a strong sense of self-rejection, with feelings of guilt, and the idea that he was perverted. He suffered a lot from feelings of inferiority, and all these things are associated with the Sun in a duet. A duet Sun (or an unaspected Sun) needs more time than usual to arrive at self-assurance, and also runs much more risk of being tossed back and forth between feelings of inferiority and self-rejection, on the one hand, and exaggerated self-conscious behavior, on the other. Both sides were not unfamiliar to Jung.

Jung's life is characterized by a repeated contact with the unconventional, the uncommon, and the unusual, whether it was the spiritism with which he experimented when he was a student, or the alchemy he apprehended psychologically. Also characteristic of yods and duets is that things always happen differently than expected—as they did after Jung's father passed away. There is no money for Jung to continue college, and pressure is placed on him to find some office job or other. Jung doesn't do this; he can borrow money to keep on studying, although this makes him go into debt. He would have preferred to specialize in surgery, but that takes too long, so he looks for a job as an assistant at a clinic. Due to his obstinate character, he was not popular with his instructors, so he harbored no hopes of an opportunity to go to the university. Maybe somewhere in a small local hospital, and then just work hard. Then there is a change at the university. A man arrives who is able to get along with Jung and who finally invites him to go with him to Munich as his assistant. Better than this seemed impossible, and Jung would be relieved of all his troubles. However, exactly at that moment he has to take his psychiatry exam, a field on which the medical world looked down (and the seminars he had taken until that time on the subject were hardly inspiring). When Jung starts studying Kraft-Ebbing's textbook at the very last minute, he starts having intense heart palpitations and feels extremely excited. In a flash it becomes clear to him that psychiatry could be the only goal in his life, and that only in psychiatry both of Jung's areas of interest, the biological as well as the spiritual side, could merge. Nobody understood why he thanked the man for the assistantship and chose instead a very lowly regarded field.

Once again we see that "side" or sideline to which yods and unaspected planets drive us and toward which Jung was driven. However, with that very yod he became the founder of one of the most important schools in that concentration!

On December 10, 1900 he started as an assistant, this time in psychiatry, in the Burghölzli Clinic. What he experiences and sees there provides the foundation for much of his later work. Neptune by transit is inconjunct his MC and is activating the world of the unconscious. This time it isn't his inner images that press on him, but he has to find a way in the strangest images and behaviors of psychiatric patients. On the morning of December 10, 1900, when he steps into the clinic, Jupiter is located at 21° Sagittarius. This is exactly over his Mars, one of the points of his radical yod.

We have kept mentioning that yods and unaspected planets are connected to themes that have already been at play for generations. Jung described this literally. He felt a remarkable solidarity with his forebears and had the strong feeling that he was under the influence of things or questions that remained unfinished or were left unanswered by his parents, grandparents, and other forebears.

> *It often seems as if there were an impersonal karma within a family, which is passed on from parents to children. It has always seemed to me that I had to answer questions which fate had posed my forefathers, and which had not yet been answered, or as if I had to complete, or perhaps continue, things which remained previous ages left unfinished.*[4]

Jung herewith wonders whether these questions have a more personal or a more general, collective nature, but has the impression that the latter is at issue. It is true that as long as you don't recognize a general pattern, it will arise as a personal problem. Think of

---

[4] *Memories, Dreams, Reflections*, p. 233.

his experiences as a child: his dream and his vision. These were personal battles and secrets for him, but finally they turned out to be archetypal images that embraced issues that are collective in nature.

A little further on he writes that both our soul as well as our body is built up of components that were all already present in our string of forebears.

> *The "newness" in the individual psyche is an endlessly varied recombination of age-old components.*[5]

He says this and then warns us not to be too forcefully swept along by the rapids called progress, considering it is swiftly tearing us away from our roots. And he also says:

> *The less we understand of what our fathers and forefathers sought, the less we understand ourselves, and thus we help with all our might to rob the individual of his roots and guiding insticts.*[6] . . .

For Jung, lack of instinct meant having lost touch with nature inside us and our capacity to survive.

> *If our impressions are too distinct, we are held to the hour and minute of the present and have no way of knowing how our ancestral psyches listen to and understand the present—in other words: how our unconscious is responding to it.*[7]

Jung does not mean anything spiritualist here, but is pointing out that in the unconscious of each person's complex-structure, the psychic inheritance of each person's ancestry also comes into play. This has become part of himself and expresses itself in images, feelings, dreams, and projections. You can only become happy if you come to terms with these messages from your unconscious. These are your own complexes, although the voice of the many generations preceding you speaks through them.

Jung also always had the feeling of living in another time, a century earlier, and experienced powerful emotions when he saw an 18th-century carriage for the first time as a young child.

---

[5] *Memories, Dreams, Reflections*, p. 235.
[6] *Memories, Dreams, Reflections*, p. 236.
[7] *Memories, Dreams, Reflections*, p. 237.

He felt it was *his* coach and that something had been stolen from him. In a rendering of one of his ancestors, he saw shoes with big buckles and he recognized them as well. In fact, he *felt* them on his feet. These kinds of experiences confused him a great deal and he was unable to talk about them with anybody, either. The image of the blurring of the boundaries of time thus plays a role already early on.

Due to the frankness with which Jung discusses his inner experiences and actualities, we can get a good image of the insecurities and the themes with which he was wrestling. Each and every one is recognizable as a part of the yod and the duet. And a feeling of being different, a feeling of isolation, and not being understood always keeps coming into play in the whole. At the same time, over the years Jung's life work has helped a great number of people, so that many of us may reach into the deeper regions of the psyche, depths he so diligently sought and simply *had* to unlock.

CHAPTER FIFTEEN

Case Files of Yods and Unaspected Planets

Helen—Temporary Yods in Transit

Helen is a sculptor and makes beautiful bronze sculptures in a home studio. When we look at aspects within signs, Helen has both an unaspected Venus as well as an unaspected Sun, so that Venus is Ruler 10 and the Sun, Ruler 1. In other words, neither of the rulers of the angles of the horoscope create a major aspect with other planets. This makes Helen extra-sensitive to the question of who she is and how she expresses herself.

The Sun and Venus also represent a great talent and a great artist. Inner doubt about her own achievements cannot take away from the fact that that unaspected Venus can provide great strength of expression regarding forms, colors, and proportions. Helen makes bronze sculptures—bronze and copper are metals belonging to Venus.

Now there is definitely more in a horoscope that has to do with art; also, for instance, the 12th house can give an artist the capacity to displace into things and the power to express something subtle, something which Helen also certainly has with her Moon-Pluto conjunction in the 12th.

With Venus and Ruler 10 unintegrated, Helen will have to manage to find her own way in the area of presenting her art objects, she has to find her own concept, apart from what others say and what she was taught. At the same time, her unaspected Venus may come to expression in an intimate relationship, and the way in which she finds a form for it, the role that it plays in her life, the way she feels in it, may be subject to instinctive extremes, insecurity, and searching, and at the same time be a very important factor. An unaspected Sun can contribute to feelings of ambiguity regarding her own strength and identity, and likewise ambiguity about what she wants and longs for regarding what is "masculine" and the men in her life.

In 1987 and 1988, a number of important transits in which these unaspected planets were involved were active in her horoscope, as well as transits that formed temporary yods. (See Chart 20, page 255.) To list a few:

Transiting Uranus trine Venus: Jan. 1987–June/July 1987–Oct./Nov. 1987 from Sagittarius;

Transiting Uranus square the Sun: Feb./May 1987, stationary!–Nov./Dec. 1987–and stationary one more time just within a 1° orb in Sept. 1988;

Transiting Saturn: Stationary at 14° Sagittarius, forming a yod with the MC, Jupiter July/Sept. 1987;

Transiting Saturn trine Venus: Dec. 1987;

Transiting Saturn square the Sun: Jan. 1988, July/Aug./Sept. 1988 (stationary!);

Transiting Saturn inconjunct the Moon and itself: Jan. 1989;

Transiting Saturn sextile Mercury: Feb. 1989;

Transiting Neptune inconjunct Pluto: From Capricorn, Jan. 1987, July through Nov. 1987 stationary;

Transiting Neptune inconjunct the Moon and inconjunct Saturn: Feb. through June 1987, stationary! But in the process of forming a yod (Neptune-Moon-Saturn) and a bit more stretched out also the yod (Neptune-Moon-Mercury) Dec. 1987, Aug. through Nov. 1988 stationary;

Transiting Neptune sextile Mercury: March/April/May 1988 (stationary), Jan. 1989;

Transiting Pluto square the Moon: Stationary July 1987 (May/Sept. 1987).

So we can see that Uranus in transit will aspect both Venus as well as the Sun various times in 1987, and the Sun has a stationary transit twice in the Spring of 1987 and in the Fall of 1988. This is palpable, uprooting, tense, and incomprehensible.

During the Summer of 1987, a stationary transit of Saturn is added in, creating a temporary yod with her MC and Jupiter, and in the Summer of 1988 is located again in a stationary square with her Sun.

Neptune starts creating a yod from Capricorn with her Moon-Pluto and with her Saturn by now, again forming inconjuncts with them, and also creates a sextile with Mercury so that another temporary yod is formed. Here, too, stationary at various times, so emphatic transits.

And for a "normal" aspect, Pluto by transit forms an equally difficult square with the Moon.

As of 1989, Saturn and Uranus take over from Neptune in forming yods with her Moon and Saturn, and her Moon and Mercury, but these two planets do it a little faster than Neptune did in 1987–1988. Neptune is the ruler of her 8th house and may therefore draw up typical fears and tensions, and make for typical confrontations.

Helen described these two years as an extremely confusing and undermining time.

> *Everything was "stuck" and there was a problem of having to choose between moving and not moving, but all kinds of things were tied into this: work, relationship, and domestic circumstances.*

At that time, Helen has a partner with whom she does not live, but whom she loves. He is also an artist. She doesn't know how she is supposed to find a form for this relationship and what she wants, exactly. She finds him to be a fine companion, but is afraid

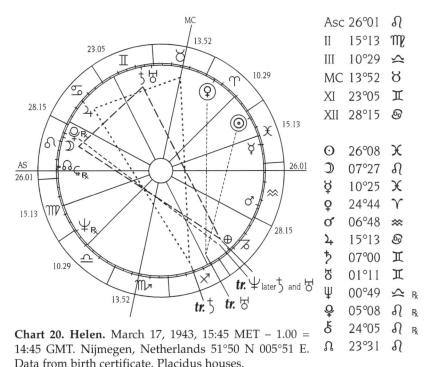

Asc	26°01	♌
II	15°13	♍
III	10°29	♎
MC	13°52	♉
XI	23°05	♊
XII	28°15	♋

☉	26°08	♓	
☽	07°27	♌	
☿	10°25	♓	
♀	24°44	♈	
♂	06°48	♒	
♃	15°13	♋	
♄	07°00	♊	
♅	01°11	♊	
♆	00°49	♎	℞
♇	05°08	♌	℞
⚷	24°05	♌	℞
☊	23°31	♌	

Chart 20. Helen. March 17, 1943, 15:45 MET – 1.00 = 14:45 GMT. Nijmegen, Netherlands 51°50 N 005°51 E. Data from birth certificate. Placidus houses.

of his possessive behavior and *knows* that after a while if he's around her too much, she won't be able to take it. So it remains a relationship at a distance. She feels that if he's around too much, she will lose her hard-fought identity.

During the first months that the Neptune yod and the transits of Uranus start coming into play, a series of events piled up, one after the other, giving Helen the feeling that her legs were totally cut out from under her. The BKR, the institution subsidizing sculptors and offering them security regarding income, ceased to exist, and all artists suddenly had to figure out how they could continue to earn their livelihood. The rent became too high for her and from all sides she was told that a move would be inevitable. Now, she had a small studio beside her apartment, but it was still makeshift and she would have preferred a smaller apartment with a big studio, but that ideal seemed more out of reach than ever.

All of a sudden, however, fate seemed to smile on her and she was offered a studio-apartment and everybody envied her. She signed the lease, but wasn't really glad about it. The apartment was located very close to where her friend and partner lived, and moving there would inevitably mean that she would come too much within his reach, and thus the threat of being spun into his possessive behavior, which would cause her to lose her independence and freedom of movement. So there she was, feeling like she was standing with her back to the wall. If she took that very desirable studio-apartment it would mean relationship and identity problems: an unaspected Sun and Venus to the hilt, and the effect of a yod. Nor did she have any assurance of an income anymore (the Venus theme plus Ruler 2, Mercury, in a temporary yod), so that she had to work very hard, had to start doing her own public relations work, manage to find new ways of deriving an income from being an artist, and so forth. Venus is Ruler 3 (PR) and Ruler 10: finding a form for new manifestations of yourself.

She had signed the lease for the new studio-apartment, but didn't dare live there. Result: she stayed in her old house and had to figure out a way to raise the rent money for two apartments instead of one at a time when she no longer had any assurance of an income! So work doubly hard.

"I postponed the move for the reason that I first had to finish an assignment," she writes, but that was an escape because she dreaded the consequences regarding her relationship and her work.

From that moment on I was living in a kind of crisis-like, panicky stage, saw myself balancing at the edge of the abyss, and no matter which step I took, one step or the other, I would somehow tumble in. Sometimes I was literally unable to stand on my legs anymore from the stress. What I finally did was to put off the move—I was paying two rents—and kept working as well as I could, until all my financial reserves were gone. I did find friends who temporarily took over the rent of the new place because they needed a place to stay.

During the summer all kinds of extra activities arose, such as designing a theme sculpture, which I brought to the attention of friends and family in a mailing; this was an unusual way for me to sell my work; it didn't start happening right away, but people wrote in on a sculpture and paid in installments spread out over a year (exactly as long as Neptune's yod effect!). This, however, did save me from "ruin."

As far as the possible move I was panicking about: every time the yod became exact, I would be confronted by the subject. The various housing organizations pressured me, saying I simply had to make a decision, or that I had to cut the knot myself. But I absolutely couldn't, and at the mere thought of it, already became paralyzed. Both at the thought of not moving, as well as of moving, I foresaw for my work (which assures me a means of survival) a huge catastrophe, or rather: total liquidation! A kind of "death sentence" I didn't know what to attribute to.

The entire duration of the yod's effect I can describe as a time during which there wasn't a moment's peace, there was always a kind of Damocles' sword hanging above my head and a lot of the time it took all my energy just to keep going. This took complete control of me and no matter how I tried to line things up, there seemed to be no possible solution. Even friends whom I had analyze the problem couldn't advise me. One would say, "Do it," and another would say, "Don't do it." So what I finally did was to stay put and not budge, but keep on working!

Seen objectively, it was a very unusual situation. I had maneuvered myself into this stalemate in such a way that there were two apartments in my name—which wasn't at all allowed in Amsterdam, but which was still the case—and that I had already given notice several months before, but because of a remarkable coincidence was still living there: the apartment management company still hadn't found any new tenants for my apartment. And when they did show up, that same day I sent an urgent letter to cancel my termination!

What we see in Helen's case is a combination of circumstances that are impossible for her and she simply sees no way out. In all respects she is under pressure and even friends can't help her. It has regularly come to my attention that if you have temporary yod configurations, even an astrologer can't give you good advice. As if it were temporarily not *allowed*. With Helen everything was mixed up and there wasn't a handle anywhere: in her work, in her relationship, and in her living situation, she felt restlessness, uneasiness, ambiguity, tension, and no way out.

We see here that there is a problematic situation concerning financial security because the government rescinded a national ruling for artists, but most of the tension Helen experienced stemmed from her insecurity, her inner conflict, her fears, and her restlessness. Thus yods and unaspected planets don't always have to do with severe external circumstances, and feeling that your back is against the wall can also come from inside. However, the experience is not any less significant because of it!

> *Only when the transit of Neptune went out of orb after a year-and-a-half, almost literally to the day, the problem solved itself. Not moving was the best thing, as turned out from the angle of declination. The apartment wouldn't be suitable for my work and would not turn out to be a material improvement. This was correct, and within a day I wrote all the letters to the organizations involved to annul the entire situation.*

> *My conclusion is that, in spite of the fact that my present apartment still has its problems, I'm not sorry about the way things ended up. Continuing with my work turned out positively in the end. New relationships came out of it, one of whom is now playing a very important role in my emotional life. This relationship, which suddenly presented itself during a transit of Neptune trine my MC, brought about a huge consciousness-raising process and confronted me in many respects with the claustrophobia of my yod period.*

What Helen momentarily overlooked was that during this transit, Uranus was creating a yod with her Moon-Pluto on one side, and Saturn on the other, and that the man who suddenly entered her life has a Moon-Pluto conjunction.

In rereading this chapter, Helen added a section at this point, which I have included word for word.

The frustrations and tensions resulting from these yod transits sowed the seed for a consciousness-raising process; since new relationships/loves (8th house) were at play, this confronted me almost obsessively with the awareness of male-female relationships. The relationship with my current partner came out of this. One striking thing about it is that, except for also having a Moon-Pluto conjunction in Leo in his natal chart, he has a yod with the Sun at its apex, to Uranus and his Ascendant. On top of this, his MC is right over my Sun in Pisces in the 8th house.

The relationship derived from work, because of the assignment "Gorilla with Young" in particular (almost a metaphor for the Moon-Pluto theme!).

In loves and relationships during that time, the "stalemate" concept was a central one. They were impossible, inaccessible, and obsessive, and didn't take shape. I had a strongly conflicting feeling of having to undertake action, but and yet not being actually able to, of wanting something for which the time is evidently not yet ripe, and not being able to see where it's all leading.

For me, this yod time seems like a time during which an extreme emphasis was placed on situations of self-preservation. Neptune in transit (my Ruler 8!) formed the apex to my radical Moon-Pluto conjunction in the 12th and my Saturn-Uranus conjunction in the 10th. It worked as a focal point to this effect—enervating and undermining. I had existential fears and constantly the image of the abyss in front of my eyes. It also meant—in spite of the attention of my friend(s)—that I felt very alone. The worst thing, I thought, was that my indecisiveness was criticized and that I couldn't make it clear to those around me that any decision whatsoever would be my downfall!

Lastly I would like to mention that it is my experience that the tension of the yod can be so great that you have to do something about it somehow, but that it's best to "lock horns" through activities in which the conflict comes into play less (in my case, work) and direct your energy at the problem that indicates the stalemate. Energy has to be able to flow, after all, in a positive sense. The tension only gets worse if the energy is fixated on the stalemate and is sucked up by it. Powerlessness is the predominant feeling associated with all this.

Helen's example clearly reveals the emotional tension that can crop up during a yod, plus the feeling of a stalemate. I have often seen that during a yod a dream seems to come true, but is accompanied by impossible circumstances, such as the longed-for studio-apartment which would have had significant consequences for her relationship. Finally her activities during this yod term led her to getting acquainted with a new man in her life, so that the relationship with her previous friend changed. They remained close friends, but he was no longer her partner. After the yod with Neptune was over, most of the inner chaos was also gone, and considering Neptune is also Ruler 8, inner confrontations would come into play as well. As Helen puts it: things resolve themselves as soon as the yod is past. The answer was lying there all the time, but it was invisible.

Jacqueline—From External Structure to Internal Flows

"I feel like I'm forever on my way and looking for something, but never get there," writes Jacqueline who has three yods in her horoscope:

- Sun sextile the Moon, both inconjunct Saturn;
- Mars sextile the Moon, both inconjunct Saturn;
- Neptune sextile Pluto, both inconjunct Mercury.

Saturn in Virgo and Moon in Aquarius are only two arc minutes out of orb, but Saturn is the old ruler of the sign of Aquarius (the nocturnal dispositor), which can give it more "stretch" in its orb. Jacqueline's life is a classic example of the effect of this yod, which also argues for making the orb a little wider than 3° (see chapter 1) and maybe extending it to a maximum of 3.5°. (Jacqueline's father also has a yod that includes the Sun, Moon, and Saturn, and her mother has the Moon opposite Saturn.) She writes me:

> It is hard for me to organize my time: no matter what plans I make for my days and weeks, it always works out differently. Usually it comes down to my doing everything except the one thing I had just decided to do. . . . With other people it seems as if their problems are caused from the outside, externally; for me it's always from the inside. The minute I think: I know what, it starts turning and churning again inside and gets uneasy, as if I fall through my own cracks from time to time, so that I feel unhappy again and have to go off looking once more. . . . It is difficult to find inner peace.

Jacqueline's words make crystal clear the kind of feeling yods give and is something I have also heard from time to time from clients and students. (See Chart 21, page 263.)

When the Sun and the Moon are involved in a yod, you can be sure that the feeling it gives you will be perceivable in every fiber of your being. Both luminaries of the horoscope are playing a central role in each other's lives. When the center of your field of consciousness, from which you derive your identity (the Sun), *and* the attitude by which you try to feel good again (the Moon) are involved in a yod, you will go through a stage in which you have a hard time finding peace and quiet. Questions along the lines of, "Who am I and what do I want?" will make for a lot of inner unrest and insecurity. By nature you call on the Moon in the horoscope so as to find calm again, both through activities that belong to the sign and house in which the Moon is located, and by the planets with which the Moon is connected. However, if the Moon is located in a yod, it doesn't offer the longed-for peace and not only shares in the unrest, but will even reinforce it.

Saturn is the apex of the yod and can be felt in two extremes. The fearful side of Saturn may lead to a tendency to stick to the rules as strictly as possible, and to fulfill patterns of expectation. Marching in step, and dutifully doing what has to be done as a kind of a handle in the world is a way of shaping this. However, because Saturn is located in a yod, it is at the same time very difficult to do this in such a way that you yourself have a feeling that you are doing it well. It is your own feeling in this, though, because with this Saturn you can come across as being very stable and calm to others who are not aware of the kinds of storms that are raging inside you. Saturn in a yod, however, can involve the risk that you try to withdraw onto safe terrain from a deep-seated fear of yourself and of life, and as a reaction hold on compulsively to particular forms and rituals, or opinions, or actions, for instance. This all comes from a need for external security because you don't experience it inside. Saturn in the yod may also work out very positively though.

The powerful side of Saturn in the yod is that you can really be steady as a rock for others, but not really be aware of this yourself. You may offer others a backbone, while to your own feeling, you're in search of your own! Always being doubtful about the format your life has, or the way in which you have to find a concrete format for activities, prevents you from seeing that you can respond very flexibly to situations in your own way. You will often find yourself in places where an old form has to disappear and a new form has to be built up. In companies this is often the department that (still) has no structure, or an existing structure that no longer suffices, and you become unnoticeably and unintentionally a part of the process of change.

With a Saturn-yod which from fear seeks certainty, I quite see that the person involved often looks for (and finds) a job that seems absolutely clear-cut: fixed actions, fixed tasks, few exceptions, and a lot of routine. However, a couple of problems arise here. A job like this can be so stifling that the person reaches his or her wits' end and may even get all kinds of psychosomatic symptoms. Or else the certainty as such is there, but there is a boss or supervisor who is absolutely impossible to work with, and who keeps pulling you out of your work or routine. Or else you enter a company at a moment that there are all kinds of unexpected problems that have to be faced because of unforeseen social changes, for instance, legal measures, economic changes, etc. People who can let the yod "flow" may play a very important role in processes of renewal and make an important contribution to the creation of a new form and a new certainty, often without being aware of it. If you give negative meaning to Saturn, you will become totally stressed out.

Saturn is also part of a yod with the Moon and Mars as its base. This connects your own patterns of activities and the need to stand up for yourself with Saturn. From a Sun in conjunction with Mars in Aries you would expect someone who forges ahead, is conquering life swiftly and with a glowing enthusiasm. Saturn in a yod with all this may suppress, push aside, complicate, or somehow stand in the way of this fiery, zesty dynamic for longer periods of time, in connection with the overall yod tendency, of course. However, this resourceful dynamic can never disappear and will sooner or later break through. Tension headaches is one of the possible expressions of this.

Saturn is also the ruler of the 12th house, so that the yod's apex is Ruler 12. This immediately brings us to the level of the capacity to actualize and empathize. This can be expressed in very diverse ways: from social to voluntary work in the third world, from hospital to shelter for drug addicts, from the monastic life to music. Neptune in her other yod (the one with Neptune, Pluto, and Mercury) underlines this again. Ruler 12 in a yod may present a deep longing for "another world" and for deeper spiritual involvement, and an almost wistful need to feel one with humanity and nature. The risk is getting lost in those feelings, and being apt to escape with regard to developing a daily life. Also in connection with Neptune and Pluto in this other yod, the ability may involve a special kind of actualizing capacity by which you can help others really well because you intuitively grasp what's at issue. Moreover, it's very possible that it may involve what we call paranormal abilities, in whatever form. This is something I often see when the Neptune-Pluto sextile participates in a yod, and it becomes even more probable if Ruler 12 is also participating, as is the case with Jacqueline. In her letter, Jacqueline goes on to write:

> *I feel safe in a structured environment, in a monastery or at a retreat, or some place like that, for instance, although I know that it isn't the purpose of this life to withdraw (again) into that kind of environment.*

Here we see one side of Saturn as well as the Saturnian need for clarity and structure in the form of a structured environment, while Ruler 12 trickles down in the examples she gives: a monastery or a place of retreat! However, Saturn also comes to the table as the "duty-planet" in a yod.

> *In daily life I am just about "addicted to perfection": everything always has to be neat and organized before I'm allowed and able to relax, and even then it is hard to let go of the constant input from outside.*

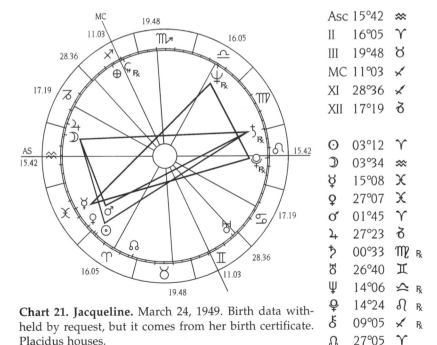

Asc	15°42 ♒
II	16°05 ♈
III	19°48 ♉
MC	11°03 ♐
XI	28°36 ♐
XII	17°19 ♉
☉	03°12 ♈
☽	03°34 ♒
☿	15°08 ♓
♀	27°07 ♓
♂	01°45 ♈
♃	27°23 ♉
♄	00°33 ♍ ℞
♅	26°40 ♊
♆	14°06 ♎ ℞
♇	14°24 ♌ ℞
⚷	09°05 ♐ ℞
☊	27°05 ♈

Chart 21. Jacqueline. March 24, 1949. Birth data withheld by request, but it comes from her birth certificate. Placidus houses.

At the time she has trouble with this, as we already saw, because when it comes down to lending meaning to this issue, everything always goes differently from the way she had planned or foreseen. She has an urge to arrange and work dutifully, so she is constantly "under fire" finding form for this.

A yod often indicates that the second half of life will look very different from the first half of life. This may be internal, through an entirely different view of and attitude toward life, but it can also be external as well—*very* different activities than before, whereby the changes are striking. Jacqueline is also a perfect example of this. In 1996, Jacqueline wrote:

> *Very slowly the 12th house is becoming more and more important in my life: after high school I started law school and worked as a social ombudsman, and as an attorney, and at the university, and after that I even studied tax law.*

Again we encounter the social (Neptune, 12th house) *and* Saturn (taxes). However, changes entered the picture.

> *Since 1989/1990 this started to change. Transiting Saturn entered the 12th house at that time, too. During the course of 1989 I had my horoscope read (for a second time) and had an aura reading. From January 1990 on, I started courses in intuitive development, was being treated by a medical intuitive, and started hypnotherapy. Since 1991 (after Saturn had passed over my Moon in 12) I have been in regression therapy and biodynamic massage, and in mid-1991 I also started studying astrology. After this: singing, yoga, swimming, meditation, healing drawing, mandala drawing, dream symbols and the interpretation of dreams, a little numerology and tarot, chakra treatments, healing workshops (based on earth energy), workshops in holotropic breathing, voice-work therapy, dance, reflexology and polarity massage. My interest was caught more and more by everything that comes into play on the level of energy inside and among people. At the moment that all these shifts were taking place, I wasn't able to oversee their scope. It all happened without my understanding what was wrong (more or less driven by headaches and a desire to find a solution to them). When I look back, my life took a different course at that time: just as if a new life were slowly beginning. I started following my inner feeling and needs more instead of answering to external expectations and demands.*

She also writes something very appropriate for all these yods:

> *During the period of time between 1986 and 1995, I had six dif-*
> *ferent people give me an astrological reading so as to get some*
> *kind of clarity in, and a handle on, all the changes that in retro-*
> *spect were, but at the time weren't at all clear to me.*

Jacqueline points out that all these changes and courses took place during the transit of Saturn through her 12th house, which is very appropriate for the subjects she started to study and the healing methods she underwent. The reason was constant headaches, which could be the tension headaches of Saturn or the churning of Arian energy. However, if we take a quick look at other transits that came into play at this time, we will see a remarkable yod emphasis.

January 1989: Transiting Uranus enters Capricorn: repeatedly squaring Jacqueline's Mars and Sun. Uranus first trines her Saturn, two legs of one of Jacqueline's yods.

February 1989: Transiting Pluto stationary at 15°11 Scorpio, squaring its own place and trining radical Mercury—two points of her radical yod.

March 1989: Transiting Saturn stationary at 13°56 Capricorn. This is within 1° orb inconjunct natal Pluto, which is already in a yod inconjunct Mercury. Transiting Saturn is thus in the process of forming a new yod. It is also square natal Neptune, another leg of Jacqueline's natal yod.

June/July 1989: Uranus by transit squares Jacqueline's Sun.

July/October 1989: Uranus by transit (stationary at 1°20 Capricorn) squares Jacqueline's Mars and trines Saturn.

August 1989: Jupiter enters Cancer and forms a temporary yod by creating a sextile with Saturn and an inconjunct with the Moon (that are already legs of an existing yod).

October/November 1989: Transiting Pluto is once again square its own place in the radix, and trine Mercury. Transiting Uranus squares the Sun.

December 1989: Transiting Saturn returns to Capricorn at 13°, 14°, and 15°. It creates a square with radical Neptune, a sextile with radical Mercury, and an inconjunct with radical Pluto. The existing yod is activated (Neptune-Pluto-Mercury) and a new yod has been added by transit: Saturn-Mercury-Pluto.

April 1990: Transiting Neptune becomes stationary at 14°34 Capricorn, the place where Saturn had only shortly before made for a yod, and creates a yod that is intensely palpable for months by creating a sextile with Mercury and an inconjunct with Pluto. Neptune is also square its own place. The stationary transit lends extra weight and emphasis. At the end of 1990 and the beginning of 1991, this aspect reappears!

March 1991: Transiting Saturn conjuncts her radical Moon and activates the Sun-Moon-Saturn and the Mars-Moon-Saturn yods.

April 1991: A stationary Uranus in transit at 13°49 Capricorn: again the formation of a new yod with natal Pluto, which is already creating an inconjunct with natal Mercury.

September 1991: Stationary Neptune at 13°59 Capricorn, again another yod with Pluto and Mercury.

December 1991/January 1992: Uranus creates a yod from Capricorn with Pluto and Mercury and repeats this once more in September 1992, when it is stationary at 14°03 Capricorn.

As the last pangs of stationary Uranus in Jacqueline's yod ebb away, we also see that Saturn by transit definitely passes over her Ascendant. It has already moved back and forth over it, but leaves the 12th house. What Jacqueline saw as the developing of the transit of Saturn through her 12th house, turned out, in fact, only to be the top of the iceberg. For, during this time her birth yods were activated by important transits, some of which were stationary, and thus significant, transits. Saturn, Uranus, Neptune, and Pluto in transit all contributed. Without being aware of it at that moment, Jacqueline turned onto a new road in her life by listening to what appealed to her and by giving in to her inner calling. It crossed her path naturally with the activated yods, which helped her on her way without it being clear as to where that road would lead. Jacqueline is now involved with areas that are *totally* different form those of working at a university and with tax law! She is now much more involved with whatever gives her a feeling of fulfillment in life.

This is a nice example of a complete turnaround and an example that reveals that a yod may include exceptional talents, even though you still aren't aware of them. If somebody had told Jacqueline when she was 18 what she was going to do later in life, she would have been incredulous.

Christina

As a child I felt I was the black sheep in my family. I argued a lot with my mother and this gave me the feeling that I was poisoning the atmosphere at home. I left home at an early age.

So writes Christina who has a yod that contains the Sun, Pluto, and Neptune. The Sun is usually seen as the father, but I have experienced all too often that it also provides information about the independent and/or dominant part of the mother, and in this yod, it can refer to conflicts with anyone in a position of authority. The Sun seeks to realize itself, and to find and develop its own inner authority. For the Sun in a yod this may quite frequently lead to trouble, considering that the feeling of self-confidence is often the object of intense doubts and undermining. On top of this you are much more sensitive to conflicting assertions made by others about you. The Sun in a yod may therefore both inwardly and externally collide with people in power and the inner doubt and undermining of the self may be projected outwardly in the form of undermining others. This has nothing to do with being mean or dishonest, it is much more what we encountered earlier with yods: these people enter a work or life situation where "the theme of leadership" is the object of change, or where something has to change. People whose Sun is in a yod may be the catalysts here, intentionally or unintentionally. Christina has Pluto in her yod, which will intensify it. Somehow, in spite of possible feelings of insecurity, this will make her want to dredge things up from the bottom, and Pluto is not shy about confrontations.

However, her yod also includes Neptune, the planet that can suck up energy, and at the same time give you a need for another dimension of experience. For the rest, Neptune also happens to be the planet that can create ambiguous situations; it indicates gossip and discouragement, or it can work in some other undermining way. On the pleasant side, Neptune can provide feelings of deeper connection and great capacity for sensitivity and sympathy, which means you really need some time to allow yourself to be in touch with your feelings.

If identity (the Sun) is at issue, and Pluto and Neptune are creating a yod with that Sun, you will see extremes from incomprehensibility to adamancy, perspicuity; from yielding and apathy to displays of power. And this is exactly what Christina experienced.

At the beginning of the 80s, she did end up in a conflict situation at work, where the theme of power and authority played an important role. (See Chart 22, page 270.) About this time, she writes:

I was working at a bank then (Summer 1979) and got caught in a heated labor and power conflict. I was aware that I was the one who got the conflict rolling, not management. For the first time in my life I felt that I was somebody with power. It gave me a

*fantastic feeling at that time. I had the feeling I had a tremen-
dous amount of energy and could take on the whole world. I was
surprised at the conservative mentality inside the banking world
and my fingers were itching to break through the ennui. I raised
some hell inside the bank and I felt like I was some sort of fresh
wind that wanted to blow down the old-fashioned structure.*

*With all my questions about the hows and whys of the way
things were done, I began disturbing the peace. At first my interest was appreciated, but at a certain point my questions got
too troublesome. In addition, with my ambition, I wanted to succeed in making a career for myself and so I began to stand up for
myself. This didn't go down well and so the struggle began. Tensions escalated and open conflict arose.*

*Later I thought, looking at my horoscope, that this could hard-
ly have anything to do with an inconjunct between my Sun and
Pluto. However, the other leg, the Sun inconjunct Neptune, was
also becoming involved. I became exhausted after a number of
years of really having manned the barricades. I was fighting authorities and this finally knocked me flat out.*

*Another stumbling block at that time (possibly due to the yod)
was that my behavior fluctuated. For instance, one week I'd be
very assertive and to the point and approach higher-ups with my
critical observations and remarks. The next week I wouldn't
have much energy and feel apathetic. If my bosses then came by
to respond, I wouldn't understand what they were getting all
worked up about. I would then simply not be capable of an assertive response and thought it was great to sit around and do
nothing. Very confusing, both for myself and for them.*

*During this conflict I sought support from a union and later
from a legal advisor. The latter advised me to leave, but I didn't
want to hear anything of the sort, that struck too close to my pride.*

*The matter lasted from 1979 to 1988. In 1988, after laborious
struggle, my contract was annulled by a lower court ruling and
I ended up being unemployed.*

In October 1978, a solar eclipse occurs at one of the legs of her yod
at 8° Libra, so exactly over her Neptune. The next solar eclipse in
February 1979 occurs at 7° Pisces, on the *other* leg of her yod, exactly over her Sun. These eclipses may very well have introduced
the entire process. The leg that was not touched, namely Pluto, set
the whole into motion. The Sun and Neptune were momentarily
"eclipsed" and started to come into play later. If we look at the
transits before the beginning of this period of time, we see the following.

In May 1979, Saturn in transit stops at 7° Virgo, in opposition to Christina's Sun, which is the apex of her yod. From November 1980 to April 1981, the Jupiter-Saturn conjunction moves back and forth in the sky in an inconjunct with her Sun, sextile Neptune and conjunct Pluto, thereby activating the yod. Both planets even stop over Christina's radical Pluto, so that they provide an extra emphasis to the temporary activation of the yod. In August 1981 they come back again.

In this fight we see a lot of extremes of the yod with regard to Christina. She starts up a fight with authorities, but at the same time has ambitions of becoming an authority herself. She wants to overthrow the structure, but wants a career in that very structure. She is alternately assertive and apathetic. In short: extremes which, if you're in the middle of it all, will be just as unfathomable and troublesome for the one with the yod as (they) were (for) her higher-ups.

> *Later I understood what the deeper background of this labor conflict was. In 1987 my mother died in a car accident, and for the first time I felt I had to learn to detach, let go. Overnight I was cured of all my feminist aspirations and was in a totally different state of mind. Only then was I able to make the decision to give up my controversial position at the bank, and my discharge was arranged in no time at all.*

In July 1987, Pluto creates a trine with her Sun by stationary transit. It stops at 7° Scorpio. Being a stationary transit, it will intensify and lengthen its effect, and it is pointing out that it's time to cope, *even* in a trine! You will see time and time again that it doesn't much matter with Pluto transits (and not at all with the stationary ones) what aspect Pluto creates. As soon as it makes a connection by means of any aspect with another planet, it stimulates deeper involvement and coping, and can be confrontational as well. For Christina, Pluto is also part of a yod, however, and may therefore by transit drag along a little bit of that yod idea. Thus Christina has Pluto in stationary trine with the Sun and it's her *mother* who passes away. Moreover, Pluto made that same transit before, it was *also* stationary in February 1986. Christina was at that time still in the middle of her conflict at work. At that time, transiting Neptune (the other leg of her yod) passed over her Moon, and this may have been the initial impetus for her bouts of apathy and lack of assertiveness. Neptune created that aspect again in November and December 1986, afterward to color the entire Spring of 1987 with a stationary transit over Christina's Sun. Not only does Neptune take along the yod effect by already being in her natal yod, it is also in the process of starting to form a new yod starting that year: from Capricorn, sextile her radical Sun, and at a later stage, approaching an inconjunct with her radical Neptune. In 1987 Pluto also keeps creating aspects from Scorpio with her radical yod, so what we see is that both the trans-Saturnian planets that are in Christina's radical yod activate their own yods several times in transit in 1987, and this is the year of Christina's internal changes. Also, in 1988 these aspects repeat, and in 1989 Saturn and Uranus by transit take the place of Neptune in Capricorn and form the Saturn-Sun-Pluto and the Uranus-Sun-Pluto yods.

So, time for coping and confrontation and time to let the hidden abilities and talents of the yod surface. Time also to break through old patterns and pay attention to the new, no matter how unsure and unclear all this may initially be.

This is how I ended up in an in-depth grieving process that lasted years. Uncles, aunts, cousins, passed away. Girlfriends got cancer, and so on. I was continually in the process of learning to let go. I did nothing but cry, but it did me good.

At 14 I almost drowned and since then I've had a fear of water and of deep places. But after giving in for thirty years to that fear of water (I made wide detours around all the swimming

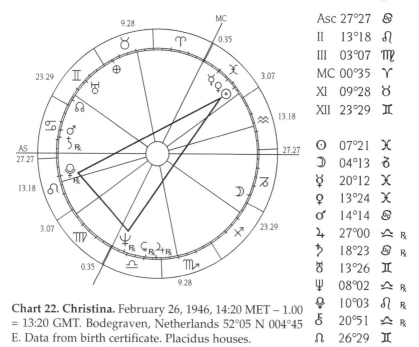

Chart 22. Christina. February 26, 1946, 14:20 MET − 1.00 = 13:20 GMT. Bodegraven, Netherlands 52°05 N 004°45 E. Data from birth certificate. Placidus houses.

pools), I decided not to be bullied by these fears anymore. A few years ago I had back trouble and was forced to do something about my physical condition. So I went to the swimming pool. Delicious, I was back in my element, water! Who knows, maybe I came close to the real intention of my Sun inconjunct Neptune: somebody with a lot of feeling for the subtle atmospheres in life. In this sense I feel I'm in a process of transformation.

Something else that preoccupied me during the first half of my life is this. I would have this earthquake dream once or twice a year. I would wake up scared and see an image of my bed over a deep rift in the earth. I would then really feel the ground shake and would lie there waiting for people to run into the streets in panic. Nothing would happen, though. Just when I started becoming uneasy about that, I would read on a dream magazine page that this kind of dream symbolizes going through major changes. After the loss of my mother (September 1987) and my work (February 1988), I also had the feeling that I was sitting in a chair whose legs were breaking off one by one, a collapsing life.

During the 26 years (1962–1988) that I was involved in the labor process, I always had the feeling there had to be something I was very good at. It wasn't coming out, I couldn't get at it. This is why I regularly switched jobs. I always felt something like, "I am working, but it doesn't fit with what I feel." These past years not having a job I've not had that feeling anymore.

Ever since taking the Jungian psychology course, I don't feel so strongly anymore about my trauma. Could my abilities be hidden away there, even? Because I now know what it is to go through pain, sorrow, and grieving, it happens that people spontaneously start talking with me about their experiences with illness and death. In a certain way I feel at home when there are issues in that borderline area between life and death. There are also my terrors, but I feel strength as well.

The feeling Christina has when she is working, namely that something isn't right, and that somewhere something as important as a talent must be hiding, I often hear from people with a yod. Their inner unrest and searching will then often be translated into frequently changing jobs or work environments, exactly what Christina did as well. Also the feeling that "won't come out" and that you "can't get at it" is very recognizable regarding yods, as we have seen several times elsewhere in this book. This doesn't mean that Christina wasn't good at the things she was doing; she might even have talent for these things, without being aware of it. However, the borderline area between life and death, for which Christina started to have increasing interest, is indeed an area with great possibilities for her: somehow independently being able (Sun) to offer assistance to people who need it (Neptune), particularly in the area of issues *concerning* problems of Life and Death (Pluto). That in doing this she is afraid, is simply part of it. Her feeling has already actually indicated a direction to her here where she has a possibility of significantly expanding.

A couple of years later she wrote me that she had entered a two-year program at the Dutch Institute for Hospice Care. "More for my own process than that I will ever pretend that I can do all that," she writes. Here again we see the insecurity and doubt of the yod, and Christina will still have to discover to what extent this theme is "written all over her"! A little further on she writes:

> *Still, I experience my process as one of individuation. For twen-ty-six years I worked in big, anonymous organizations and en-joyed the colossal. Now I'm going through a very individual process and I often have the feeling anyway that I have some-thing else to "lay down," as they say. The past nine years I have also had the feeling that I'm somebody who's fulfilling a family karma or unfinished family business. It has sometimes felt as if this concerned some age-old family burden. But I don't know the how and what of it exactly. . . ."*

Precisely the feeling a yod often gives, as we have already seen in various instances.

Now Pluto is involved in a square to her natal Sun (just before the completion of this book), and with it the yod relationship with the Sun will be repeated and the yod activated, she is in the mid-dle of a Plutonian time. Again she is closely involved with cases of death and dying, including one she experienced as being truly ex-traordinary. A girlfriend of hers also had a yod, at exactly the same place as Christina. While Christina has a yod that includes her Sun in Pisces (at 7°) inconjunct Pluto in Leo and Neptune in Libra, her friend has a yod with the Moon in Pisces at 7° incon-junct her Sun in Libra (over Christina's Neptune) and Pluto in Leo very close to Christina's Pluto. Thus overlapping yods.

> *The last year and a half we were in very exceptional contact. We helped each other. We knew about our mutual yods and that lent something special to our friendship. In the fall of 1998 my friend passed away. At the top of the bereavement card: "dying is being*

reborn." We always talked about the process of dying in this way. Her transformation to the spiritual world and my going through my changes in life here. This is how we exchanged experiences. . . ."

It is evident just from this description how naturally Christina can deal with Life and Death. Maybe this activation of her yod will be the one that gives her a last push into a new destiny. She hasn't had the earthquake dreams in a long time. . . .

"Where things are all going to end up for me, I simply don't know. That's actually pretty scary!" she writes in a recent letter.

If you know how yods work, there is but one piece of possible advice: follow the voice in your heart and take up the things that cross your path. Realize that your insecurity is greater than it needs to be, and that you are able to do a lot more than you first think. So, just take a step, in the direction of the things that appeal to you. The rest will follow of its own accord.

CHAPTER SIXTEEN

Gemma—Your Own Form within the Generational Theme

In Gemma's horoscope, Mercury is located in Aquarius sextile Venus in Aries, and both form a yod with her MC in Virgo. Considering Mercury and Venus always rule more than one house in the horoscope, a good number of houses are participating in the thematic of this yod. Mercury is Ruler 8 and Ruler 10 and Venus is Ruler 6, Ruler 7, and Ruler 11. Gemma has put a number of her feelings connected with her yod down on paper, and expresses it thus.

I experienced the latent, vague uneasiness very obviously, even as a child. I experienced that I had fallen out of unity: I realized that very painfully because I was different from the way I was expected or desired to be. I dropped "difficult" remarks. I kept having the feeling of being abandoned by my mother. I had to achieve and get confirmation as the model child. The expression and cultivation of my personality seemed to be hampered by barriers. I had the feeling that I wasn't put together right, that I can't be who I am. I experience strong emotions because of this: fear, rage, and sorrow struggle for priority. . . . I clearly had the oddball role in my family and was "the child who was different." I had and still have very different opinions, different religious ideas. Back then, I often used to think I was some kind of exchange child, from another part of the world, not Dutch, often not even Western (Asian or South American).

I felt a bond with nature and with the universe that nobody else in the family had.

My ideas about being a woman you might call progressive. In that respect, too, I didn't measure up in any way to the traditional image of women in our family: kind and gentle, "properly" married to a man of social consequence, placing the husband on a pedestal, always at work for the family like a good, self-effacing mother. My (very happy) marriage with a former RC priest created a big flap at the time. My parents had a very clear image in mind of the type of man with whom it would be best for me to marry: my husband didn't fit into that picture. In our marriage he wasn't the boss, nor was I the docile woman: the division of roles for us was based on equality and space for our own activities. This wasn't customary in my family! I kept using my last name (something my husband was totally for): this, too, was a factor that stumbled into the usual criticism.

What's more, I do not present and behave myself according to the codes that rated in our family. In my husband's family, in fact some of them call me "respectable." I have always called up contradictory reactions that often had a confusing effect on me as well.

Gemma hereby puts into words the familiar feeling with a yod configuration: the feeling of not belonging, the feeling of being different, and the like. (See Chart 23, page 278.) Her 10th house participates twice in the yod: both the MC as well as the ruler of the 10th are involved. So no wonder that Gemma places so much significance on the problem of conceptualizing externally. Gemma's family identified with the upper classes, and her parents did everything to make sure they met the external demands that were associated with their "position." In addition, they were:

. . . Catholic and they tried to practice their faith entirely by the rules as well. They were very definite, dogmatic, and conservative in this, and had a lot of trouble with anything that deviated from that.

Her mother is a Virgo with her Sun in the 12th house and Neptune at the MC, her Moon squares Saturn, and her Sun trines Saturn.

At an early age she was dealt the role of the victim and had no trouble accepting it. Her own mother was a very dominant woman and her sisters ordered her around as well, and were always at her about something. She quite often allowed herself to be maneuvered into the role of the scapegoat: she cushioned my father's bad moods, shushed family arguments, and would get all upset because uncles, aunts, acquaintances, preachers, and nuns thought her youngest daughter (me) was a strange child. She could be very depressed, but also had a sparkling and creative side to her personality. It slowly but surely disappeared, though, under the burden of her feelings of guilt and her religious fears.

Gemma's mother totally identified with opportunities for sacrifice and religious experience her horoscope offered her, although of course a Sun in the 12th and Neptune at the MC could also have produced an inspired musician. Instead she remained stuck in the role she had played from early childhood on, and continued it in her marriage.

However, Gemma's mother also has a number of very different energies in her horoscope. She has the Moon in Aries trine Mars in Leo, trine Uranus in Sagittarius, and sextile Pluto in Gemini. Pluto and Uranus are in opposition, and both are square her Sun. What a dynamic and what a love of freedom!

Only now do I understand that she was troubled by depression, because she was never able to realize a bubbling and adventurous life.

Gemma writes about this. (See Chart 24, page 279.)

Gemma's mother had to repress a considerable portion of her horoscope, thus her aptitude, in order to continue being able to shape that other portion which included sacrifice and withdrawal. Only by identifying with a higher reality, such as through faith, was she able to keep this up.

Plain tragic it was that she started seeing God more and more as a strict father who was going to pass negative judgment on her faults. Maria, she saw as an example of a woman who was always self-effacing. This notion contributed, however, to depressions arising in her psyche because she didn't live the fullness of her character.

Gemma's father had a number of very strict basic assumptions that determined his life. Foremost, you had to come from a good family, preferably with lineage and a family coat of arms. You had to be above average intellectually, get high grades at school and preferably undergo a scientific education. You also had to be musically adept, and provide proof of this by being able to play an instrument well, and lastly you had to be dogmatically Catholic. Thus achievement, honor, and respect, and with this he must also have repressed a livelier and looser part of his horoscope. (See Chart 25, page 280.)

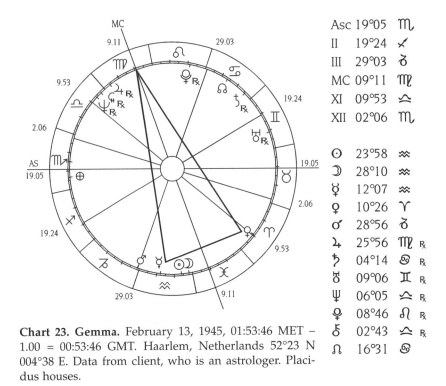

Chart 23. Gemma. February 13, 1945, 01:53:46 MET – 1.00 = 00:53:46 GMT. Haarlem, Netherlands 52°23 N 004°38 E. Data from client, who is an astrologer. Placidus houses.

Asc	19°05	♏
II	19°24	♐
III	29°03	♑
MC	09°11	♍
XI	09°53	♎
XII	02°06	♏
☉	23°58	♒
☽	28°10	♒
☿	12°07	♒
♀	10°26	♈
♂	28°56	♉
♃	25°56	♍ ℞
♄	04°14	♋ ℞
♅	09°06	♊ ℞
♆	06°05	♎ ℞
♇	08°46	♌ ℞
⚷	02°43	♎ ℞
☊	16°31	♋

Gemma's parents received these convictions from their own childhood and were not able to break through these patterns. Still, something was "rumbling" around already in the undercurrent of the family. Gemma's father's mother's (so, her grandmother's) horoscope is riddled with yod configurations. Gemma's grandmother has the following yods: (See Chart 26, page 281.)

- Pluto-Mars-Jupiter
- ASC-Pluto-Mars
- MC-Pluto-Jupiter
- Mars-Saturn-ASC

Gemma's grandmother has her Sun in the 12th, and an unaspected Neptune! She transferred her religious values to her son, Gemma's father. Gemma's father has his Sun in the 12th, and his Moon in Pisces, and so he resonated flawlessly with this. What Gemma's grandmother must, however, have repressed is a sturdy dynamic and her independence. When you see children today with connections between Mars, Jupiter, and Pluto you're looking at a substantial chunk of assertiveness and decisiveness. These are children who won't let themselves be talked into things easily, who want to fight for their own way in life, and choose their own goals and concentrations, and also they particularly want to have their own opinions. They can go far. As it happens, a well-known woman with a T-square that includes Mars, Jupiter, and Pluto is Margaret Thatcher, just to name an example. Even when these three planets are in a yod, this does not take away from the tremendous strength that is contained in this interconnection. There will only be more tension regarding it.

So Gemma's grandmother had a yod to which the themes of freedom, space, assertiveness, and a personally formed opinion were central, and her other yods emphasize this thematic even more. We know that yods arise particularly when there has already been some kind of imbalance regarding these themes for several generations. In most cases, masking things and repressing them substantially come into play. In other words: already with Gemma's grandmother it was very likely that in her birth family there was a "churning of psychic energies," as it were, regarding

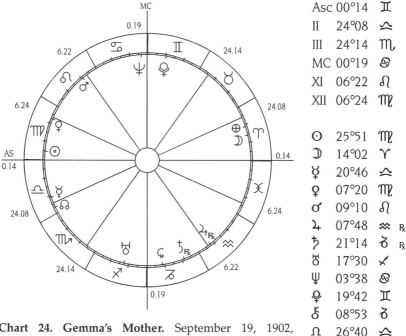

Chart 24. Gemma's Mother. September 19, 1902, 05:53:57 GMT. Etten-Leur, Netherlands 51°34 N 004°39 E. Data from birth certificate. Placidus houses.

these themes, and Gemma's grandmother might have been a turning point in this. The insecurity of the yod and the unaspected Neptune made her choose for the "religious line," however, which was continued by her son.

Gemma's father then marries a woman who, just like his mother, has her Sun in the 12th house and who reflects the unaspected Neptune of his mother in having Neptune at her MC. And just like his mother, she had a substantial dynamic in her horoscope, with much need for space and freedom, so his wife also has this firmly anchored in her horoscope. Neither of these women found a form for this dynamic in any way in daily life, however, and repressed these themes.

There is yet another factor of importance. Gemma's grandmother has her Venus in the 12th house, which (as I showed in my book on the 12th house) is often an indication that there were relational problems in the parents' marriage which were covered up by the so-called "devout lie," or where they acted as if nothing were wrong and repressed the dynamic. Or else there are artistic or artistically-oriented talents that were not allowed a chance, or the theme of femininity, enjoying beauty and the pleasant things in life was hidden away by her parents. Gemma's mother also has Venus in the 12th house!

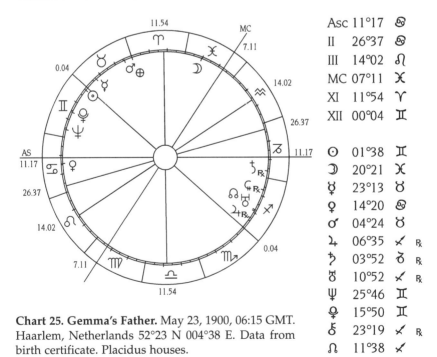

Chart 25. Gemma's Father. May 23, 1900, 06:15 GMT. Haarlem, Netherlands 52°23 N 004°38 E. Data from birth certificate. Placidus houses.

Asc	11°17	♋
II	26°37	♋
III	14°02	♌
MC	07°11	♓
XI	11°54	♈
XII	00°04	♊
☉	01°38	♊
☽	20°21	♓
☿	23°13	♉
♀	14°20	♋
♂	04°24	♉
♃	06°35	♐ ℞
♄	03°52	♍ ℞
♅	10°52	♐ ℞
♆	25°46	♊
♇	15°50	♊
⚷	23°19	♐ ℞
☊	11°38	♐

In studying whole family lines, it has been confirmed for me more than once that if a particular planet is located in the 12th house for several generations, this repression will start to come out in the family line in the form of an unaspected planet or a yod. Well, Gemma has Venus in her yod!

From the entire picture of her family that derives from the above, a couple of matters seem to step into the foreground:

- Problems regarding outward conceptualizing: The family wants to keep "up" the family name. Gemma has her MC and Ruler 10 in her yod.
- Exaggerated emphasis on intellectual achievement: Gemma has Mercury in her yod.
- Emphasis on also being something musically/artistically, on the one hand, while all pleasure, or a hearty enjoyment of life, and such, weren't appreciated: Gemma has Venus in her yod.
- Exaggerated emphasis on everything religious: This is not reflected by Gemma.
- Enormous repression of assertive and freedom-loving personality traits on the part of her paternal grandmother and her mother. We see this return in part in the rest of Gemma's horoscope,

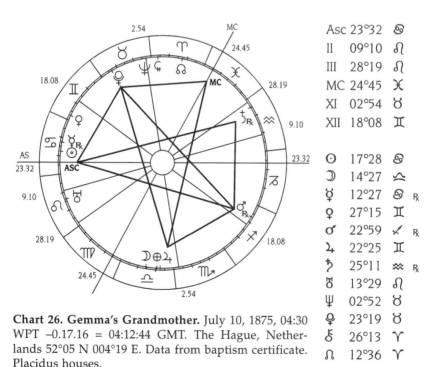

Asc	23°32	♋
II	09°10	♌
III	28°19	♌
MC	24°45	♓
XI	02°54	♉
XII	18°08	♊

☉	17°28	♋	
☽	14°27	♎	
☿	12°27	♋	℞
♀	27°15	♊	
♂	22°59	♐	℞
♃	22°25	♊	
♄	25°11	♒	℞
♅	13°29	♌	
♆	02°52	♉	
♇	23°19	♉	
⚷	26°13	♈	
☊	12°36	♈	

Chart 26. Gemma's Grandmother. July 10, 1875, 04:30 WPT –0.17.16 = 04:12:44 GMT. The Hague, Netherlands 52°05 N 004°19 E. Data from baptism certificate. Placidus houses.

like Venus in Aries sextile Uranus and trine Pluto, but strikingly enough, it comes out in the yods Gemma's daughter has. (See Chart 27, below.)

Gemma's daughter has Pluto at her MC, in a yod with Mars and Neptune, and a yod that includes the Sun, Moon, and Uranus, and if we take a little more than a 3° orb, also a yod that includes Mars, Saturn, and Neptune. The yods that Gemma's daughter has seem to reach back to the yods Gemma's grandmother had! Here are the themes regarding Mars, Pluto, Saturn, and Neptune, her grandmother's themes, and the Sun, Moon, and Uranus are also involved. In other words: Gemma seems to pick up part of the thread of the family dynamic in her yod and her daughter picks up *another* part.

I have often seen themes skip a generation and then continue to work full force for several generations. In Gemma's case, her grandmother has a yod, but it seems as if her parents momentarily remained "on the sidelines." This is only relative though, because they had a child and a grandchild with yods, and in those yods the themes that included matters they had repressed were extremely recognizable.

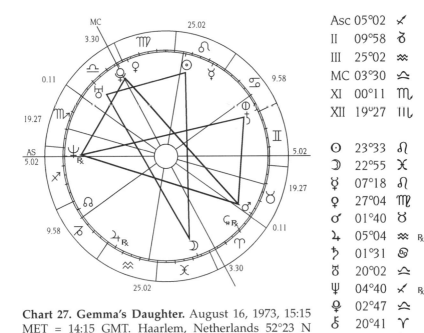

Asc	05°02	♐
II	09°58	♑
III	25°02	♒
MC	03°30	♎
XI	00°11	♏
XII	19°27	♏
☉	23°33	♌
☽	22°55	♓
☿	07°18	♌
♀	27°04	♍
♂	01°40	♉
♃	05°04	♒ R
♄	01°31	♋
♅	20°02	♎
♆	04°40	♐ R
♇	02°47	♎
⚷	20°41	♈
☊	05°12	♉

Chart 27. Gemma's Daughter. August 16, 1973, 15:15 MET = 14:15 GMT. Haarlem, Netherlands 52°23 N 004°38 E. Data from birth certificate. Placidus houses.

Back now to Gemma's situation. We see great potential that wasn't realized by her parents, nor was it realized farther back in the family line. An attitude of avoidance was assumed and that basically comes down to living a life that complies as much as possible with "what's fitting." Gemma, with her MC and the ruler of her 10th house in a yod, simply *can't* do that and is thus a life-size translation of her parents' shadow. In a way, she is acting out the parents shadow, which in turn can feel very threatening to the parents.

Her parents accepted the teachings of the church without thinking. Gemma has Mercury in a yod and that is a Mercury that will always pose uncomfortable questions and see things differently. *Also* it's confrontational for her parents. Gemma was able to learn well and was initially the apple of her father's eye. She writes:

> *He saw in me a kind of miracle child. Quickly, though, it turned out that my remarks, certainly those about religious matters, caused him discomfort. He thought me "strange" and "typical."*

In other areas Gemma also seemed to be developing into the opposite of the ideal her father had in mind.

> *I did not realize the promise of the "miracle child": I didn't become a famous soloist, or a brilliant scientist. In looks I don't represent the ideal type for the family, which is slender, blond, and aristocratic. On the contrary: I am stocky, dark, and seem to be able to enjoy the sensual side of life. I have pretty progressive ideas about the Catholic faith and moreover started getting involved with astrology and Jungian psychology. My father placed great value in the fact that both topics named were not accepted by the scientific community and he therefore rejected them. In the last year of his life, though, he was able to admit that if I saw something in them they couldn't be* complete *nonsense. But his resistance remained strong.*

It is all too evident that Gemma did cause her parents a lot of unrest with her yod mirroring their shadow and this quite often came down on her head. Her mother also had trouble with the way in which Gemma gave meaning to her life.

> *She didn't understand that I was no longer adapting to the norms that were sacred to her.*

The man whom I married was, as I mentioned, a former priest. Both my father, as well as my mother, had trouble with this. My father had the holy conviction that as a good Catholic you have to turn to what the pope and the bishops hold up for you. This conviction was undermined by me and this caused him anxiety. My mother believed that on account of this step, I would fall out of God's grace and this, too, became a source of great anxiety. In addition, she was afraid that family, friends, and acquaintances, as well as the parish, would look at her as if she were the one to blame for it. In this way she came to bear a burden she really couldn't carry, which expressed itself in deep depressions.

What we also see is the reversal in her father's attitude: if at first Gemma was the apple of his eye of whom he expected a lot, she was later quite often dealt the role of scapegoat. Extremes in approach, so characteristic for a yod! And Gemma was troubled by terrible feelings of guilt for a long time—toward her father because she realized she had disappointed him in just about every area, and toward her mother because her mother became seriously ill and in her presence it was let on now and then that all the misery Gemma had caused her no doubt had something to do with it.

One of the assignments of the yod is to gain clarity about feelings of guilt. In by far the most cases they are not justified. Nevertheless you can still have a good case of them, and they can keep you from expressing the creative side of the yod. Gemma, however, managed nicely to liberate herself from these impossible emotions and finally was really able to make peace in her heart with her mother.

Mercury in the yod is essentially interested in things other than the norm and so it isn't strange that when Gemma becomes involved with the psyche, she doesn't choose to take mainstream academic psychology, but Jungian psychology. And in the eyes of our society, astrology is of course still a "sideline."

Because I began to get involved in astrology I am regarded with some suspicion by some in my family. Fortunately there are also family members who look at it positively!

Among my friends as well, though, people have drawn the line because of my astrological activities. Among some colleagues in the music world I rate, for the same reason, as somebody who landed on a slippery slope.

It doesn't touch Gemma anymore. She wants to:

> *show herself in the social world as the woman she is,*

and:

> *absolutely according to the book as an air sign I rationalized away emotions for a good deal of my life. For this reason as well it was a direct blessing that psychological astrology crossed my path!*

Gemma's husband has plenty of inconjuncts in his horoscope and an unaspected Pluto. With that Pluto he may have to face tremendous and deeply defining changes in his life. The step to leave the priesthood and to marry was, at the time, a very big one, and as we already saw, his wife's family had considerable trouble with it. However, his marriage with Gemma is excellent. They give each other all the space they need for their own development, are able to discuss absolutely everything with each other, and after almost thirty years of marriage are still crazy about each other. They are thus living proof that you can have a very happy marriage even with yods or unaspected planets in your horoscope. I have definitely seen this in a number of cases. Every time, however, it struck me that both partners had found an attitude toward life where searching for tangible security had drifted into the background and the urge for openness, honesty, and to be allowed to find your own way and shape it, no matter what the cost, had come to the forefront. This attitude toward life also characterizes Gemma's marriage.

As I pointed out earlier, Gemma has a daughter who also has a number of yods. Even though you are working on your yod or unaspected planet, once they start appearing, they can continue for several more generations. Gemma noticed that her daughter is touchy about the aforementioned family dynamic. Fortunately, both seem capable of supporting each other and fortunately they have no trouble discussing anything. Gemma's daughter has always been given the space by her parents to be herself and she let it clearly be known that this space shaped her in a positive way.

Still, her daughter will have to make a number of choices, partially in the domains inherent to the yod she shares with her mother, but largely in other domains that reach back to her mother's grandmother, her great-grandmother. If we look at Gemma's, her grandmother's, and her daughter's zodiacal points, planets, and house rulers, we see the following similarities. (Also note Table 3 for a detailed list.)

Gemma's grandmother: ASC, MC, Mars, Jupiter, Saturn, Pluto: Rulers 5, 6, 7, and Co-Ruler 10 in yods; Neptune, Ruler 10, unaspected;

Gemma: MC, Venus, and Mercury: Rulers 6, 7, 8, 10, and 11 in a yod;

Gemma's daughter: MC, Sun, Moon, Mars, Saturn, Uranus, Neptune, and Pluto: Rulers 2, 3, 4, 8, 9, and 12 in yods.

Thus, finding your own way, your own structure, your own religiosity, and your own identity are important themes for Gemma's daughter. By showing how you can live creatively with a yod, Gemma can be a good example for her daughter.

Gemma intellectually goes her own way and every year has succeeded in becoming more the woman she wants to be, and to accept who she is. In the area of music she is able to engage herself totally: she plays the organ excellently and does it with heart and soul. For years this produced a new conflict, namely the feeling of wanting to do something with her knowledge and insights

Table 3. Gemma's family tradition.

GRANDMOTHER	GEMMA	DAUGHTER
MC AND RULER 10	MC AND RULER 10	MC
MARS	—	MARS
JUPITER	—	RULER 9
SATURN	—	SATURN
PLUTO	RULER 8	PLUTO AND RULER 8
RULER 5	—	SUN
RULER 6	RULER 6	—
RULER 7	VENUS AND RULER 7	—
NEPTUNE	—	NEPTUNE AND RULER 12
—	MERCURY	RULER 3
—	RULER 11	—
—	(VENUS)	RULER 2
—	—	URANUS
—	—	MOON/RULER 4

(Mercury), notably in the areas of astrology and psychology for which she also has talent (Mercury is Ruler 8), and also wanting to do something with music and musical expression (Venus, among others). Practicing both concentrations at the same time is hard, considering her need to *surrender* totally to her immediate involvement. And with Ruler 6 in a yod, it is pretty tricky to find the right direction right away, or if you have found it, to maintain it in proper proportion and to stay on track. Not that this doesn't ever work, it just needs some time to get going and will be accompanied by uncertainty about choices made or to be made.

For years she not only wrestled with these two focuses, but also worked on them with great pleasure—until she opted to withdraw into herself for a while and do just about no paid work in the outside world. She wanted to be on the sidelines, away from the busy outside world. She wanted to take coping with her childhood and her past a step further and to come to terms with herself on a deeper level. Her husband supported her in this, as always. So Gemma went through a significant period during which she learned to bend with life, to relax, and to let things come more as they will.

And so she discovered an important requirement to allow a yod to develop creatively, namely: go with the flow and live totally in the here and now. Enjoy what there is and be who you are. And precisely at that time Gemma received an offer she could only have dreamed about: to be the successor to a great and much loved organist at a major church—a considerable honor. She accepted the offer and the year that Uranus by transit connects with her yod, everything is arranged. This means that the field of tension regarding the choice she "had" to make regarding her work resolved itself. And as if Life were giving her family a little wink: honor and respect as the organist at a major church!

CHAPTER SEVENTEEN

Living with a Number of Yods— Esther's Experience

Esther has an advanced degree in psychology and is an astrologer. She is familiar with the interpretation of inconjuncts and yods. She has a number of yods in her own horoscope and summarized her experiences with them for one of my workshops. Her Moon is at the apex, inconjunct Pluto on the one side and inconjunct Mercury, the Sun, and Neptune on the other, so that in fact we have three yods:

- Moon, Pluto, and Mercury;
- Moon, Pluto, and the Sun;
- Moon, Pluto, and Neptune.

She writes:

One of the most characteristic expressions of these yods in my view is that no matter what happy or painful experiences I undergo, my feelings concerning them are never unequivocal. Always, no matter how angry, happy, or sad I may be, there is something somewhere that tells me that this feeling doesn't really fit. This is why I can never completely surrender myself to a particular emotion, although it may seem different to outsiders, even in an inferior mood—as an air sign, water is my inferior element.

So I never feel totally angry, sad, or happy. In a psychodrama group I gained some perspective on this. My fellow group members, though, just like my husband and current friends, were really driven up the wall by all the ambiguity. I was asked the question ad nauseam as to what I really felt and each time there were at least two feelings that presented themselves at the same time.

When Esther let it be known that she was both angry with someone as well as feeling sympathy for that person, this was invariably interpreted by those around her as defensiveness. Esther
writes the following about this.

> *And yet I knew that no matter how twisted that feeling might
> seem, it had nothing to do with defensiveness. I wasn't afraid,
> but felt precisely unreal if I opted for a single feeling. This is my
> reality in which I often feel insecure, although I seldom show
> this. I am unable, it seems, to make sure that others really un-
> derstand me and I always feel different. I have meanwhile taught
> myself to present myself unambiguously or else they won't know
> with whom they are dealing. With my intimates, this doesn't
> work very well, and quite often leads to pretty subtle distur-
> bances in communication.*

These disturbances in communication always have these mixed
feelings as a foundation, in the form of wanting something and at
the same time not wanting it, wanting to choose the other and
yourself at the same time, and so on. In the end, Esther doesn't
know what she wants, is annoyed at both the situation as well as
at her reaction to it. This creates inner tension which causes her to
behave in a forced manner and *therefore* she asks the other person
if there might be something wrong. This in itself creates another
problem, because Esther can't explain exactly what's wrong. Not
that she doesn't know, and she wouldn't at all mind sharing these
feelings with the other person (as long as they aren't her deepest
feelings), *"but my experience has taught me that this person won't understand, so that it's best for me to keep it to myself,"* Esther explains.
The result, however, is that there is a big chance that both Esther,
as well as the other person, don't feel as much at ease.

> *This is why I feel the most comfortable when I'm by myself, a
> place where sorrow may be happiness at the same time. Being
> alone too long I don't like, either, though. The balance between
> being with other people and being alone is very hard for me to
> find because I never know to what extent I can be myself with
> others.*

People who know Esther intimately and who accept her as she is,
will become acquainted with her warm-hearted side, and will find
out that they can really have a good laugh with her. She herself
doesn't write about this, but this relaxed side can sometimes

spontaneously break through. The outside world, however, never gets to see how Esther *really* feels inside at a moment like that, although I have the distinct impression that she has become more easy-going. However, what she writes clearly articulates the internally felt conflicting tendencies of yod configurations. (See Chart 28, page 292.)

Mercury in a yod with the Moon as Ruler 3 are also responsible for all kinds of upsets in communications resulting from "a doubling up" of feelings. However, Esther also has a similar kind of doubling in her thinking, without this spoiling her clear and keen intellect, as it happens. A yod says nothing about the *quality* of somebody's capacities, but it says a lot about the *way* in which this will take shape and manifest itself! Another participant in the yod is Pluto, a planet that often tries (from insecurity or fear) to maintain control of the situation. In a yod, that's tricky! She writes:

> *On the mental level I can never be satisfied with a straightforward statement. The other facets don't very easily drift far enough into the background for me to be able to involve myself exclusively with a particular facet, which I have to do in day-to-day life, of course, otherwise I wouldn't get anywhere. The effort I suffer in order not to pay attention to the other thoughts and feelings, results in a substantial amount of tension for me. According to a physical therapist, my shoulder muscles are permanently so tensed that total relaxation is hardly possible anymore. Even though I try to keep things under control, I know at the same time that I can't do that. I really don't like it when things don't go the way I want them to, but at the same time I know that whatever it is, I want it more than you could ever actualize. No matter how I try to be in control of the situation, it somehow slips out of my hands even as I watch. If I do succeed at something, I'm usually dissatisfied with the results, or think it's not important.*

The famous "is-that-all?" feeling of a yod! Mercury and Ruler 3 in a yod also come out in another way.

> *Recently it has become clear to me that all kinds of reporting activities will suffer significantly from this attitude. Although I am very capable of thinking logically and love outlines and models, I find it difficult to describe them. I am able to draw them out entirely, but words fall short in describing the experience of the whole, which is, after all, greater than the sum of its parts.*

*At every step I take, I sense the restriction and the incomplete-
ness. The structure may be logical, but this still doesn't make it
true for me. Although I know very well that restriction is the basis for formulating a theory and that I attach a lot of value to
theory and logic, there is still always something that rattles in
any conclusive argument whatsoever.*

Questions will *always* remain for Esther, deriving from that inner
unrest. By nature somebody with a yod will say, and undoubtedly
if Mercury or Ruler 3 are located in it, "Sure, but—." If other people don't understand, this may result in misunderstandings or irritations that don't particularly contribute to a feeling of certainty
and safety for the possessor of the yod! One reaction is to clam up,
as it were, or to lock things inside and not say anything anymore.
The tension will still be tangible though. Or else he or she makes
an extra effort to arrive at clarity. Unfortunately you see attempts
like this end up quite often in increasing ambiguity.

A lot depends on the way in which the other person responds
and the maturity of the other person's reaction. Mercury plays an

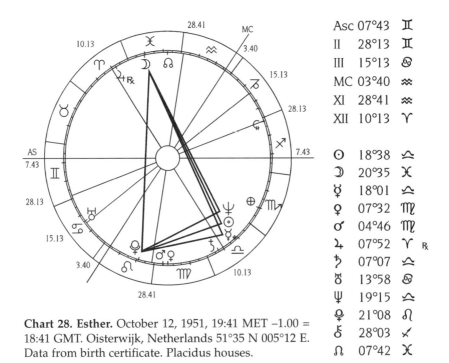

Asc 07°43	♊	
II	28°13	♊
III	15°13	♋
MC 03°40	♒	
XI	28°41	♒
XII	10°13	♈

☉	18°38	♎	
☽	20°35	♓	
☿	18°01	♎	
♀	07°32	♍	
♂	04°46	♍	
♃	07°52	♈	℞
♄	07°07	♎	
♅	13°58	♋	
♆	19°15	♎	
♇	21°08	♌	
⚷	28°03	♐	
☊	07°42	♓	

Chart 28. Esther. October 12, 1951, 19:41 MET –1.00 =
18:41 GMT. Oisterwijk, Netherlands 51°35 N 005°12 E.
Data from birth certificate. Placidus houses.

important role in teaching situations. If you're teaching a child with Mercury in a yod, the child will ask troublesome questions and even though the child *completely* understands what you mean, he or she may still occasionally come out with a sticky point. If teachers have problems with their own self-worth or authority, a child like this can be seen as being exceptionally troublesome and nasty, and of course the child will be blamed. However, teachers who are internally balanced will not interpret this as a personal attack, but feel that there is both an insecurity as well as a hunger for something deeper behind it, and accept that this child has a very different approach and also needs a lot more attention than the average child. If the child, while still a child, is understood in this way by someone, the child will reap the benefits of this later on in life. Esther offers a nice example of this from her own school days.

> *I kept on asking and asking until, when I was 9 I was sent out of class because I asked, "But how can I tell that our God is the only real one?" "That's written in the Bible," was the answer. "But how do I know the Bible is true?" was my next question. The teacher had enough of this and told me I had better go out in the hall and ask the Lord our God to forgive me for my unbelief. That's right, it happened to be a school with the Bible. Of course I left the classroom, but I lost any respect I had for her for good. And I've had innumerable other experiences like this.*

Young children can think and philosophize in a delightful way, and they have a playful, unique logic. Adults tend to dismiss it as "immature," but innocent children are often excellent at finding room for conflicting and remarkable paradoxes. An adult with Mercury or Ruler 3 in a yod will, if this person has gained a perspective on the meaning of it, have a fabulous capacity to understand and evaluate the world of thought of children and stimulate children creatively in the area of thinking, logic, and the big questions in life.

Esther went into education to be a teacher, then studied psychology and worked at a university, and also studied astrology. She became both an astrologer as well as a teacher, and enjoys the children she teaches. She understands their world and deals with it in a very natural and relaxed manner. Here the ability of Mercury and Ruler 3 in a yod manifests itself very clearly: she's a natural when it comes to the worlds of children's thoughts and lives and can therefore link this up very directly in her way of teaching.

She also likes to do research, however, and at the time she was working at the university as a psychologist, she did plenty in this area. The yod manifested itself here as well, as she writes.

In many situations in which I learned what the rule is, I stumble on the exception as soon as I want to apply the rule, so I have to find another solution. This solution usually presents itself, too, so that you get pretty resourceful, but don't learn to walk well-trodden paths very well so that you sometimes simply can't apply something trivial. It always takes extra effort, which will result in a brief "aha experience," but doesn't offer any certainty regarding the future. Other people often praise me for such solutions and tell me I really should do something with them sometime. If I try this consciously, the difficulties I encounter are again of an unforeseen nature. Since I then get the feeling of having to prove myself to that other person, however, I'm no longer open to the solutions that would otherwise come from somewhere outside my conscious mind. A failure for which I have only myself to blame will then be the result. I don't feel myself totally guilty, though, because I know very well that this involved an unfortunate combination of circumstances.

With a yod you run a greater risk than the average person would of arriving precisely at the spot where the business is running amuck or stagnating. The background of this is that yods often pop up at moments that involve a turning-point, even if its aim and the why are still unclear at that time. Esther calls this an "unfortunate combination of circumstances." This is exactly what it is and feelings of guilt are not justified in this case. For somebody with a yod, this is very important to realize! So it doesn't *really* have to be related to your qualities and capacities.

It is also true that you will encounter the exception to the rule sooner with yods and unaspected planets, or you are there precisely when the reliable pattern doesn't work and the rare deviation appears. And then see if you can get out! However, it would also have to be *there* that unsuspected talents appear, regardless of whether this involves organizing (to get things running again with a yod Sun), or inventive solutions (Mercury in a yod), or in some other way feeling, seeing, grasping, "comprehending," or in some way catching the drift in order to smooth things out again (Neptune in a yod). Esther illustrates this nicely with "solutions that would come from somewhere outside my conscious mind." This only works well, however, if an important requirement has been met: no pressure and not too much tension. If there is pressure, regardless of whether it comes from inside by wanting to achieve at all costs, or from insecurity, or from outside by expectations or deadlines, there is a greater risk you'll be blocked. Esther has also experienced this.

> *The problem is just that somebody who has taken me on board for the inventiveness I exhibited in situations with no strings attached, will be cheated in the end because in a permanent employment situation little remains of it. This sometimes gets me down. The only things left for me are the moments of sheer wonder in situations where I somehow, without consciously trying to reach that state, all of a sudden feel and realize why things are the way they are, and that I am part of it.*

Here we see Neptune's help in the yod briefly break through. By relativizing the boundaries for a moment, and sojourning in a different, roomier atmosphere, everything is momentarily placed in an entirely different perspective.

> *In practice various things have led me to experience many failures and disappointments in family, education, and work. Looking back, though, each failure also meant another chance to be able to pick up again the things that I frequently had no choice but to drop. I only understood this later, however, when I was actually already on my way to another failure on another front.*

Here Esther gives a description that actually grossly underrates her abilities and talents, but the person with a yod often experiences this feeling. For a particular period of time (longer for one person, shorter for another) this clearly involves the feeling that the things you're doing fail anyway, or that you aren't good enough, and such. I have spoken with various people with yods who got good grades as students, but responded to this with a feeling that the grades were a mistake, or they accidentally received good scores, and inside they wrestle with the idea that in some way or other they were a failure. If something did go wrong, this was a sure confirmation of their feeling, while they didn't seem to see, hear, or comprehend the things they did do well, or for which they received compliments. The children whom Esther teaches, for example, worship her, so it's impossible to speak in terms of a failure.

From early on, Esther noticed that whenever she got sick, she would get really sick, such as measles with complications, mononucleosis with complications, often high fevers, and as a child she had stomach and intestinal complaints for years. The first physical problems, in the form of stomach and intestinal complaints, arose when she was 2 or 3 and her father was diagnosed with cancer. Before Esther was even 5 years old, he had passed away.

Esther's Sun is located in a yod with Pluto and Neptune and with this she is very sensitive to anything that happens in her environment regarding the theme "male" and "strength." The death of one of your parents at such a young age, of course, makes a very deep impression, but with somebody with that theme in a yod, it will hit extra hard. Her Moon is also located in a yod with Pluto and Neptune, which also makes Esther very sensitive to how various things are picked up by and coped with by those around her. With a Moon-Pluto connection she is very sensitive to both the positive as well as the negative influence of nurturing and security, and along with this she will unconsciously have very keen antennas for whoever takes care of her, certainly in difficult times such as after the death of a parent. The Moon in connection with Pluto can then have an almost insistent need for attention, unnoticed and unintentional, to be able to stand up to the glaringly uncertain feeling. However, in a yod that gains expression through situations where attention can't be paid, or is asked for at the wrong moment, the one with the yod shuts herself from these fears and acts as if there's nothing wrong. In Esther's case it gives her great inner, emotional unrest, fear, and insecurity, and an added sensitivity to the way in which her mother deals with her father's death.

I couldn't express my sorrow over the loss because I felt that my mother, who herself no longer cried or laughed, couldn't handle it. Instead, I kept acting tougher and tougher. The lump I regularly felt in my throat, I would swallow away.

It is hard to figure out whether Esther's mother really couldn't have given her support. The fact is, though, that a child with a yod involving the Moon and Pluto will be very sensitive to fears and repressed matters in the domestic environment and Neptune as part of the yod will add an almost paranormal dimension to this. There is also the chance, though, that precisely because of that sensitivity, the reaction becomes exaggerated and a mechanism for self-rejection arises, something we see happen more often with yods.

Esther then goes through a difficult period. She and her mother temporarily lived somewhere else where she didn't feel at home and was teased terribly and even physically attacked (like being kicked into a canal). Nobody helped her, not even her mother. "Through all these experiences I had gotten the idea that whatever I did, I'd still be the one who got hit," Esther wrote, and even in her dreams the strength left her arms if she wanted to fight for herself.

From about the time of her father's death up until she was 10, her life was characterized by "illness, feelings of fear and loneliness, and the relentless teasing," and during this period we see the yods become activated from time to time by progressions and transits. The relationship with her mother is difficult. Esther had already decided very early on not to bother her mother with her problems and fears, and did not let her mother share in her life because of this. Esther also had a lot of trouble with her mother at the times when she was sick. Her mother would insist on very strict bed rest and dietary rules, from stinging nettle juice to sweats and fasting cures, and rigorous quarantine, while Esther would really be longing for some attention and doing little things like simply being read to or playing a game. However, that wasn't allowed and Esther got the feeling that you were also being punished if you got sick and you weren't a person anymore, but utterly reduced to "body."

Everything that is nurturing and caretaking is a lunar theme and the contact you have with your own body often has to do with the 2nd house. Both the Moon as well as Ruler 2 are located in Esther's yod. And what we see in this summary of her first ten years is a feeling of loneliness and being rejected and teased, as well as problems in communicating with and being with her mother. Result: both the building of feelings of self-worth (Sun) as well as feelings of confidence in life (Moon) and in her body (Ruler 2) were problems or didn't happen smoothly.

After 1966, the yods were once again activated by a good number of transits and progressions. At this time I wondered what purpose my life had anyway, and whether it wouldn't have been better for my father to have died a few years earlier, then at least I wouldn't have been around. I didn't know what I wanted anymore and didn't want to do anything. Normal symptoms of puberty nevertheless made me feel very lonely. Fortunately my

Dutch teacher noticed in an essay that I was really in the dumps. She started up a conversation with me, which saved me, not because she addressed my personal problems directly, but because for the first time I was meeting somebody who, in my mind, knew the key to the secret of life. She was Indonesian and a Rosicrucian, and she knew a lot about mythology and literature. With her small shape and her mysterious voice, she was the embodiment of Isis to me. Because of her I became exceptionally interested in mythology and literature. Magic realism in particular appealed strongly to my imagination. In touch with this mythological world, I began to experience life as something that made good sense.

The picture Esther sketches here lends wonderful meaning to a Moon-Pluto-Neptune yod: coming again to yourself and to the reason for life through mythology and something that is "magic," brought your way by a woman! It is and will remain a yod though, and so precisely because of this positive development, Esther came up against an emotional dilemma.

My mother couldn't stand it when she noticed that I had more contact with this teacher than with her. She always felt, she said, distance between herself and me, but now she had the feeling of having lost me for good. When she said this, I felt sorry for her. I felt like I was standing in between a rock and a hard place. On the one side, I had hidden my feelings from her because I always thought she wouldn't be able to handle my grief, while on the other side, I felt a kind of embarrassment for her in this respect. Besides this, I was afraid of losing my deepest self if I were able to share it with her. She did not have the right to trespass into my world. And yet I didn't want to hurt her.

This portion of Esther's feelings fits with a connection between Pluto and the Moon (and can also appear with Ruler 8 in aspect with the Moon, or with the Moon in the 8th house). With these three combinations, many times I have encountered a fear of sharing deeper emotions and feelings with those who are close to you, such as a mother. There is a fear that "something" will be taken from you if you share it with someone else, but this isn't immediately an action directed at the *other* person, as it is rather a result of a personal fear. If Pluto and the Moon happen to be involved in a yod, there is more probability that this theme will come out in a sticky and pronounced manner. So, too, with Esther who ended up in a kind of dilemma, but who resolved it well by finding a form in which she still, it's true, did not share her deeper inner stirrings with her mother, but did manage to give her the feeling that she meant something in Esther's life.

The duality of the situation was that Esther came into contact with a world that fascinated her: that of mythology, magic realism, mystery, and something that elicited deep feelings, and precisely because of this she had to come to terms with her mother. When there seemed to be more openness, her mother shared with Esther her fears, doubts, and grief, and whole diatribes about how wrongly she had probably done everything. In short, her mother saddled Esther with her own dynamic and that, for a pubescent teenager, is not easy.

I have also seen this happen to others with the Moon and Pluto in a yod. A woman, for instance, who told of how, just after she entered high school, she was doing her homework one evening, when her teary mother came into her little room extremely upset. Sobbing, her mother informed her that she had the feeling that another family member, with whom her daughter got along very well, was in the process of stealing her daughter away from her. The woman with the Moon and Pluto yod understood nothing of this; that wasn't how it was at all, according to her. However, she felt so awkward about the situation that she started paying more attention to her mother. She expressed this particularly by starting to take care of her mother, so that she became her mother's mother as it were, and in fact *because* of this, psychically speaking, lost her mother. For Esther such a process was also at play. She writes:

> *My mother saw herself as immature and told me that I was actually more mature in everything than she was. She also told me that, in spite of everything, it was really better for me that my father was no longer alive because he would really have stood in the way of my development. He hadn't wanted a child because he was already pretty old. Her bookcase, meanwhile, had filled up with popular psychological literature by mostly followers of Adler. I really didn't know what I was supposed to do with all this, but I finally tried to live up to her image. Evidently she set high score by my advantage and I knew how to say the things she wanted to hear. That I became more motherless than ever before because of this is something I realized only later.*

March 1968 is the beginning of an important turning point for Esther. By transit, Pluto is stationary with her Moon: Pluto stops at 20° Virgo in Spring 1968 and remains in orb until August. Also, her MC has arrived opposite Pluto by primary progression. Deservedly time for coping and a turnaround. Esther recounts:

I get measles for the second time, followed by mono and other complications. The illness ritual now became an honest to goodness battle. Being forced to stay in bed made me so furious that I kicked the footboard off my bed. None of the cures and diets worked. I rolled from one illness into the next, until rescue showed up from an entirely unexpected quarter. A girl with whom I was slightly acquainted came to visit me and said she was going to go on vacation to a boating camp. Suddenly she asked me if I wanted to go with her. Very symbolic for the Moon in Pisces in the 11th house in a yod. After a lot of begging and pleading, I convinced my mother. On the day of departure I was still tiring quickly and covered with hives. After two days of sailing on the rivers, though, all my symptoms had disappeared. As if reborn, I came home. For the first time I had felt good in a group. Evidently I had changed so much that one of the girls at school commented that when I returned to school after my illness it was as if I had stepped onto the stage, drawn back the curtain, and said to everyone, "Here I am." At school, too, I now felt as if I belonged, even though I inwardly still felt different. I paid little emotional attention to my mother anymore, although the conflicts about what I did and didn't do hadn't completely cleared up. The stifling situation from before was over.

Transits and progressions of Pluto can be true releases and often announce a period of powerful psychological growth if the message has been well received. You will never have any certainty about this though. One time it can be a giant leap forward so you can leave a lot of the mire behind you, whereas another time it may be precisely a leap *into* the mire. This last was the case when Esther's Pluto by primary progression arrived in opposition to her Moon in 1975. The squares by primary progression of the Sun and Mercury with Pluto that were exact in 1974, as it happens, were also still having an effect.

In 1972 Esther moved in with someone and they married in 1975, also during the time when primary Pluto was opposite her Moon. A week after their wedding, she found out that her spanking new husband cared more for one of her girlfriends than for her.

*This was such a huge shock that it seemed as if my whole world
had collapsed. That week I cried more than I had my whole life
put together. I wasn't able to handle my job as a school teacher
and flute teacher. I resigned, asked for a divorce, and dove into
the cafe scene.*

Here she had a brief relationship with someone who turned out
later to be a psychopath, and who cleverly managed to trick her
out of a lot of money and valuable things. During that same year
she met a much older man with whom she had a very emotionally
intense relationship.

*The more dependent on him I became, however, the more he
would withdraw, so that I started to understand, as painful as it
was, that I was looking for a father in him. This man was very
important for me. He stimulated me to go to college and into
psychotherapy, which gave me some perspective again on my life
and could give it some direction. Mythology, literature, music,
and also astrology with which I had preoccupied myself for a
number of years already, moved aside to make room for a causal,
scientific approach to reality and a quest for more deep-seated
motives in myself and others, stripped of all their fluff.*

Esther calls 1975 a disastrous year, a year in which Pluto not only
aspects her yod Moon by primary progression, but transiting Pluto moves back and forth over her natal Saturn (the older man
theme!) in opposition to Jupiter, the ruler of her 7th house. We see
turbulent developments regarding the theme of partner (Jupiter is
Ruler 7), the theme of studies (Jupiter, and Saturn as Ruler 9), and
the unconscious quest for a backbone, for structure, and the father
theme (Saturn). A transit of Pluto over Ruler 9 may decisively
change an existing concept of life, particularly if this concerns a
theoretical vision. Pluto is part of Esther's yod by nature and may
therefore in all its transits drag along the unpredictable and incomprehensible elements of the yod. This year also turned out to
be a pivotal year for her, just like 1968, with the transit of Pluto
opposite her Moon. This time, however, it carries more complications and confusing experiences.

She let go of the mythological world and entered the world of
science. Such turnarounds are not unusual with yods, but precisely with yods you often see at a later stage, if the thread is picked
up well, that all the experiences, even the most extreme, in some
way or other, come together in a natural way. So, too, for Esther,

who is now having a lot of fun setting up and structuring her own astrological research and that of others as scientifically as possible. Astrology, psychology, music, mythology, and the mystical, have just as much space as statistics and science, and she succeeds in combining these things in fruitful ways. Another stunt by an "impossible" combination, which for somebody with a yod is actually very normal, natural, and to be taken for granted, precisely because with a yod you contain so much diversity inside. Mainstream psychology still has little equipment to deal with this, as many people with a yod have experienced. Esther also noticed it.

> *This period of time made deep inroads into my whole life and my concept of myself, and was the remarkable crisis facet which is so typical of a yod, more there than ever. According to the IMP intake person, various aspects of my personality weren't really integrated, which in my opinion can also be related to the yod. After all, in a yod, seemingly incompatible elements and methods of coping must still work together in a subtle way that is difficult to trace, which can't come to light in a less subtle psychological diagnosis.*

In 1979 and 1980, transiting Pluto moves back and forth over her Sun-Mercury-Neptune conjunction in Libra: one leg of the yod transits over the other! Pluto, from this position, of course is also regularly creating inconjuncts with her Moon.

Her life is turbulent. The year before she started living with a man who had a lot of personal problems; there were problems with money and residence, and actually the only thing that was still going well was her school work. In this situation she becomes pregnant, while the relationship with her boyfriend is becoming almost intolerable due to his problems. The pregnancy is a difficult one, the birth as well.

> *It was a long, excruciating delivery during which they thought the baby wasn't alive anymore and they were also afraid I might die. As it happened, I would have preferred nothing more than being dead, because everything was really unbearable, something I'd never want to go through again. My boyfriend, however, discovered that the baby was alive, but that the recording equipment wasn't functioning properly, so that he succeeded in rescuing me in the nick of time from an at that point in time still life-threatening Caesarian section. In the end, our baby daughter was born alive anyway.*

Questions of life and death, matters that balance on the edge, I have encountered all too often with Pluto in a yod; the most, though, when both Pluto as well as Neptune are present in the yod, or one of the two luminaries (Sun or Moon). Esther is also an example of this, but I want to state emphatically (as I have elsewhere in this book) that you shouldn't turn things around. I also know women with Pluto in a yod for whom pregnancy and childbirth took place just fine. Sometimes other meanings for that Pluto appear, such as a falling-out with a parent at the birth of a child, or witnessing various deaths among your intimates while you're pregnant, just to name a few examples.

Esther has Pluto inconjunct the Moon in her natal yod and we have seen what she felt and experienced concerning security and care when she was a child: a mother with whom she was unable or unwilling to share anything and a father who passed away when she was very young. When in 1968 Pluto has shifted in the sky and arrives by transit in opposition to her Moon, she experiences a kind of rebirth and manages to free herself internally from her mother's influence.

When Pluto arrives, by primary progression, in opposition to her Moon in 1975, she is thrown back harshly on her own devices and it seems as if life is experimenting to see where the bottom is to her emotions and feelings. She discovers that she is in search of a father, and reviews her life in a different way to work out that theme.

By transit, Pluto arrives at an inconjunct with her Moon and is conjunct her Sun, and both previous themes come together in a new experience. Just as in 1975, this involves a relationship and not a particularly easy one. It does not become a divorce, as in 1975, nor a psychopath, nor a father figure, but it is a relationship that Esther experiences as threatening, and which concerns a man who has a lot of problems. The husband/father theme is once again in the forefront. And as she managed in 1969 to release herself from her mother, the fact that Esther became a mother herself and gave life to a beautiful daughter means that in short order she will manage to free herself of her own fear of being nurtured.

I discovered that I loved to hug her and take care of her and so I came into more frequent contact with my own need for nurturing, with which I had always had a lot of trouble. For instance, I was nauseated as long as I can remember by my mother's touch, and I stiffened at the well-intentioned and comforting physical touch of other women and also girlfriends. I noticed, though, to my surprise and joy that I was able to fulfill the mother role very naturally. Along with this I think it's also much easier now to lay an arm around somebody's shoulder on top of a comforting word, and I can think it's very pleasant from others toward me, with the exception of my mother. In the earlier mentioned psychodrama group I wasn't able to learn that. Maybe during the prior period of time "I" was first supposed to figure out a piece and then withdraw so that I would be able to experience this piece in myself.

Although the relationship with her friend was anything but pleasant, Esther assessed very soberly that the state of marriage offered more rights and legal advantages than the state in which she was now with her child. Her friend really wanted to get married, so she gave in. They were consequently married. Shortly afterward his problems became so overwhelming, and he became so inaccessible and unapproachable that Esther couldn't take the pressure and psychic threat any more and asked for a divorce. It almost appears like a repetition of her previous marriage: barely wed and she wants a divorce. However, this time things went differently. When her husband received the divorce papers, he decided to go into therapy, because he also realized how destructive he was being. He had himself admitted, and Esther was involved in the therapy as well.

I came to the discovery that I really did care for him very much and that there were quite a few areas where we got along well. I withdrew the petition for a divorce and from that time on, everything went a lot better, although certainly not without difficulty.

Along the way I came to the realization that I always looked for my partners among poets, dreamers, magicians and mystics who would all too often enjoy one too many.

Esther writes that this insight helps her take a significant step forward.

I understood that this had something to do with me, but that I don't necessarily have to project this into a partner. My feeling of being dependent has disappeared. So maintaining the relationship with my husband was therefore a free choice. My attitude in it I can determine for myself and I can decide for myself whether I will pay any attention to his criticism and tyranny. I see things with much more nuance now and so I am not afraid to dare see my own poor ways because I am no longer afraid of being rejected. Emotionally I am also better able to distinguish what belongs to him and what belongs to me, so that he can't really chase me into a corner anymore. I maintain my own sense of things, no matter how paradoxically they may fit together.

Esther now knows to combine the previous themes from previous crisis years and to move ahead on a new, internally far more stable level.

After receiving her degree in 1987, she got a job at a university and was to do research on which she worked with a lot of pleasure. However, when it came to the point of making the research findings publishable, Mercury and Ruler 3 in the yod started acting up again and she had to struggle with her fear of failure, which blocked her. Gradually she also felt:

. . . a growing inner refusal to deal so selectively with the data in order to make the small points of significance appear to be more important than they were. Besides this, I had again taken up my old love, astrology, and began to realize increasingly that my reality looked a lot more colorful than the boring gray of the social psychology research group.

Esther draws the line and decides to go back to her old vocation— teacher. This is what she writes.

Transiting Saturn was at that time in a stationary square with my Sun/Mercury/Neptune conjunction, just as it was in October 1974 when I got my first teaching job. By being able to teach again and be involved with children, I began to feel more upbeat. It was a big step backward, but I don't think that's bad anymore. The work doesn't take up so much of my time that I don't have any for my hobbies, astrology and music. The scientific climate at the university made it impossible for me to be able to live in the world of the inexplicable as well, and to be able to marvel. Although I think a scientific method of thinking is still very valuable, it is my experience that there is still a level of understanding that goes beyond it. This is a world I already knew in my teenage years but which I couldn't reconcile with the world of causality to which I was also attached. In the meantime I am satisfied that both have their own framework of elucidation and it is sometimes fun to be able to translate concepts from one framework into the other, but that they can also exist side by side as totally different ways of approaching the world of appearances.

Esther concludes:

> *In my opinion, the thread running through this whole story is situations getting out of control, or letting them get that way, when they weren't assessed properly in the first place. I kept getting trapped, knowing that various things weren't right, but where it concerned my own life, I didn't have any solutions. They would present themselves, inevitably through a crisis, so that I would lose something that was important to me. Strangely enough, I realized only recently that all these remarkable crises did keep bringing me a bit closer to myself. These situations, which I would never consciously opt for, have not made my life any easier, it's true, but have given it more meaning.*

A number of people played critical roles in the most important crises in Esther's life.

> *They personify, in a certain sense, the activating of my yod, because I have a very strong although odd connection with them, which, as such, turned my life or theirs upside down.*
>
> *Comparing their natal charts with mine provided surprising results. Two points, notably about 20 degrees Capricorn and 20 degrees Taurus seem to jump out. These people have either their Sun or their Moon located here. These points form a sextile with my Moon, so that Pluto, or the Sun/Mercury/Neptune conjunction, respectively, which form the base of the yod in my radix, now start functioning as the apex, while they square the other leg of my yod.*
>
> *What is striking in all these relationships is that they have never been enabled to become what one of the parties hoped or hopes, and at first there was an element of repulsion present. For my mother, whose Moon is 20 degrees Capricorn, I didn't at all resemble the child she had wished for either. They also always involve a remarkable connection or bond that can even stand up to the breaking up of a romantic relationship.*

Esther also had romantic relationships with a couple of the men with whom she had one of these "yod relationships." And although these relationships failed, the deep bond remained in another way, and the relationship with these people is for Esther still very meaningful. For Esther, her Ruler 5 and Co-Ruler 5 (the Sun and Mercury, respectively) and Co-Ruler 11 (Neptune) are located in the yod. Her 7th house is not involved in the yod, and Esther has noticed this very directly. She writes about the relationships in which a yod comes into play in synastry.

> *They are also connected with pretty drastic changes in my life or in the other person's life, which in retrospect, with the exception of my mother's antics, I still experience as an enrichment. With my ex-husband and my current spouse, this repulsion element and the impossible nature of the relationship never came into play—although other difficulties did. There also isn't the same kind of friendship. Except for starting to run a household together, these relationships changed nothing in the way I run my life and I would also feel great resistance if this were asked of me. What is telling about this is that my 7th house is not involved in the yod, but my 5th and 11th houses are.*

When Esther began studying psychology, she fell in love with a fellow student.

> *The type I never fall for. For that matter, nor am I his type. It all started with a couple of chess games at the canteen that were battled out as if they were a question life and death because he couldn't stomach the fact that I kept beating him. Meanwhile, a kind of sucking attraction developed from which we couldn't free ourselves. His Moon at 18 Taurus creates a square with my Pluto, a sextile with my Moon, and an inconjunct with my Sun/Mercury/Neptune conjunction. Our mutual yod is thus formed by both our Moons at the base and my Sun/Mercury/Neptune conjunction as the apex.*

The relationship developed very quickly and intensely and an entirely new theme entered Esther's life: meditation, absolutely appropriate if your Moon in Pisces and your Sun and Mercury are conjunct Neptune, and undoubtedly so if these are located in a yod.

> *In addition to his studies, he was a very active member of a meditation group. His experiences in this area strongly appealed to me and I joined the group myself. This altered my entire lifestyle. We studied according to a tight schedule during the day— before I studied mostly during the evening— and spent almost all our evenings in this group, where we shared our meditation*

*experiences with one another. We didn't sleep much, but spent
our nights mostly talking. I became a vegetarian, drank no alco-
hol anymore, and turned my back on the bars. The meditation
techniques for the first time gave me some peace from the
thoughts constantly running through my head, while I was able
to lose myself in this group together with him. We even traveled
to Miami to meet this guru and kiss his feet. I would never have
reached this point by myself. I attach enough importance to my
own individuality to find this kind of devotion ridiculous. Still,
it was a beautiful experience. All warm, radiant light, which we
encountered again in each others' eyes. Mercury, the endless
talk, Neptune, the meditation thing, the devotion, and the Sun
as the radiant experience of light, at which it happened the most
important meditation technique was directed, are recognizable
here. The sixth house position of these planets possibly also
played a part. Being a practicing member also involved doing as-
sorted tasks for the group so that you were also able to have meditation experiences in practical activities. Normally I detest such
commonplace tasks. Still, a number of times I experienced that
working in this way can be very nice and that it doesn't even
matter what you're doing. It all took a considerable amount of
time. Still, I achieved the most in my studies at this time. I was
the first to complete the core courses and later a bachelor's degree. It was simply a question of discipline that I can otherwise
never muster.*

*Little by little our relationship got more difficult, however.
The power struggle that at first had only taken place on the
chess board slowly started to extend to the academic domain. He
couldn't take my getting better grades. Finally he started a relationship with my best friend. So I lost two friends at once and
didn't even have a place to have a good cry. My Moon in the
11th house, which was a component of our mutual yod (in which
my Co-Ruler 11 was also involved), was now showing its difficult side. I tried to meditate, but the light I saw was ice-cold and
I no longer felt at ease in the group. Nor could I find a place of
peace within myself. I had actually felt a certain resistance earlier to worshipping gurus and to the somewhat ascetic way of life.
In particular, the idea that everything that was "mind" should
be inferior and that you can only see the light when you are free
of your attachments was hard for me to tolerate. I was no longer
able to identify internally with the idea that one part in myself
would have to fight the other. I completely submerged myself in
my studies, and two months later met the man to whom I am*

now married. After six months I no longer found it necessary to steer clear of my former boyfriend. It turned out that we still felt a lot for each other and a friendship has developed between us in which we can truly say anything to each other.

If you want to deal with a yod in a positive way, then it is very important that conflicting needs and traits are each allowed their own space. Then it will be impossible to "swear off" one and to repress it in favor of another part. Somehow it eats at you, otherwise, and will contribute to inner unrest and doubt. This is also true of the meditation group's strict rules for living. Esther already clearly pointed this out: her yod brings her to the awareness that there are always several sides to an issue and that nothing is completely true or unequivocal.

The disciplined experiences she gained in the meditation group, aside from the meditation experience itself, are, however, also experiences that are once again pushed into the forefront at a particular moment in her life by the yod. Then it will turn out that these experiences are a separate piece of the puzzle, and when that piece falls into place, Esther will notice that she is getting closer to her inner destiny. When I sent Esther this chapter for approval, she wrote the following about it.

Actually, I think this has already happened. In 1993, when Uranus and Neptune by transit were square my Sun-Mercury-Neptune conjunction, I started the Jungian psychology course. In active imagination I have actually, besides feeling deep emotions, still always experienced the same kind of peace as in my meditation. To empty myself of my thoughts I still happen to use a number of these meditation techniques. In doing them, I don't have to free myself from attachment, though, and repress my "mind," but am able simply to experience my whole self. Here, too, a certain discipline is necessary in order to create the circumstances for me to isolate myself. This also taught me to pay attention to all kinds of subtle synchronistic signals so that finally many pieces of the puzzle have fallen into place. The most important thing, I think, is that I have learned to deal a lot better with my feminine emotional side.

The people with whom Esther forms new yods, turn out to create them either from Taurus or Capricorn with her existing yod. Those who add their bit from Capricorn are forming a sextile with Esther's Moon, and the top of the yod is then Esther's Pluto. For those who form the yod from Taurus, Esther's Sun-Mercury-Neptune conjunction is the apex of the yod. In looking back on these relationships, Esther noticed a number of important things.

> *Where Pluto functions as the apex, the factor of death plays some kind of role. With my mother (Moon at 20 Capricorn) it was the death of my father that set matters in operation and the struggle is now about inheritance rights. The older man who played such an important role in my life in 1975 (he has Sun and Mercury around 19 Capricorn) asked me in case he dies to represent his personal affairs, while a member of a psychodrama group (Sun 20 Pisces and Moon at 19 Capricorn, just like my mother!) confronts me with her suicidal behavior and expects help from me regarding the recent death of her girlfriend.*

Where the other yod possibility, the one from 20° Taurus, is concerned, Esther has only had the relationship with the meditating friend. In the yod that was thus formed, Neptune is also located at the apex, along with the Sun and Mercury.

> *With this, in my view, I am also touching the crux of my family dynamic, namely religion and death. The horoscopes of my mother's side of the family that I am familiar with also seem to emphasize this theme. . . . My mother's father descends from Huguenots who fled France. The religious war in all its fanaticism still hasn't subsided among their descendants. Along with this, the premature death of parents or children, which is systematically kept quiet, runs through this family like a thread. Taking all this into consideration, it looks as if I, who have these remarkable yod relationships, have at any rate been working out something of my family dynamic in an unconventional manner, and no matter how much I might have wanted to, I often wasn't able to keep a straight face. In the eyes of my religious family, my study of psychology, worshipping gurus, and study of astrology, not to mention all those relationships with men made a straight connection with the devil. Yet, uncles, aunts and cousins nowadays have a certain kind of respect for me, and I am treated with all due courtesy by them, in spite of my totally differing opinions and way of life.*

A yod simply doesn't involve any guarantee of peace, but inside, Esther has undeniably arrived in more calm waters, and many bits of her varied experiences have fallen in place, or are in the process of doing so. Her increasing inner stability is also reflected in being accepted by those family members for whom she is clearly a piece of shadow. Esther's life and experiences in relationships turn out to be associated with a deeper family dynamic; evidently this thread in the generations preceding her is due for a change—a turning-point. This is where Esther will play a role with her yod, whether she wants to or not. The themes of the generations before her, religion and death (Neptune and Pluto), are the themes Esther keeps stumbling across in all their variations. However, she can also give her own, creative, and renewing meaning to them: getting involved with other dimensions, away from restricting, traditional opinions, and moving toward psychology, music, the mystical, and the magical, to name a few studies Esther referred to in her story.

Esther also keeps encountering turning-points, and the familiar exception to the rule. However, she now recognizes it, and is capable of getting through it and even looking at it with a good amount of humor. She has accepted and found space for the different worlds in herself. The searching hasn't stopped because of this, but it is no longer a disturbing factor. She has gotten fun out of "searching just to search."

CHAPTER EIGHTEEN

In Conclusion

We are part of a chain of human experiences running far back into the past. The questions our ancestors had live on in us and are still seeking an answer. We are inclined to see ourselves as separate individuals. In the West we usually don't realize how much we are part of a whole—part of a family line, part of a society, of the culture in which we grow up and live, part of the circle of people around us, from anonymous fellow town and city dwellers, to co-workers, to the circle of our own friends.

It is the yods and the unaspected planets that connect us, albeit usually in a somewhat uncomfortable fashion, with the past that once was, and still is, and that inside us still wants to take shape. Like churned-up energy, it breaks through and presses on us, particularly when it appears in the larger context of a family line, or even a society, or culture, to be "time" to change. In these processes of change, people with unaspected planets or yods often play critical roles, both on a small scale as well as on a large one. They are the ones who mark the turning-points.

However, changes often require several generations, and so we also see that people with yods or an unaspected planet in many cases aren't around anymore to see the consequences of what their life released. When you study the struggle of the yod and the unaspected planet only in the light of a single lifetime, what happens seems so laborious and oftentimes also unfair. Because, why should connections among the same planets for people who have yods happen to be so much more turbulent than for people who are connected by square or opposition, the other tension aspects? Only when you study yods and unaspected planets from the perspective of a larger whole, of turning-points in family lines and social processes, do you start seeing what a deeply defining and important role these horoscope factors play, and what kind of a special role those who have these horoscope factors can play. This may be the case also on a small scale.

Erich Neumann goes into this process wonderfully in his book *Depth Psychology and a New Ethic*. He argues that developments of the collective are always decades behind the developments of individuals. So it is up to the individual to find solutions to problems that are felt individually, but that are also part of a larger whole. Neumann writes:

> *The individual who is brought up against the overwhelming problem of evil and is shaken by it, and often driven by it right up to the brink of the abyss, naturally defends himself against destruction. In order to survive at all, he needs . . . the aid of the forces of the deep unconscious; in them and in himself he may be able to find new ways, new forms of life, new values, and new guiding symbols.*[1]

Neumann also ascertains that if the individual has to come to terms with "evil," that the individual not only is involved with an individual reality, but also with the personal expression of a collective situation. Thus the creative energies of the unconscious, which hint at new possibilities, are not personal, but an individual form of the creative aspect of the collective, that we call the universal human unconscious.[2]

In other words, if the individual can use these positive and creative forces to tackle and solve his or her problems, the individual is thereby making a new beginning. It only seems to be for the individual, but this is not the case: The individual holds the future of the collective, according to Neumann. He says that the person who is involved in dealing with his or her own problems, which can be considered to be part of the collective, and the way he or she copes with the problems, reflect on our future.[3]

> *Both the problem and the level at which the solution emerges are manifested in the individual; both, however, have their roots in the collective. It is precisely this that makes the experience of the individual so significant. What happens in him is typical of the whole situation, and the creative stirrings which enable him to find his own solutions and salvation are the initial stages of future values and symbols of the collective.*

---

[1] Erich Neumann, *Depth Psychology and a New Ethic*, Eugene Rolfe, trans. (New York: G. P. Putnam's Sons, 1969), p. 29.
[2] *Depth Psychology and a New Ethic*, p. 29.
[3] *Depth Psychology and a New Ethic*, p. 30.

> *The individual (and his fate) is the prototype. . . . He is the re-*
> *tort in which the poisons and antidotes of the collective are dis-*
> *tilled. This is why the deep psychic happening which seizes hold*
> *of an individual and reveals itself in him in a form that can be*
> *experienced has a special meaning for a period of transition and*
> *of the collective disintegration of standards.*[4]

It is the inner struggle in the individual person that may result in
solutions for the society of the future. Neumann ascertains that
particular people are more sensitive to contents from the collective unconscious. For them particular problems become urgent,
while for the collective this still is not yet the case. I have the
strong impression that this applies particularly to many who have
yods and unaspected planets and that the pressure from the "up-
permost layer" of their collective unconscious, the layer where the
experiences of their ancestors are found, is involved with those
problems. The trouble now is that people with yods and unaspected planets can be bothered by problems that don't seem to be
problems (yet) for most people. In fact: the problems with which
this group of people wrestles, particularly the way in which they
wrestle with them, is not really recognized as a problem. How often with a yod or unaspected planet don't you get a reaction of
disbelief, or something along the lines of, "Oh don't be so difficult!" Neumann's continued analysis is very worthwhile for yods
and unaspected planets; he could have written it applying directly to them! He says:

> *. . . A sensitive person [has to deal with] a future problem of hu-*
> *manity which has confronted him and forced him to wrestle with*
> *it. . . . This explains the lack of contemporaneity, the remoteness*
> *and the eccentric isolation of these people—but also their pro-*
> *phetic role as forerunners. Their fate and their often tragic*
> *struggle with their problems is of crucial significance for the col-*
> *lective, since both the problem and the solution, the criticism*
> *which destroys the old and the synthesis which lays the founda-*
> *tion for the new, are performed by these same individuals for the*
> *collective . . .*
>
> *The connection between the problems of the individual and*
> *those of the collective is far closer than is generally realized. . . .*
> *The marital tragedy of the individual is the arena to which the*

---

[4] *Depth Psychology and a New Ethic*, pp. 29–30.

problem of the changed relationship between man and woman is brought for settlement by the collective—a problem which has a collective meaning and relevance transcending the marital conflicts of the individual.[5]

People with a yod or unaspected planet lack a fixed orientation, in a certain sense. This is to say: the example they experience in their childhood is in the most cases not enough for them, with the odd exception where a parent understands the child with the yod or unaspected planet and helps that child on its way. However, the example that these children usually get is inadequate, or an example such children *can't* follow. The problem these children experience is by nature one that doesn't have a "normal" or "easy" answer. There is no simple, ready-made solution, so quieting these children with a cookie or a little present helps very little. These children will have to find a solution themselves, and under their own steam, in order to be able to shape their personal destiny, and this usually means by trial and error.

With those personal, unique solutions you also get your own feeling for what is good and what is evil. And in many cases this may deviate partially or completely from traditional opinions. Courage is needed in order to live that personal feeling, that personal judgment about what is good and evil in actuality, to dare to express it. In doing so, you will touch sore spots and you will definitely not receive any thanks for it. However, if you manage to live with a yod or an unaspected planet in a positive way, you will, by being who you are and through the solutions you find, together with "companions in fate" everywhere in the world, be the quiet trailblazers for new norms and values in the future.

Even if you don't have a yod or an unaspected planet in your natal chart, you will be part of this process. After all, you will inevitably be involved with temporary yods by progression and transit, and will then be just as much a part of the process as those people who have them in their natal charts. The questions and problems that temporarily reveal themselves inside you, and the stalemates in which you find yourself might be related to a larger and deeper thematic than you are able to surmise prior to the experience.

We are all part of a larger whole. We are part of the past because we are part of a family whose roots go back to a gray past. We are a part of the future, regardless of whether we have or will

---

[5] *Depth Psychology and a New Ethic*, pp. 30–31.

have children, because we are the retort in which the future is taking shape. At important crossroads in time, at major turning-points and through necessary changes, people with yods and unaspected planets, if they succeed in finding creative form for these contents in their horoscopes, are in the deepest sense pioneers of the future, regardless of whether their role is played on a large or small scale. In their inner fight lies the seed of the new ethic and of the norms of the future. The yod has always been called "the finger of God"—and rightly so, in my view. We may rely in the deepest sense on the road that yods and unaspected planets show us.

Bibliography

Devold, Simon Flemm. *Morten 11 jaar*. Zeist, Holland: Indigo, 1997. [Conversations about life with a child who is going to die.]

Dossey, Larry. *Recovering the Soul: A Scientific and Spiritual Search*. New York: Bantam Doubleday Dell Publishing Group, 1989. [The connection between mysticism, religion, physics, and the healing arts.]

————. *Space, Time & Medicine*. Boston: Shambhala, 1982.

Duff, Kat. *The Alchemy of Illness*. New York: Crown Publishing Group, 1994.

Epstein, Alan. *Understanding Aspects: The Inconjunct*. Reno, NV: Trines Publishing, 1997.

Franz, Marie-Louise von, and J. Hillman. *Lectures on Jung's Typology*. Zürich: Spring Publications, 1971.

————. *Shadow and Evil in Fairy Tales*. Boston: Shambhala, 1995.

Furth, Gregg M. *The Secret World of Drawings: Healing through Art*. Gloucester, MA: Sigo Press, 1989.

Greene, Liz. *The Art of Stealing Fire: Uranus in the Horoscope*. London: Centre for Psychological Astrology Press, 1996.

Hamaker-Zondag, Karen. *Aspects and Personality*. York Beach, ME: Samuel Weiser, 1990.

————. *Foundations of Personality*. York Beach, ME: Samuel Weiser, 1994.

————. *House Connection*. York Beach, ME: Samuel Weiser, 1994.

————. *Psychological Astrology*. York Beach, ME: Samuel Weiser, 1990.

————. *The Twelfth House*. York Beach, ME: Samuel Weiser, 1992.

Hand, Robert. *Planets in Composite: Analyzing Human Relationships*. Atglen, PA: Whitford Press, 1975.

Jacobi, Jolande. *The Psychology of C. G. Jung*. New Haven, CT: Yale University Press, 1973. [An introduction to his work.]

Jung, C. G. *Answer to Job*. Princeton: Princeton University Press, 1972.

————. *The Collected Works*. 20 volumes. Bollingen Series XX. Princeton: Princeton University Press, 1953–1979; and London: Routledge & Kegan Paul, 1953–1979.

————. *Memories, Dreams, Reflections*. Aniela Jaffe, editor; Richard and Clara Winston, trans. New York: Pantheon, 1961; New York: Vintage Books, 1989.

————. *Man and His Symbols.* New York: Dell Publishing, 1964.

————. *The Psychology of the Unconscious,* B. M. Hinkle, trans. New York: Dodd, Mead & Co., 1952.

Koch, Walter. *Aspektlehre nach Johannes Kepler* [The Study of Aspects According to Johannes Kepler]. Hamburg, 1952.

Lewis, Marcia. *The Private Lives of the Three Tenors: Behind the Scenes with Placido Domingo, Luciano Pavarotti, and José Carreras.* Secaucus, NJ: Carol Publishing Group, 1996.

Morton, Andrew. *Diana: Her True Story.* London: Pocket Books, 1992.

Neumann, Erich. *Depth Psychology and a New Ethic.* Eugene Wolfe, trans. New York: G. P. Putnam's Sons, 1969.

————. *The Origins and History of Consciousness.* R. F. C. Hull, trans. Bollingen Series XLII. Princeton: Princeton University Press, 1954.

New Larousse Encyclopedia of Mythology. Introduction by Robert Graves. London: Hamlyn (1959) 1977; London: Prometheus Press (1959) 1974.

Sakoian, Frances and Louis S. Acker. *That Inconjunct-Quincunx: The Not-So-Minor Aspect.* Washington, DC. Privately Published, 2nd ed., 1973.

Index

Acker, Louis S., 9
Aesculapius, 239
a]-Fayed, Dodi, 165
al-Fayed, Mohammed, 165
annoyance, 107
Aquarius sextile Venus in Aries with MC in Virgo, 275
Aries–Aquarius–Virgo yod, 152
aspects, 1, 15, 20
  major, 19
  minor, 19
aspect patterns, backgrounds of, 7
  aware, daring to become, 136

Beethoven, 98
Brandt, Willy, 115, 116

Cancer–Virgo–Aquarius yod, 152
Capricorn, 209
Carter, Jimmy, 98
case files, 251
change, processes of, 313
Charles and Diana, composite for, 176, 177
Charles, Prince, 112, 158, 161, 165, 170, 171
child with yod or unaspected planet and shadow projection, 109
choices, impossible, 55
Christina, 266, 270
churinga, 240
Clinton, President William Jefferson, 110, 183, 191, 201, 203, 214, 216, 217
  and impeachment, 183, 205
composite chart, 156
compulsion, 155
confidence, 297
conjunction, 1
consciousness, 103, 104

death, 119
  theme of, 163
dependence, 148
Diana, Princess (Lady), 54, 73, 112, 158, 161, 162
Dossey, Larry, 119
dreams, 63, 137
duet, 33, 37
  between Saturn and Venus, 96, 97
  interpreting, 93
  unaspected, 93

Edward VII, 170
ego, 104, 107
egotistical displays, 143
element, 4, 10
Elizabeth II, Queen, 54, 173, 180
emotions, 135
emphasize planetary meanings, 93
Epstein, Alan, 9
Esther, 289, 292
events out of the blue, 52
evil, 103, 117, 118
  archetypal, 120

fairy tales, 118
faith, 245
family
  dynamics, 47
  patterns, 37, 39
  themes, 35, 38
fate, 118
fixed orientation, 316
Foster, Vincent, 194

Gemma, 275, 278
  daughter of, 282
  grandmother of, 281
  mother of, 279
generation problem, 35
generational dynamic, 78
God, 121
  finger of, 242, 317
  hand of, 62
Goldberg, Lucianne, 192, 195
good and evil, 119, 121
grand cross, 1

grand square, 7, 8, 10
grand trine, 1, 7, 8, 9

Hades, 169
Harry, Prince, 178
Havel, Václav, 65, 66, 111
Helen, 253, 255
Henry VIII, 181
houses, 92
  rulers of, 90

identity, 267
inconjunct, 1, 2, 11
  and yod, 8
individuation, 104
insecurity, 23, 52, 86, 98
  personal, 146
integrity, 136
Isikoff, Michael, 192

Jacqueline, 260, 263
Jannette, 219, 225
jod, 1
Jones, Jim, 137, 138
Jones, Paula, 193, 205, 215
Jordan, Vernon, 192
Jung, C. G., 73, 88, 89, 90, 103, 117, 237–250
Jungian
  study of elements, 11
  typologies, 4
Jupiter, 74, 88, 163, 237
  unaspected, 98, 111
  in yod, 244

Kepler, Johannes, 2, 9
Keppel, Alice, 170
Khomeini, Ayatollah Rubolia, 111, 112
kite, 7
Koch, Walter, 2, 9

leadership functions, 99
let things take their course, 140
Lewinsky, Monica, 97, 101, 110, 112, 155, 183, 184, 187, 201, 205, 211, 212, 214
  relationship theme in family of, 185

Lewis, Marcia, 185
life
  change, complete, 64
  second half, 88
life and death, 219
  questions of, 303
love and marriage, 80

Mahatma Gandhi, 111, 113
mana, 240
Mars, 88, 94, 176
  unaspected, 22, 23, 27,
    28, 57
Mercury, 85, 93, 132
  in Aquarius sextile
    Venus in Aries, 275
  in Aries, 3
  in Cancer, 75
  in a composite, 157
  in Gemini, 74, 75
  in a yod, 74, 84, 294
Mercury, Moon, Neptune
  yod, 84
Mercury, Neptune in a
  yod, 85
Mercury–Pluto duet, 111
Mercury, unaspected, 21,
  111, 149, 157
  in a composite, 176
Mercury–Venus–Uranus
  yod, 111
misunderstandings, 84
mode, 4, 5
  cardinal, 5
  fixed, 6
  mutable, 6
  negative, 7
  positive, 6
Moon, 85, 297
  in Pisces in the 12th
    house, 176
  and Pluto in a yod, 299
  progressed, 126
  unaspected, 23, 49, 72,
    99, 100, 133
  unintegrated, 99
  in Virgo, 3
  in a yod, 71, 86
Moon–Jupiter duet, 213
Moon, Pluto, Mercury
  yod, 289
Moon, Pluto, Neptune
  yod, 289, 298
Moon, Pluto, Sun yod,
  289

Morton, Andrew, 211
Mountbatten, Lord, 166,
  170
music, 2

Neptune, 74, 81, 85, 209,
  237, 238, 267
  in Sagittarius, 126
  unaspected, 111
  in a yod, 294
Neumann, Erich, 104, 314
nodes, 17
numerology, 2

opposition, 1
orbs, 15, 19, 20

pain, learning process of,
  244
parents and shadow, 109
Parker-Bowles, Camilla,
  161, 165, 173, 174
Part of Fortune, 17
Persephone, 169
phallus, 242
planets
  in 8th house, 196
  insecurity and
    unaspected, 23
  in same mode, 6
  in single element, 5
planets, unaspected, 19,
  20, 26, 28, 29, 30, 32,
  37, 40, 63, 64, 78, 93,
  108, 172, 220
  and ambivalence, 26
  in a composite, 156
  dealing with, 135
  in a duet, 172
  effects of, 47
  emphasize planetary
    meanings, 93
  and fate, 95
  and houses, 100
  interpreting of, 93
  involves searching,
    94
  isolated, 21
  and power, 97
  by progression, 132
  by progression and
    transit, 123
  and reception, 33
  and synastry, 30
  by transit, 132

Pluto, 72, 74, 81, 88, 91,
  124, 132, 163, 164,
  237, 267
  aspects, temporary,
    169
  in a duet, 147
  in the 8th, 197
  in Libra, 126
  transits and
    progressions of, 300
  unaspected, 111, 147
  unsuspecting, 115
  in a yod, 242
points, 16
premonitions, 63
pressure, 155
problems, religious,
  philosophical, 244
progression, 63
projections, 86, 106, 204
psyche, 105
Ptolemy, 2

quintile, 2

reception, Aquarius and
  Cancer, 33
relationship dynamic for
  the British royal
  family, 181–182
relationships, 145
religious
  teachings, 209
  thought, 138
Reno, Janet, 205
repressed contents, 36
ruler of the 8th house,
  unaspected, 101, 173

Sagittarius–Aquarius–
  Cancer yod, 152
Sakoian, Frances, 9
Saturn, 74, 209
  transit, 126
  unaspected, 95, 98, 178
Saturn, Uranus, and
  Neptune yods, 51
Saturn–Venus duet, 155
Saturn–yod, 262
Self, 103, 104, 119
self-confidence, 107
self-worth, 297
semi-sextile, 2
serpent, 243
sextile, 1, 11, 126

shadow, 40, 41, 42, 103, 106, 107, 108, 110, 114, 115, 198
archetypal, 110
collective, 108, 111, 112, 113
collective family, 127
sign, 1
background, 2, 4
Solzhenitsyn, Alexander, 111, 114
spirit stone, 242
square, 1
stalemate, 54, 79, 117
standing at crossroads, 54
Starr, Kenneth, 155, 183, 193, 203, 208, 212, 214, 215
stones, magical, 240
Sun, 267, 297
in a duet, 246
and Moon in a yod, 261
unintegrated, 99
Sun–Saturn square, 76
Sun–Saturn–Uranus yod, 75
Sun, unaspected, 25, 26, 94, 95, 98, 99, 133
in a composite, 157
Sun in a yod, 294
with Pluto and Neptune, 267, 296

T-square, 13
taboo, 243
image, 242
Telesphorus, 239, 241, 242
temporary aspect, 133
tension, 52
theology, 245
transit, 63, 123
trine, 1
Tripp, Linda, 155, 183, 184, 191, 192, 194, 199, 212, 214

turning-point situation, 115
type
feeling, 5, 11
intuition, 5, 11
sensation, 4, 11
thinking, 4, 11

unconsciousness, 103
collective, 103
personal, 103
Uranus, 35, 74, 209

Venus, 81
Venus–Pluto–Neptune yod, 51, 79, 80, 82
Venus and Pluto with yods, 53
Venus–Saturn duet, 213
Venus, unaspected, 23, 24, 220, 221
in a composite, 176
visions, 137
Voorhoeve, Joris, 56, 57

Willey, Kathleen, 192, 214
William, Prince, 79, 165, 178, 180
wronged, to be, 58

yods, 1, 7, 12, 13, 16, 37, 58, 63, 64, 78, 108
activated by Pluto, 124
activated by progression or transit, 58
and backstabbing, 58
in a composite, 158
configurations, 35
deal with each planet separately, 70
dealing with, 135
effects of, 47
forming new, 126
and houses, 90
incomprehensible

circumstances, 50
interpreting
temporary, 125
Moon, 72
period, 127
by progression, 123, 125
searching, 59
several temporary yods by progression or transit, 131
sextiles become yods by transit, 126
stretched out, 129
in synastry, 151, 154
and talent, 65
temporary
configurations, 123
temporary, in transit, 253
by transit, 123, 125
as turning points, 92
we don't see ourselves, 49
we're not really aware of them, 48
working with children, 60
yod interpretation, 69
check creative ability, 87
consider signs involved, 74
and fate, 78
houses connect to rulers, 90
misunderstandings, 84
Pluto, 73
restlessness, 75
risks, 86
yod and duet, 87
yod and unaspected planet, 313, 316
in action, 183

Karen Hamaker-Zondag is the author of fifteen books, many of which are published by Weiser, including *The Twelfth House* and *Tarot as a Way of Life*. She gives workshops and lectures in Europe as well as in the United States, where she is a very popular speaker. She is the recipient of the 1998 Regulus Award for Education from the United Astrology Congress.

She is a founding member of two schools: Stichting Achernar, an astrological school; and Stichting Odrerir, a school of Jungian Psychology. Since 1990, she and her husband Hans, have published *Symbolon*, a popular astological journal. Karen lives near Amsterdam with her husband and two children.